The Pubs of Haverfordwest, Milford Haven & Mid-West Pembrokeshire

The Pubs of Haverfordwest, Milford Haven & Mid-West Pembrokeshire

by

Keith Johnson

Logaston Press

LOGASTON PRESS
Little Logaston Woonton Almeley
Herefordshire HR3 6QH

First published by Logaston Press 2006
Copyright © Keith Johnson 2006

All rights reserved. No part of this publication
may be reproduced, stored in a retrieval system,
or transmitted, in any form or by any means,
electronic, mechanical, photocopying, recording
or otherwise, without the prior permission,
in writing of the publisher

ISBN 1 904396 63 1
(978 1 904396 63 5)

Set in Times New Roman by Logaston Press
and printed in Great Britain by
Oaklands Books Services, Glos.

Contents

Acknowledgments		vii
Chapter One	Introduction.	1
Chapter Two	Haverfordwest: Cartlett & Salutation Sq.	19
Chapter Three	Haverfordwest: Prendergast	35
Chapter Four	Haverfordwest: Bridgend, Old Bridge & Swan Sq.	43
Chapter Five	Haverfordwest: Holloway, North St., Queen's Sq. & Church St.	55
Chapter Six	Haverfordwest: Bridge St., Castle Sq. & Quay St.	61
Chapter Seven	Haverfordwest: High St. & Dew St.	75
Chapter Eight	Haverfordwest: Mariners' Sq., Dark St., St. Mary's St. & Tower Hill	91
Chapter Nine	Haverfordwest: Market St. & Hill St.	105
Chapter Ten	Haverfordwest: St. Thomas' Sq.. Merlin's Hill & Shipman's Lane	117
Chapter Eleven	Haverfordwest: Barn St., City Rd., Portfield & Portfield Gate	125
Chapter Twelve	Slebech & Uzmaston	133
Chapter Thirteen	Merlin's Bridge	137
Chapter Fourteen	South of Haverfordwest: Freystrop, Hook, Llangwm, Burton & Rosemarket	141
Chapter Fifteen	Neyland, Honeyborough, Llanstadwell & Waterston	159
Chapter Sixteen	Haverfordwest to Milford Haven: Johnston, Tiers Cross, Steynton, Priory & Dale Road	179
Chapter Seventeen	Milford Haven: Hamilton Terrace & Victoria Rd.	191
Chapter Eighteen	Milford Haven: Pill, Charles St., Robert St. & Priory St.	207
Chapter Nineteen	Hakin & Hubberston	231
Chapter Twenty	West of Milford Haven: Herbrandston, St. Ishmael's, Dale & Marloes	251
Chapter Twenty-one	West of Haverfordwest: The Havens	265
Bibliography		277
Index		279

HAVERFORD WEST CASTLE,
(With the Priory.)
Pembrokeshire.

Acknowledgments

This is the third in a series of four books on the history of Pembrokeshire pubs. The south of the county has already been covered, and I am grateful to all those who bought the first two volumes in this series. This book covers the towns of Haverfordwest, Milford Haven and Neyland, together with a large chunk of countryside bounded on three sides by the Cleddau, the Haven and St. Bride's Bay. As you will discover, there were lots of pubs in this area – more than 50 in Hakin alone – so be prepared for a very long pub crawl ...

As with the first two books, this history of the inns of the central part of the county has been cobbled together from a wide variety of sources, some of them more reliable than others. Primary source material about old pubs is notoriously difficult to find, so as well as census returns, I have had to rely on old newspapers, travel journals and trade directories for most of the information. This has been augmented by the personal memories of many local people, often jotted down on the back of beer-mats, and I am grateful to all those who have helped me with my researches and pointed me in the direction of a long-forgotten Royal Oak or Masons' Arms. I should point out that dates in the text are at best a rough guide to when licensees were in charge; memories can play tricks and trade directories can be inaccurate, to the extent that one licensee was still appearing in a trade directory 14 years after his death!

Numerous books have been written on the history of Haverfordwest, and fortunately two of them were compiled by gentlemen connected with the licensed trade. John Brown, the Market Street wine merchant, wrote *Haverfordwest and its Story* which was later revised and expanded by J.W. Phillips and Fred Warren as *The History of Haverfordwest with that of Some Pembrokeshire Parishes*. And William D. Phillips, author of *Old Haverfordwest,* was born in the Bull Inn, Prendergast, and later ran the Salutation Inn. Both books have proven invaluable in compiling this account.

There is also a useful, but far from complete list of old Haverfordwest pubs to be found in G.D. James' *The Town and County of Haverfordwest and its Story.* This appears to be a copy of a handwritten sheet, dating from 1882, which once hung in the Dragon Inn. The late Mr. Wyn Jones, architect and historian, researched the old pubs of the town for Haverfordwest Civic Society and I am grateful to Mrs. Elfrida Jones for permission to use his notes, while Bill Richards' book *The Changing Face of Haverfordwest* was another important source.

Neyland's relatively brief history has been well documented, and both Simon Hancock and Desmond Davies have much to say about the pubs of the town; I am particularly grateful to Mr. Hancock for his help with the Neyland chapter. The pubs of Milford Haven, on the other hand, have rarely been mentioned by the town's historians who tend to be more interested in the history of the docks than the town itself. The exception is the Lord Nelson Hotel, and even then the writers have followed each other in perpetuating the error that the name was changed to Lord Nelson in 1802 following the visit of the Hero of the Nile. (In fact the name was changed to Nelson Hotel nearly a decade later and didn't become the Lord Nelson until the 1850s).

I owe a particular debt of gratitude to all the staff at the County Reference Library and the County Records Office for their unfailing help and encouragement. Thanks also go to Andy Johnson and Ron Shoesmith of Logaston Press for their guidance and patience, to Katy Shoesmith who produced the maps and to Jennifer Shoesmith for her help with the index.

Very many people have provided information and illustrations for this book and it would be impossible to list every one; my thanks go to them all. In particular I would like to thank the following for their special contributions: John Ambrey, Barrie Burgess, Barbara Chester, Edgy Cooper, Margaret Copley, Beryl Davies, Maureen Dytor, Sybil Edwards, David Faulkner, Joy Fuller, David Griffiths, Bill Griffiths, Simon Hancock, Mr. and Mrs. Jimmy Murphy, Ian Norman, Bernard Prettyman, Maxine Rolls, Martin Rowland, Kay Scourfield, Jasper Slater, John Smedley, John Stevenson, Roland Thorne, Owen Vaughan, John Warren, Brenda Williams, Roger Worsley, Haverfordwest Civic Society, Haverfordwest Museum, Coastlands Local History Group,

> Now since we're met, let's merry merry be,
> In spite of all our foes,
> And he that will not merry merry be,
> We'll pull him by the nose.
> And he that will not merry merry be,
> With a generous bowl and a toast,
> May he in Bridewell be shut up
> And fast bound to a post.
> And he that will not merry merry be,
> With a company of jolly boys,
> May he be plagued with a scolding wife,
> To confound him with her noise.
> (Traditional song)

CHAPTER ONE

Introduction

A survey carried out in 1899 revealed that Pembrokeshire had exactly 500 pubs out of a Welsh total of 8,124. Neighbouring Cardiganshire had 314 licensed houses and industrial Carmarthenshire had 782. However, the real significance of these figures became apparent when the number of pubs was set alongside the population figures of each county, because with one pub for every 164 inhabitants, Pembrokeshire was firmly at the head of the Welsh drinking league. (By comparison Merioneth had one pub for every 450 inhabitants, and it was calculated that Glamorgan would need an extra 2,000 pubs to match Pembrokeshire's ratio!).

It wasn't a new phenomenon. Pembrokeshire people have always enjoyed a drink. As far back as the 6th century, St. David himself – a confirmed teetotaller and mortifier of the flesh – was forced to issue the following edict to his fellow monks: 'Those who get drunk through ignorance must do penance 15 days; if through negligence, 40 days; if through contempt, three quarntains' (a quarntain – from which we get the word 'quarantine' – being a period of 40 days).

Ironically, perhaps, it was the shrine of St. David which brought many thousands of pilgrims flocking to the county in the Middle Ages, resulting in numerous hostelries being opened up along the pilgrim ways. But the concept of the inn can be traced back to a period long before the Age of the Saints. It is thought that the Romans introduced the idea to Britain, setting up *tavernae* along their network of roads where travellers could rest and perhaps enjoy alcoholic refreshment. This was predominantly wine, which the Romans imported from other parts of their empire for the benefit of their legions in Britain, but it is thought that they also brewed a kind of beer from cereals. This idea caught on, and by Saxon times there were houses in every village where the men would gather to hold petty courts and to quaff ale out of drinking horns – the real fore-runner of the modern pub.

The earliest ale-houses in Pembrokeshire would probably have been fairly primitive affairs, thatched wooden huts where the inhabitants owned a cauldron capable of boiling up a brew of sweet ale. None of these would have been 'full-time' pubs; they would simply have rustled up a brew when there was a demand – perhaps for a feast day. By the 6th century these ale-houses had become slightly more sophisticated, to the extent of offering a choice of alcoholic beverages. Mead – made from fermented honey – was a well-established favourite of the Celtic people; one early Welsh law specified that a cask of mead should be nine palms high and wide enough to serve as a bathtub for the king and one of his court. And in Wales there were two types of ale – *cwrwf*, which was an everyday kind of ale, and the highly-flavoured (and more expensive) *bragawd* which was spiced up with cinnamon, ginger and cloves.

By AD 745, ale-houses were so widespread – and had gained such a low reputation – that the Archbishop of York had to issue a Canon: 'That no priest go to eat or drink in taverns'. And there were so many inns by the time of King Edgar (959 – 975) that he tried to limit them to one per village.

The arrival of the Normans in Pembrokeshire and the creation of castle towns such as Pembroke, Tenby, Haverfordwest and Newport meant the establishment of permanent ale-houses in the county. These were often found alongside the market square and close to the church – the historic link between the monasteries and the brewing industry being a strong one. Outside the protection of the towns there were fewer ale-houses – especially in the disputed countryside. These were sometimes known as 'hedge ale-houses' because, with their thatched roof and low walls made out of 'clom' (mud or clay strengthened with straw), they were barely distinguishable from the surrounding vegetation. But as time went by and St. David's began to gain a reputation as a shrine of international importance, so rather more substantial wayside inns were opened to provide hospitality for the pilgrims and later for travelling merchants.

A 14th-century inn with its pole and bush

Moves to regulate the pub trade began at an early date. The Magna Carta included a decree designed to standardise the measurements of wine, ale and corn throughout the land, while in 1266 the Assize of Bread and Ale recognised that these items were the necessities of life and sensibly linked their retail price to the current price of grain. Breaking the assize of ale became an offence which was to keep the manorial courts busy for centuries to come. In

1606, for example, Caria Tanner, a resident of Newport, Pembrokeshire, 'broke the Assize of Ale, selling small measures in illegal measures, therefore she is in mercy 12d.'.

The widespread introduction of hops in the 15th century meant that ale slowly began to give way to a new, bitter drink called beer. Despite considerable opposition to this 'pernicious weed' – it was even prohibited for a while – the hop proved very popular with brewers and eventually with drinkers, beer having a sharper flavour and better 'keeping' qualities than the traditional ale. There seems to be no record of large scale hop-growing in Pembrokeshire, although hops were grown in the Carew area at one time (as the name Hop Gardens testifies) while the name Hopshill at Saundersfoot might indicate another area where the vines were cultivated successfully.

A 14th-century tavern with a cellar for keeping the ale

As the number of common ale-houses increased, so did the number of regulations controlling them. It was Henry VII – a son of Pembrokeshire – who introduced Acts in 1495 and 1504 giving local Justices the power to suppress ale-houses which were badly run or which were responsible for keeping men from their all-important archery practice. A further Act in 1553 made a legal distinction between the different kinds of hostelry; ale-houses sold only ale and beer, taverns were restricted to towns and cities and sold only wine (though later they sold beer as well), while inns also offered accommodation. Most of these places would have brewed their own beer, although in the smaller houses, where the part-time ale-house keeper had a trade which occupied most of his day, it was the practice to buy beer from better-equipped inns and later from full-time brewers.

A 16th-century brewer.

Although both Tenby and Haverfordwest were notable wine-importing centres at one time, it seems unlikely that there were too many taverns in Pembrokeshire that offered only wine – ale and beer were the order of the day for the Welsh lower classes. However a complaint to the Star Chamber in 1602 stated that an Irish priest who visited Pembroke was 'a comon haunter of alhouses and wintaverns', so there must have been wine bars in the town 400 years ago. Even so, most of the wine that the merchants shipped into the county was destined for the castles and manor houses of the gentry; according to the bards who sang his praises Tomas ap Phylip of Picton Castle once took delivery of a shipment of 20 tuns of wine – about 5,000 gallons.

Despite this impressive statistic, the Elizabethan historian George Owen thought that heavy drinking was rare in Pembrokeshire. However he did concede that an influx of Irish settlers into the county in the days of Henry VIII had given the locals a taste for whiskey. As Owen explained:

> Those Irish people here do use their country trade in making of Aqua Vitae in great abundance which they carry to be sold abroad the country on horseback and otherwise, so that weekly you may be sure to have Aqua Vitae to be sold at your door, and by means thereof it is grown to be an usual drink in most men's houses instead of wine.

By the beginning of the 17th century, there were plenty of licensed alehouses in Pembrokeshire – and more than a few unlicensed ones as well. In 1606, the Court Leet and View of Frankpledge in Newport dealt with the case of a tailor named Richard ap Ievan and ten others who 'kept taverns in their houses and sold ale without licence'. And in 1615, Hugh Johnes of Llanychaer and Thomas Price of St. Dogmael's were separately presented at the Great Sessions for 'keeping without a licence a common tippling house and for selling ale and beer'. What was unusual about the this case is that as well as running an illicit shebeen, Price was better known as the Rev. Thomas Price, vicar of St. Dogmael's!

In the towns, the inns and ale-houses tended to cluster around market squares and harbours where there was always a lively trade. Quay Street in Haverfordwest and the area around Tenby harbour would have had their share of rough and ready 'sailortown' pot-houses, while the pubs on Fishguard Square, Narberth Square and the East End of Pembroke came alive on market days and fair days. Out in the countryside, wherever there was hard work to be done, ale-houses – legal and otherwise – sprang up to provide refreshment for the labouring man. Bread, cheese and 'table beer' – as opposed to strong ale – sustained the quarryman and labourer, ploughman and collier throughout the long working day.

Many smaller country ale-houses had names designed to encourage the passer-by to enter – some of which live on in the name of Pembrokeshire localities. There were several ale-houses called 'Step Inn', as well as a 'Venture Inn' (now Venterin) near Lampeter Velfrey, the 'Stop-and-Call' at Goodwick and the 'Step Aside' near Kilgetty. With the Cleddau River carving its way through the heart of the county there were numerous ferry crossings, and all of these had an ale-house on at least one side of the river – usually run by the ferry-man and his wife and usually called 'Ferry Inn' or 'Waterman's Arms'.

In the towns, inns of a more substantial nature had been established, perhaps following the dissolution of the monasteries when pilgrims could no longer seek shelter in abbeys and other religious houses. The sadly-demolished Swan in Haverfordwest was said to date from the 16th century, while there are references to both the King's Arms in Pembroke and to the King's

A mid-18th-century brewhouse.

Arms in Tenby in 1617. These inns offered reasonable accommodation for travellers, stabling for their horses, and a ready meal, but the golden age of the inn – the era of the stage-coach – had yet to arrive and they were far from the bustling establishments they were to become.

The 18th century saw a further development with the arrival of purpose-built public houses. Where ale-houses were basically cottages with a room in which refreshments could be enjoyed, the public houses might have several rooms to cater for the different classes of drinker (but without offering the accommodation which would have turned them into inns). This competition had the effect of dragging many ale-houses 'up-market', although this increased respectability didn't prevent the criminal classes – the pickpockets, prostitutes, smugglers and highway robbers – from continuing to frequent the seedier houses at the bottom end of the scale.

Another change in the 18th century was in the amount of spirits being consumed, particularly cheap brandy and gin. While duty had to be paid on beer, spirits remained exempt for a good many years, so that the consumption of spirits increased from about half a million gallons in 1684 to eight million gallons in 1743 – an increase of well over a gallon per person per year. It took a succession of 'Gin Acts' to curb the dram shops and gin palaces and persuade people to turn back to the relatively healthy consumption of beer, ale and – increasingly – porter.

Porter was a specially blended mild beer which took its name from its popularity among London's market porters, and porter breweries soon sprang up all over the country – notably that of Samuel Whitbread in Chiswell Street in the City of London. This also led to another new development – the brewer's dray. Where once the ale-house keeper would have been expected to fetch the casks from the brewery himself, now the brewer made regular deliveries to all the pubs on his patch – a practice which eventually led to the 'tied house'. Although brewery-to-pub delivery was initially confined to the larger centres of population, horse-drawn brewer's drays inevitably found their way onto the streets and country lanes of Pembrokeshire.

Up to this time, and for many years to come, the easiest way to travel to Pembrokeshire was by sea, and little in the way of coaching inns had developed in the county. This changed in the late 18th century with the establishment of a packet service to Ireland from Hakin Point and also the emergence of Tenby as a fashionable sea-bathing resort. The coach road to Hakin Point ran by way of St. Clears, Llanddowror, Tavernspite, Narberth and Haverfordwest and several coaching inns were established as posting stages along this route, including the Picton at Llanddowror, the Plume of Feathers at Tavernspite, the Golden Lion in Narberth, the Coach and Horses in Robeston Wathen and the Castle in Haverfordwest. On the road which

Published for Bettering the Condition and Increasing the Comforts of the POOR.

C*AUTION*

To Alehouse Keepers, & their Guests.

It is better that Offences against the Laws should be Prevented, than that Offenders should be Punished.

THE PROPER USE OF INNS, &c.

THE proper use of Inns and Alehouses, is to furnish Refreshment and Lodging to Travellers, upon a reasonable profit; to accommodate persons meeting on *necessary* business; Soldiers in his Majesty's service; and some whose occupations require a frequent change of residence, or who cannot provide themselves with meat and drink in a more convenient manner.

 The neighbouring Justices of the Peace have the Power of granting a License for keeping a Publick House, and they have the like Power of refusing to grant a License, without giving any reason whatever for such refusal, which is entirely at their discretion; it is therefore the Interest as well as the Duty of an Alehouse keeper to take care, that he conduct himself and his House in a becoming manner, lest he forfeit the good opinion of the Justices and be deprived of his License.

 A principal duty of an Alehouse keeper is to prevent Artificers and Labourers from drinking more than for their necessary Refreshment; and not to allow them to lose their time and spend their money to the injury of themselves and their families: therefore, almost all debts (commonly called Ale Scores) are incurred in an improper manner; and are such, as the lawful means (if any) of recovering such debts would often discover bad conduct in the Alehouse keeper, and hazard the loss of his License.

 The Law protects the Alehouse keeper from losses, by giving him the power of detaining the Person of any Guest who refuses to pay the reasonable charges for the meat and drink which have been furnished him: Debts are seldom incurred by Travellers, who are generally Strangers, and when they are incurred by Artificers and Labourers, great blame will attach to the Alehouse keeper from the manner in which such Ale Scores must have been contracted.

 An Alehouse keeper is liable to heavy penalties for allowing Tippling, Drunkenness, or disorderly behaviour in his House, extending to the Forfeiture of his Recognizance, and that of his Surety or Bondsman, and the loss of his License.

 The Guests who are guilty of Tippling, Drunkenness, and disorderly Behaviour are also liable to heavy penalties; and Artificers and Labourers who waste their time and their money at Publick Houses, ought to consider that although they may avoid punishment from the forbearance with which the Laws are executed, yet their Wives and their Families cannot escape from the miseries of Poverty, the certain consequence of their Husband's misconduct; and that the wholesome restraint which the Law lays upon a man in this respect, gives the best assurance of protection to his Family and to Himself, when it forbids him to waste his time and his money in a Publick House, and disturb the peace of others by his intemperance and bad example.

To   *Alehouse keeper.*

You are desired to have this Paper pasted up in your Kitchen, or some other usual place where your Guests take their Refreshment.

SIGNED

Should this notice still be posted in landlords' kitchens?

branched south to Pembroke, there were the Milford Arms in Saundersfoot, the White Lion in Tenby and the Golden Lion and Green Dragon in Pembroke itself. These were all substantial buildings with good rooms and plenty of stabling, and as often as not had been built at the instigation of the local squire.

Many coaching inns were well-run establishments; some weren't. According to John Byng, writing in the 18th century:

> The innkeepers are insolent, the hostlers are sulky, the chambermaids are pert and the waiters are impertinent; the meat is tough, the wine is foul, the beer is hard, the sheets are wet, the linen is dirty and the knives are never clean'd!

It is to be hoped that Pembrokeshire's inns were run to a better standard, though most late 18th century travellers settled for describing them as 'middling' or 'tolerable' at best.

While the number of larger, well-appointed inns and public houses continued to increase, approved and licensed by the magistrates, there were still large numbers of smaller and humbler houses which operated in the grey area between ale-house and unlicensed 'shebeen'. In 1779, several people in Steynton, Pill and Hubberston were convicted of 'selling ale and strong beer without being licensed so to do', and as time went by it became apparent that gin drinking was once again on the increase and that the dodgier ale-houses were turning into dram-shops.

Various Acts were passed in the 1820s in an attempt to reverse this trend, culminating in the 1830 Beer Act. This was designed to encourage the consumption of beer at the expense of spirits – a move which would boost the country's agriculture and brewing industries and also improve health. Beer was widely considered to be a wholesome and health-giving drink, much more so than water which was often of a dubious quality – especially in the towns. For example, when Milford Sunday School held a New Year's Day treat in 1818, nearly 200 children enjoyed a meal of roast beef and plum pudding 'and afterwards ale supplied by Mr. G. Starbuck and Mr. R. Byers' – Byers being the local surgeon.

The 1830 Beer Act duly abolished all duty on beer and brought into being the 'beer-shop' or 'beer-house'. For the cost of two guineas, any householder could obtain a beer-house licence which would permit the sale of beer and cider only – as opposed to the fully licensed public houses which could also sell wine and spirits. The result of this new legislation can be easily imagined – beer-houses by the thousand opened up all over the country. Former 'shebeens' entered the fold of legitimacy, while masons and blacksmiths, farmers, coopers and carpenters took the opportunity to sell beer as a sideline to their regular trade. Within a year of the Act coming into force there were 24,000 new beer-houses in Britain and the figure had reached 46,000 by 1836. In the twin towns of Pembroke and Pembroke Dock there were 45 beer-houses in 1840, while Milford Haven had 24. 'Everybody is drunk', reported Sydney Smith soon after the Beer Act came into force. 'Those who are not singing are sprawling'.

These new drinking premises were often called 'Tom and Jerry shops' after a pair of dissolute characters in Pierce Egan's serialised novel *Life in London,* or sometimes 'Kiddleywinks'. They were often badly run, and as the Haverfordwest weekly newspaper *Potter's Electric News* noted: 'Beer-shop owners prey upon labouring men who earn their money like horses – and then spend it like asses'. They also attracted a seedy clientele.

> The beer-shop keeper collects about him the very dregs of society. It is in these places that robberies are planned and crimes committed. The beer-shop keeper is too frequently the banker of the thief.

Because of their very nature, beer-houses are difficult to research. The Beer Act made no provision for the keeping of records of licences, and numerous 'Kiddleywinks' came and went without leaving any trace other than a vague folk memory. Several of these were *ad hoc* affairs which opened to take advantage of such things as the arrival of gangs of navvies to build a road or railway and which closed again following their departure. Others lasted much longer, and there was hardly a street in Pembroke Dock which didn't have a beer-house or three to cater for the town's hard-drinking population of shipwrights, seamen and soldiers.

Running parallel with the spread of the beer-shop came the rise of Nonconformity and also the growing influence of the temperance movement. This movement had become organised as far back as 1828, and – ironically perhaps – had strongly supported the Beer Act and its aim of getting people to stop drinking gin. Its members pledged themselves to abstain from all spirits – except for medicinal purposes – and only to drink beer and wine 'in moderation'. This wasn't enough for some of the hard-line reformers who went even further and advocated total abstinence. These teetotallers, who often clashed with their more 'wishy-washy' temperance colleagues, embarked on a high-profile campaign aimed at persuading people to give up the demon drink altogether. Meetings were held up and down the country at which reformed drunkards in their Sunday best were paraded in front of the audience as living examples of the benefits of total abstinence.

One such character who addressed a meeting in Ebenezer Chapel, Haverfordwest in January 1839 was introduced as 'a reformed drunkard from Milford'. He gave what was described in the *Welshman* newspaper as 'an

"Good Words'" Gospel Temperance Services for the People
Haverfordwest Temperance Council
Sat., April 4, to Thurs., April 9.
Christian Temperance
Campaign
Will be conducted by MR.
JAS. GILLESPIE
Musical Missioner and Temperance Advocate.
Composer and Hymn Writer, Editor of "Mission Melodies"

Saturday, April 4th, at 7.30 Temperance Hall—Great Temperance Demonstration & Welcome Meeting

Sunday, April 5th, Three Great Meetings in the **TEMPERANCE HALL.**
3 p.m. Subject, "Wanted a Man." Open to all.
6 p.m. Special Meeting for Boys and Girls.
8 p.m. Great United Meeting. Subject, "Drink the Destroyer."

Monday, April 6th at 7.30. **Albany Chapel.** Subject—'**EXCUSES EXAMINED**'

Tuesday, April 7th, at 7.30. **Hill Park Chapel** Subject—'**THE CRY OF THE CHILDREN**'

Wednesday, April 8th, 7.30. **Bethesda Chapel** Subject—'**THE POWER OF DRINK.**'

Thurs, Ap.9th, 7.30. **Wesleyan Schoolroom** Farewell Lecture and Musical Recital, entitled '**LOVE COURTSHIP & MARRIAGE.**'
Admission on this special night by Ticket 6d. each.

Mr. GILLESPIE will sing at every Meeting.
The Singing begins earlier than advertised time of Meeting.
Come and hear the Soul-stirring Solos and Choruses.
A WELCOME FOR YOU
Admission Free *Questions Invited*
Ask at Hall Door for a copy of "GOOD WORDS."

---

exciting, though melancholic' account of himself, explaining that for 17 years he had 'served the monster intemperance'. During this time he had been notorious for his habitual drunkenness, but he had signed the pledge 12 months before and was now 'in every respect more happy than when he was in the habit of indulging in the intoxicating draught'.

In Narberth, a Total Abstinence Society was formed in 1837 and in 1841 the *Welshman* reported that there were 'numerous' total abstainers in the town of Pembroke whose battle-cry was: 'Honour to the Welsh water-drinkers! Destruction to the publicans and sinners of Cymru!' To begin with they were fighting a losing battle. The number of pubs and beer-houses continued to grow, and although the coaching inns were badly hit by the arrival of the railway, this was more than offset by the number of pubs created to serve the new form of transport, with Railway Inns and Railway Taverns being opened in every town and nearly every village on the line – from Johnston and Wiston to Jameston, Lamphey and Penally. Quarrying villages such as West

Williamston, Ludchurch and Cilgerran were awash with pubs and beer-houses and it was said that every house in Hakin that wasn't a licensed pub was an unlicensed one.

Gradually, however, the tide began to turn. The Lord's Day Observance Society had been founded in the same year as the British and Foreign Temperance Society, and the two movements soon found plenty of common ground on which to campaign. They achieved some early success with the passing of the Lord's Day Act of 1848 which prevented pubs from opening before 1pm on a Sunday. Attempts to restrict Sunday opening still further in 1855 led to street riots in London; even so an Act was passed soon afterwards restricting Sunday opening to the hours of 1pm to 3pm and 5pm to 11pm. In

Drinking a yard of ale at the Masons' Arms, Priory, near Milford Haven. Landlord Fred 'Firpo' Hoggins is assisting Harold 'Baski' Spriggs to steady the glass, while those looking on include Ronnie 'Bambi' James, Ronnie Ormond, Jimmy Reynolds, John Boswell, John 'Gypsy' Jones and an open-mouthed Billy Davies.
(Picture courtesy of Mr. John Stevenson)

Pembrokeshire, as in the rest of Wales, the campaign against Sunday drinking was spearheaded by the Nonconformists. Each wave of religious revival which swept across Wales was accompanied by a wave of temperance activity – in Cilgerran it was claimed that the thunder of one revival had turned the beer sour.

In 1860 came the first movement towards 'early closing' – a laudable scheme designed to give shop-workers in the towns a mid-week half-day holiday. Sports clubs – most famously Sheffield Wednesday – were formed in many places to provide 'healthful and innocent amusement' for young men with time to kill. Cricket clubs were formed all over Pembrokeshire; as one of the founders of the Pembroke club pointed out:

> If these young men are not on the cricket field, there will probably, many of them at least, be found in the pursuit of some vice or sensual pleasure – perhaps guzzling like brute-beasts in the pot-houses with which the town of Pembroke unfortunately abounds.

By the end of the 1860s there was a growing consensus that the beer-house had long outlived its usefulness and that the number of pubs in the country needed to be curtailed. The 1869 Wine and Beer-house Act brought all licensed premises under the control of the magistrates. This effectively meant that no new beer-houses were opened while many of the existing ones closed down, their trade not being sufficient to warrant the cost and effort of applying for a justices' licence. The Aberdare Act of 1872 added to the burden of legislation on the drinking trade, curtailing drinking hours, increasing fines for licensing offences, prohibiting the sale of liquor to

---

An Act to prohibit the Sale of Intoxicating Liquors on Sunday in Wales.
[27th August 1881.]

WHEREAS the provisions in force against the sale of fermented and distilled liquors during certain hours of Sunday have been found to be attended with great public benefits, and it is expedient and the people of Wales are desirous that in the principality of Wales those provisions be extended to the other hours of Sunday:

Be it therefore enacted by the Queen's most Excellent Majesty, by and with the advice and consent of the Lords Spiritual and Temporal, and Commons, in this present Parliament assembled, and by the authority of the same, as follows:

1. In the principality of Wales all premises in which intoxicating liquors are sold or exposed for sale by retail shall be closed during the whole of Sunday. *Premises where intoxicating liquors sold to be closed on Sundays in Wales.*

2. The Licensing Acts, 1872–1874, shall apply in the case of any premises closed under this Act as if they had been closed under those Acts. *Application of Licensing Acts. 35 & 36 Vict. c. 94. 37 & 38 Vict. c. 49.*

3. This Act shall commence and come into operation with respect to each division or place in Wales on the day next appointed for the holding of the general annual licensing meeting for that division or place. *Commencement of Act.*

4. Nothing in this Act contained shall preclude the sale at any time at a railway station of intoxicating liquors to persons arriving at or departing from such station by railway. *Sale of intoxicating liquors at railway stations.*

5. This Act may be cited as the Sunday Closing (Wales) Act, 1881. *Short title.*

The 1881 Welsh Sunday Closing Act.

under 16s and generally making life difficult for the landlord. (This Act was so unpopular that it was blamed for the fall of Gladstone's government two years later; Disraeli's administration increased the opening hours by 30 minutes as a mark of appreciation).

In Wales, Sunday opening remained the biggest bugbear of the temperance brigade. In Calvinist Scotland the pubs had been closed on the Sabbath since 1853, and when Ireland introduced Sunday closing in 1878, the Welsh campaigners were determined to be next. Temperance and chapel leaders claimed (with some justification) that the majority of people in Wales were behind them – although a public meeting held in Tenby in February 1880 to press for Sunday closing was 'miserably attended'. In the industrialised areas of Wales, the sabbatarians received powerful support from the iron-masters and the coal-owners who were fed up with half their workforce turning up for the Monday morning shift still drunk from the excesses of the previous day. Wales was ripe for Sunday closing, and when a private member's Bill, introduced by Flint MP John Roberts, received its third reading in August 1881, the Welsh Sunday Closing Act duly entered the statute books.

In Pembrokeshire, many of the big landowners were also active supporters of temperance – among their tenants, if not on a personal level. As a result, estates like Stackpole, Marloes and Lawrenny were without a public house for many years – to the great benefit of pubs in villages like Dale, Hundleton and Landshipping which were just over the border in neighbouring estates.

Towards the end of the 19th century and in the first part of the 20th century, efforts continued to be made to reduce the numbers of public houses and also to standardise their lay-out. Magistrates found themselves with the power to take away licences for petty offences or because the lay-out of a pub did not meet their approval. And since many of the magistrates were chapel deacons and temperance-supporting landowners themselves, they did not hesitate to use this power.

Ironically, perhaps, the closure of village pubs, whether by the local squire or by the magistrates, often led to increased consumption of alcohol as more and more shebeens appeared in the rural areas. Obviously these places didn't have to abide by the licensing laws and the drink flowed at all hours of the day and night. Herbrandston didn't have a pub in 1899 but it did have a thriving shebeen run by a widow named Mary Sutton; on one occasion a watching policeman counted 23 men – locals and militia – entering the cottage for an illegal pint of home brew. Recognising this problem, the police and magistrates tended to spare village pubs, even going so far in the case of Herbrandston as to allow a new pub, the Foxhounds, to be opened in 1901.

CARRIERS TO AND FROM HAVERFORDWEST.

Tu., Tuesday; W., Wednesday; Th., Thursday; S., Saturday.

From and to	Put up at	Name or Description.	Days in Town.
Croesgoch	Mill Inn	S James	S
Fishguard	Commercial Hotel	Mail Cart	Daily
Hazelbeach	Plasterer's Arms	M. Willams	S
Johnston	Mr. Crabb Dew st	Venables	W & S
Little & Broad }	Lamb Inn	Read	Tu & S
Haven }	Lamb Inn	Jenkins	Daily
Marloes	King's Arms	M. Edwards	S
,,	,,	R. Hooper	S
Mullock bridge	,,	M, Edwards	S
Milford	Mr. Crabb Dew st	Venables	W & S
Middle Hill	Castle Hotel	J, John	S
St. David's	Milford Arms	Moriarty	Tu, Th, & S
,,	Mill Inn	Butler	Tu & S
Solva	,,	Joseph Davies	Tu & S
,,	Carmarthen Arms	J. Evans	Tu & S
Steynton	Mr. Crabb Dew st	Venables	W & S
St. Ishmael's	Fox & Hounds	Reynolds	S
,,	Plasterer's Arms	Thomas	W & S
Treffgarne	Farmer's Arms	E. Thomas	W & S
Waterston	Plasterer's Arms	M. Williams	S

The pubs of Haverfordwest acted as departure points for carters and carriers serving the villages of mid and north Pembrokeshire. This was the weekly schedule for 1909.

In 1904 a new Act was passed which established the principle of compensation for any publican whose house was considered 'redundant' and whose licence had been suppressed through no fault of his or her own (although in practice most of the compensation went to the owner of the property, rather than the publican who was usually a tenant). The first pub in Pembrokeshire to be axed under the compensation scheme was the St. Dogmells in Hakin, and the Act was eventually responsible for the closure of nearly 100 pubs in the county, among them noted houses like the Albion on Tenby Harbour, the Tower Inn in St. David's, the Gun Tavern in Pembroke Dock and the Sailors' Arms in Lower Fishguard. However, the publicans did not go down without a fight. Pembroke Dock Licensed Victuallers Association was formed in 1909 'for combination to combat the forces acting against them' and the Pembrokeshire LVA followed a year later with about 50 members. One of their aims was to obtain an 'impartial bench of magistrates' to adjudicate on the renewal of licences. All too often the magistrates would instruct the police to object to a certain licence, and then rule on the objection themselves – a 'disgraceful' situation according to Mr. S. McCulloch, the first president of the Pembrokeshire LVA.

The Defence of the Realm Act – DORA – took a toll on Pembrokeshire pubs following the outbreak of the First World War. The Act meant the introduction of even tighter licensing laws aimed at preventing drunkenness among servicemen, dockers, munitions workers and the like. In Lloyd George's opinion: 'Drink is doing us more damage in the war than all the German submarines put together' – but as someone who had once pressed for total prohibition in Wales, he might not have been entirely objective. Opening hours were curtailed, while one of the daftest rules brought in by the Act was the 'no treating' law. Under this rule no-one was allowed to buy a round of drinks or even buy his mate a pint; this was thought to encourage excessive drinking. In 1916 James Gray, landlord of the eminently respectable Avondale in Hakin, was fined ten shillings for allowing 'treating' in the pub.

He was lucky not to lose his licence. With a mass of new rules and regulations to fall foul of, it was inevitable that many landlords found themselves in court. And when they appeared before the bench there would be the inevitable clamour from the temperance brigade for the pubs to be shut. Many were, and when the troops returned from the trenches it was often to find that their favourite local had been forced to close. Wartime 'casualties' in Pembroke Dock alone included the Foresters' Arms, the Albert, the Sun and the Duke of York.

Licensing restrictions were gradually lifted following the end of the war – although Sunday closing remained sacrosanct. The number of pubs continued to fall, both as a result of the still-active redundancy committee and the economic depression, while changing social habits (and weaker beer) meant the number of drunks on the street fell dramatically. In 1908, 99 people had been convicted of drunkenness in Pembroke Borough; by the 1930s the figure was down to half a dozen each year.

As attitudes changed, and people began to look upon the village pub as a convivial social centre rather than a den of iniquity, so support for the temperance movement began to wane. By the time the Second World War came, the tide had turned to the extent that calls for a return to the licensing restrictions of 1914 were dismissed out of hand. In his excellent history of brewing in Wales, *Prince of Ales*, Brian Glover quotes Quintin Hogg (later Lord Hailsham) as stating in 1939:

> The Temperance Council must clearly understand that the national emergency is not a moment to introduce temperance propaganda under the cloak of national necessity. Beer is the innocent pleasure of many millions, especially those who bear the brunt today.

Such a sentiment – a million miles from that of Lloyd George 25 years earlier – shows how much attitudes had changed. The temperance movement was in retreat, although the redundancy committee continued to pick off pubs well into the 1950s – the Crown and Anchor and the Bell and Lion in Pembroke Dock were both closed in 1953.

The interior of the Three Crowns in Waterston – a typical pub refurbishment in late '60s style.

With the post-war growth of tourism, inns began to be seen as an amenity and Sunday closing in Wales became increasingly regarded as anachronism and a hindrance to the industry. A new Licensing Act in 1961 paved the way for each county to decide by a referendum (held every seven years) if it wanted Sunday drinking. The three west Wales counties of Pembrokeshire, Carmarthenshire and Cardiganshire voted to stay 'dry' in 1961, but in November 1968, alone of the three, Pembrokeshire voted to become 'wet'.

The late 1960s and early '70s also saw the opening of a number of new pubs in the tourist areas of the county – the Lobster Pot, the Lawrenny Arms, the Galleon and the Miracle Inn among others – and the enlargement and refurbishment of many more. Sadly, this refurbishment was often at the cost of the character of the old inn, and a pub guide of the time called *The Inn Crowd* shows (unintentionally) the widespread damage that was caused by the over-enthusiastic application of formica, leatherette and fake beams covered with equally fake horse-brasses.

Fortunately a good number of old Pembrokeshire pubs managed to avoid this kind of tasteless 'scampi in the basket' seventies makeover, so that the county still has a wide range of unspoilt taverns – from 'Bessie's' in the Gwaun Valley to the Charlton in Pembroke Dock and the Old Point House in Angle. And although well-established pubs continue to close – the Railway in Milford Haven, the Carmarthen Arms in Haverfordwest and the New Anchor in Hook are all recent victims – a glance at the pages of this book will show that this is simply part of an on-going process that has seen pubs come and go throughout the centuries as taste and circumstances changed with the passing years.

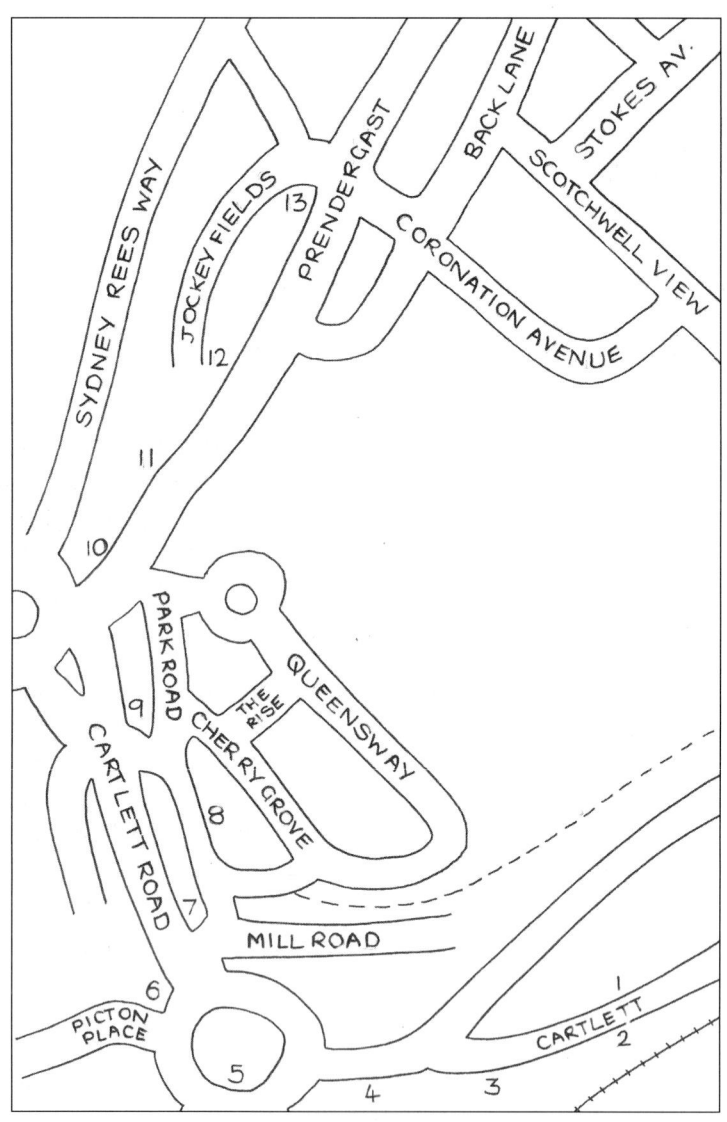

HAVERFORDWEST
CARTLETT, SALUTATION SQ. & PRENDERGAST
CHAPTERS 2 & 3

1	Masons' Arms	8	Ivorites' Arms
2	Queen's Hotel	9	Bridg End Inn
3	Carmarthen Arms	10	Wellington
4	Milford Arms	11	Fountain
5	Mill Inn	12	Horse and Groom
6	County Hotel (formerly Salutation)	13	Bull
7	Plough and Harrow		

CHAPTER TWO

Haverfordwest
CARTLETT & SALUTATION SQUARE

Its strategic position in the centre of the county and at the lowest bridging point on the Western Cleddau ensured that Haverfordwest would become an important commercial and administrative centre. Occupying the highest navigable point of the river, the town also developed into a busy port. The prosperity this trade created can be seen in the wealth of fine Regency and Victorian buildings which still survive, many of them the fashionable town houses of the Pembrokeshire gentry.

Hidden behind these elegant terraces are steep, narrow streets which reveal the medieval origins of the county town, the oldest part of which is the area around the castle hill. The castle itself, said to date from the 12th century, is now an impressive ruined shell. There are three parish churches, of which the 13th-century St. Mary's is the most imposing, while the ruins of a substantial priory can still be seen alongside the river.

Haverfordwest also stands at the heart of the county's road network. At one time this was a source of great benefit to the town, bringing trade to the fairs and markets, while numerous coaching inns were opened to accommodate travellers on the Mail Coach road from Carmarthen to Milford Haven. In more recent years this advantage has turned into a headache, with motorised traffic pouring into the town from all directions and becoming snarled up in the bottleneck of narrow streets. New roads, roundabouts and by-passes have had to be built, and a certain amount of the town's charm and character has been lost as a result.

Researching the history of the town's many pubs presents a few problems, since the early licensing records of the old Borough are lost, with the fortuitous exception of the year 1826. In fact, more is known about the pubs of Cartlett, Prendergast and Merlin's Bridge, much of which once lay outside the Borough boundary and for which the surviving records are more comprehensive. The 1826 records reveal that there were 58 ale-houses in the three parishes of the Borough, to which could be added 12 in Prendergast, four in

Cartlett and a couple in Merlin's Bridge, making the town very well supplied for drinking houses even before the days of the beer-shop. In fact the number of pubs dipped a little in the 1830s as several of the old, narrow streets and 'Rows' were demolished as part of the 'gentrification' of the town following the building of the New Bridge.

The busiest time for the pubs – busier even than market days and fair days – was election time. The Orange party, usually headed by the Owen family of Orielton, used the Castle Inn as its headquarters during the often bitterly-fought campaigns of the 18th and early 19th centuries, while the Blue faction, usually led by the Philipps family of Picton, took over the Mariners'. This election rivalry reached a peak in 1831 when the Whig candidate Col. Robert Fulke Greville and Sir John Owen contested the county seat. According to David Williams, writing in *The Welsh History Review*:

> Conditions had become tumultuous in the streets of Haverfordwest which were packed with Orange (Tory) partisans and their Blue (Whig) opponents. Sir John's headquarters were at the Castle Hotel and Greville's at the Mariners. They were the only tolerable inns in the town.

It was common practice for the opposing parties to treat voters to food and drink at these elections as a means of enticing them into town and into the polling booths. Greville and his supporters took over no fewer than 31 inns and ale-houses where Blue voters (and their wives) could obtain refreshments for free during the two weeks that polling took place. The huge bills that the Blue party ran up in each pub are still preserved in the National Library of Wales, each account carefully itemised down to the last feed of hay for the horses and glass of cider. Some licensees were still petitioning to be paid by both parties three years after the event and Mrs. Jane Thomas of the Fishguard Arms was heard to remark when news spread that one of the candidates was to fight a duel: 'I hope Mr. Greville will not be shot as I will lose my bill'!

Strangely the surviving accounts include two substantial inns which appear nowhere else in the records – the **Apollo** where William Kemp was in charge and the bill came to a staggering £987 7s. 11d. and the **Royal William** run by a Mrs. Thomas who on one day alone provided dinners for 115 visiting voters from different parishes and put up 20 people at a shilling a head.

By 1848 there were 70 inns and ale-houses in the Borough, which by now included Prendergast and Cartlett, while the pubs would have been filled in the 1850s with navvies building the railway and militia men billeted around the town during the Crimean War. A military survey in 1856 reported that Haverfordwest inns were capable of billeting 300 militia and 250 horses, and every night a picket, in the charge of an officer, would go round the town and endeavour to ensure that all the militia men were safely tucked up in their billets by nine o'clock.

In 1856 the following letter appeared in the *Haverfordwest and Milford Haven Telegraph*:

> Passing through the streets of this town the past week, I observed cases of gross inhumanity on the part of public house keepers in selling, or allowing to be sold on their premises, intoxicating drinks to those persons who, having drunk to such an extent are incapable of using themselves properly, thereby (in cases which too often occur) destroying the happiness of their families and ruining both father and children.

Not surprisingly this kind of activity and the great number of pubs in town had prompted a reaction from the temperance movement. Haverfordwest Teetotal Society was established in April 1837 and a Temperance Festival was held in the town each Whitsun. It must have had some effect, because after peaking in the 1850s the number of pubs began to fall slightly in the 1860s to around 60 licensed premises. This figure managed to stay fairly constant over the next few decades, despite the demise of the beer-houses in 1869, and it wasn't until the early years of the 20th century that numbers began noticeably to dwindle. As usual this had quite a lot to do with the Redundancy and Compensation Committee which – while recognising that the many fairs and markets justified the need for a good supply of inns and ale-houses in the town – was obviously concerned at the number of drunks on the street.

An article which appeared in the *South Wales Daily News* in August 1912 described Haverfordwest as 'the most drunken town in Wales' – and produced the statistics to prove it. The newspaper had studied the number of convictions for drunkenness per 10,000 of population and discovered that Haverfordwest topped the table with a score of 172.30, with Carmarthen – famed for its hard-drinking habits – well down the list on 105.66. And with 102 people having been convicted of drunkenness in the town in 1911, there was no getting away from the fact that Haverfordwest with its numerous alehouses was something of a honey-pot for thirsty labourers and farm-hands with a shilling in their pocket and an evening to kill. In her pictorial history of Haverfordwest, Sybil Edwards noted that the Castle Hotel had a hand-drawn trolley which the porter used for moving luggage. 'In the evenings the police would borrow the trolley to pick up drunks and take them to the police station'. By 1921 the town still had 43 public houses for a population of 6,000, a figure which contrasted sharply with Bridgend where 28 pubs served a population of 9,000.

However Haverfordwest made a determined effort to sober up in the 1920s, and while there were 65 cases of drunkenness reported in 1925, this had fallen to 33 in 1927. The number of pubs was dropping as well – there were 38 licensed houses in 1928, plus two licensed clubs – and this figure has continued to diminish ever since.

This book's historic pub crawl starts in Cartlett, which is the name given to the area of Haverfordwest lying to the west of the New Bridge over the Cleddau. For centuries this was the main gateway to Haverfordwest as all road traffic from Narberth and Carmarthen entered the town by way of this little suburb. There was a flour-mill here, while set back from the Cartlett bank of the river stood an impressive string of lime-kilns. Thus the numerous hostelries in the area had to cater for a varied clientele, from well-to-do travellers to lowly boatmen and labourers, but each seems to have found its niche in the market.

This area of town has altered dramatically over the years, first with the opening of the New Bridge in 1833, then with the arrival of the railway 20 years later. But the major changes have taken place over the last 30 years as new roads and a vast roundabout have completely altered the landscape, sweeping away a number of old buildings and altering the course of the Cartlett Brook in the process. The new by-pass also had the effect of taking the passing traffic away from the pubs at the entrance to town, no doubt contributing to the fact that two have since closed.

Arriving in Haverfordwest on the turnpike road from Narberth, the first pub the Victorian traveller would have encountered was the **Foresters' Arms** on the right in Bethany Row, or Foresters' Row as it was once known. David Lewis ran the Foresters' in 1851, John Evans was the landlord in 1854 according to a court case in the *Welshman*, and Benjamin and Mary Jenkins were there from 1858 to 1861, after which it seems to have closed.

Near here was the less than successful **Square and Compass** where William Bowen was the innkeeper in 1820. He changed the name to **Carpenters' Arms** in 1821, but this doesn't seem to have improved matters and the pub closed the following year.

The *Carmarthen Journal* for 1825 mentions a **Masons' Arms** kept by the Griffiths family. However, stonemason James Lamb was landlord of this substantial Cartlett pub from 1826 to 1841 and Thomas Williams had charge in 1844. Thomas Hunt was there throughout the 1850s and early 1860s, shoemaker James Morgan kept the pub from 1867 to 1871 and his widow Mrs. Margaret Morgan was the landlady from 1874 to 1893. Writing in 1925, W.D. Phillips noted:

> The Masons' Arms has always been a well-conducted and popular house, especially with workmen. Mr. James Morgan, a former holder of the licence, was for some years choir leader in Bethesda and a respected citizen, as is Mr. Phillips, the present landlord.

Henry Phillips – the 'respected citizen' – was landlord from 1895 to 1932, his trade being boosted by thirsty residents of the 'dry' Picton estate who made it their local. Mr. and Mrs. Charles Howells took over in the mid 1930s and were still there in 1941 and Teddy Collins was the well-remembered licensee in the 1950s and '60s. Charlie Elliot was in charge in 1984, but the pub closed in the 1990s and is now a shop.

The **Narberth Arms** in Cartlett seems to have been opened in about 1834 by Thomas Thomas, and it was a successful enterprise because he was still pouring the pints in 1852 helped by his wife Jane. The *Pembrokeshire Herald* reported in 1846 that a dinner had been held here, at which the remarkable figure of 509 tradesmen enjoyed a substantial meal. The following week a tea-party took place, this time with 100 females partaking. John Lloyd took over the Narberth Arms in 1853, followed by Benjamin Jones in July 1854. He was still there the following year when he found himself in trouble for refusing to accommodate soldiers from the Royal Artillery who had been billeted on the inn after arriving in the town by train late one night. There is no mention of the inn after this date.

The Masons' Arms may no longer be a pub, but its sign is still in evidence.

It is difficult to determine exactly where the Narberth Arms stood, although it may have been on the junction with the old road to Uzmaston which was rendered impassable by the building of the railway in 1853.

Possibly the Narberth Arms was pulled down during work in connection with the station approach, and it may even have been demolished to make way for the new **Railway Inn**. Work began on this inn in 1862, only for a mysterious fire in June 1863 to destroy the building before it could be opened. According to W.D. Phillips:

> A workman was arraigned on the charge of arson, it being alleged that the premises were wilfully set on fire so as to secure the insurance money.

The inn was subsequently rebuilt as the **Queen's Hotel.** Benjamin Davies was granted a licence in 1866 and celebrated the opening with a banquet for 50 guests the following February. Davies was still the landlord in 1897 and he was also a proud member of the United Kingdom Bill Posting Association, advertising his willingness to carry out 'bill posting in all its branches'. Mrs. Mary Davies was in charge by 1900 and Robert Haslett ran the inn from 1906 to 1920. Cora Reynish was the licensee in the early 1920s and Edward Nutt in charge from 1929 to 1934. It had become a James Williams house by the time Mr. and Mrs. John Thomas were running the Queen's in the late '30s. In 1948 the tenancy was taken over by David Ernest Lewis who had previously run the Prescelly Hotel (now Tafarn Sinc) at Rosebush and also the Picton Inn at Clarbeston Road. Thomas Davies was one of the last to run the Queen's in the 1970s, the name of the inn being perpetuated by the Queen's Function Centre which superseded it.

The Queen's Hotel is on the right and the Masons' Arms on the left of this view of the station approach.
(Picture courtesy of Haverfordwest Reference Library)

For many years the Morgan family pub, the **Carmarthen Arms** seems to have been opened by Thomas Williams who ran the inn from 1816 until the early 1830s. Mary Williams was in charge in 1835 and William Morgan, who was there from 1844 to 1855, must have rubbed his hands in anticipation when it was announced that the railway station was to be built almost on his doorstep. However he didn't live to reap the full benefit of this windfall, dying in 1855, at which time the licence passed to his widow Mrs. Maria Morgan. In 1857 she was called on to provide breakfast for 42 tenants of the Picton estate and other mourners on the occasion of the funeral of Baron Milford, and she was still running the pub ten years later. Her son, another William Morgan, was there from 1871 to 1892 and his widow Mrs. Margaret Morgan was landlady from 1895 until her death, aged 78, in 1924. She was followed by her daughter, Miss Elizabeth Morgan and then Matilda Morgan who seems to have been there until 1949. Alexander Morgan took over, followed by Thomas Murray in the 1950s and former naval commander John Cox and his wife Mary (herself a former officer in the Wrens) in the 1960s and '70s. Ex-footballer John Collins then ran the Carmarthen Arms for several years, but sadly this historic old pub closed in 2005 and there are plans to convert the building into flats.

An early photograph of the Carmarthen Arms, presumably with Margaret Morgan in the doorway.
(Picture courtesy of Mr. Roger Worsley)

The short-lived **Tylers' Arms** seems to have been in this area. John Lewis was the landlord in 1827-1828.

The Carmarthen Arms was still open for business in 2002.

The name of one Cartlett pub has recently, and rather misguidedly, been changed to **Mill-Ford Arms**. This was previously the **Milford Arms** which would have proudly displayed the coat of arms of landowner Lord Milford of Picton Castle on its sign. From 1809 until his death in August 1811 William Powell was the innkeeper; he had formerly been a sergeant in the Royal Pembroke Militia. Maria Powell – presumably his widow – then ran the pub for about four years and the landlord from 1816 until his death in 1832 was Edward Powell. This was a very busy pub during the wild days of the 1831 election; on one day alone Powell provided 154 breakfasts and 240 dinners for voters as well as feeding 101 horses and accommodating 50 lodgers at a shilling a head. He was succeeded by Mary Mathias who was there between 1835 and 1844. Her son Joseph Mathias was licensee in 1850 and Frederick Philp, farmer and innkeeper, was in charge from 1851 to 1861; he too had to provide refreshments on the occasion of the funeral of Baron Milford in 1857 with 55 mourners calling in for breakfast.

By 1865 the landlord was Robert Richards and he was still there in 1876. The Milford was a popular place for farmers to meet up after a day at the mart, and the stabling was regarded as first rate. Mrs. Maria Rowe was land-

Javelin men – escorts to the Assize Judge – outside the Milford Arms in the late 19th century.
(Picture courtesy of Mr. Roger Worsley)

lady from 1881 to 1895, but John James was in charge from 1900 to 1906. William Fitzgerald was landlord from 1910 to 1925 followed by Victor McKenzie, while Arthur and Elizabeth Codling were in charge for much of the 1930s. There were various licensees in 1940s and '50s, while more recent landlords have included Stan Healey and Des Davies. In the 1970s the

The Milford Arms has become the 'Mill-Ford' Arms in recent years.

Milford was acquired by Mr. Jasper Slater of Haverfordwest Coin Machines, since when it has been run successfully by various managers.

Cartlett coachmaker Richard Mathias opened the **Coachmakers' Arms** in 1823 and ran the pub until his death in 1833. The name appears (incorrectly) as the **Mail Coach** in the accounts submitted after the election of 1831, during which fortnight the Blue party ran up a bill of £577 at the inn. Mathias was succeeded by Benjamin Griffiths and then by William Rodney, but the pub had closed by 1844.

In W.D. Phillips' book *Old Haverfordwest* he says that the **Lamb and Flag** was situated on the road 'formerly leading to the level crossing for Uzmaston, now partly covered by Mr. Evan Jones' yard'. The landlady apparently went by the nickname 'Mary Marryboro', but other than that nothing is known. The New Road to Uzmaston, which superseded the one blocked by the railway, still leaves Cartlett by way of Cambrian Place. Local writer Charles Sinnett had this to say in 1976:

> The old **Cambrian** Inn once stood upon the site now occupied by the three centre houses in Cambrian Place which was, in 1829, outside the town. Parts of the old structure can still be seen in a bar window in one of them and a cellar in another. Tom Crunn, the genial landlord, was 'mine host' for a number of years. The river at high tide flowed immediately past its front gate. Its clientele were those of the shipping fraternity who plied their craft up and down the river.

Sadly it has proven impossible to find any mention of this pub or its affable landlord in any of the official records going back to the 1790s, although that does not mean that they did not exist at some stage in the dim and distant past.

Again according to W.D. Phillips, writing in 1925:

> The present Mill Inn is a comparatively modern structure. The original building stood on the ground now covered by the Cheese Factory.

This must have been just over the border in Prendergast parish, which is where the **Mill Inn** appears in 1805, kept by William Ormond. He was still there in 1817, while William Williams kept the pub from 1818 to 1851. Presumably the pub was relocated during the redevelopment of the area during the building of the New Bridge. In May 1837 the freehold of the Mill Inn was up for sale, together with the nearby water-powered corn grist-mill which gave the pub its name. Prospective buyers were informed that the Mill Inn was on the London Road, fronting the approach to the town and the New Bridge. The pub seems to have been bought by William Fortune. Sarah Williams was the licensee from 1855 to 1871, paying a rent of £13 a year. The pub was subsequently kept by her daughter Ann

Cartlett has changed almost beyond recognition since this photograph was taken, with the Mill Inn on the right among the buildings demolished.
(Picture courtesy of Haverfordwest Reference Library)

who married Richard Charles Harding, and he was licensee between 1874 and 1895.

In 1880 the cottages around the Mill Inn were demolished to allow for the widening of the bridge over Cartlett Brook, but the pub survived this early piece of road tampering in the area. At the time this was the registered office of the Gleddy Lodge of Odd Fellows Friendly Society. It was also the regular venue of social events connected with the Scotchwell Harriers, the beagle pack run by Admiral Stokes of Scotchwell House. John Beet, drill instructor to the Pembrokeshire Yeomanry Cavalry, held the licence for a couple of years in the 1890s, as did Robert Thomas. Isaac James was landlord from 1902 to 1914 and Mrs. Margaret A. Jones was the landlady from 1919 to 1923. She was followed by Ishmael James who purchased the freehold from the Picton Estate in 1929 and remained in charge until 1932. From 1933 until the 1960s the licensee was Miss Louisa James whose occasionally foul-mouthed parrot was one of the characters of the town. According to Sybil Edwards:

> Miss James was of Romany origin. Her Gypsy caravan was kept behind the inn and in Romany tradition was burned when she died.

The Mill Inn, too, has perished, disappearing during the building of Freeman's Way in the early 1970s. However it was a much earlier redevelopment of this part of town in the 1830s which led to the opening of the **Salutation**. The building of the New Bridge prompted the opening of this substantial coaching inn, and the first licensee was a horse-trader named Fenwick.

SALUTATION HOTEL,
HAVERFORDWEST,

(Three Minutes' Walk from the Railway Station.)

THE above old-established Hotel, which for many years has been successfully carried on by the late Miss Caroline Reynolds, is now entirely under New Management, and both Private Families and Commercial Gentlemen will find every comfort with prompt attention and moderate charges.

Wines and Spirits of Superior Quality and of the Best Brands. Guinness's Extra Bottled Stout. Bass's Mild and Pale Ale on Draught and in Bottle.

POSTING IN ALL ITS BRANCHES. AN OMNIBUS FROM THE HOTEL MEETS EVERY TRAIN.

310

LEVI HARRIES, Proprietor.

Patronised by H.R.H. the Duke of Edinburgh.

SALUTATION HOTEL & ROYAL POSTING HOUSE, HAVERFORDWEST.

Horses & Carriages of every description. Bus meets every Train.

L. HARRIES, Proprietor.

Top: Levi Harries announces his arrival at the Salutation Hotel in 1892. Bottom: Levi Harries was able to claim royal patronage after supplying a carriage and horses to the Duke of Edinburgh.

In 1838 the Salutation was taken over by Walter Reynolds who declared in an advert in the local paper that he 'hoped to be favoured with that support which his predecessor so liberally received'. He evidently was, because he was still the landlord in 1865. An auctioneer by profession, Reynolds was also a leading figure in the Odd Fellows movement in Haverfordwest, a town councillor, and the official Welsh interpreter for the local courts. The Misses Caroline and Mary Reynolds held sway here from 1868 to 1874, but from 1881 until her death in 1892 Miss Caroline had charge on her own. She was followed by Levi Harries, formerly mine host at the Commercial, who ran the inn until about 1908.

The County Hotel – formerly the Salutation – in 2002.

Prendergast-born journalist William D. Phillips succeeded Harries and was still there in 1912 when the Salutation was described as a 'family and commercial hotel and posting house'. He was followed by Mrs. Mabel Condy and Lewis H. Thomas, while Lavinia Hookway was the licensee from 1922 to 1935. Charles Grey, a former market trader and fruiterer, took over the Salutation in 1940, changed its name to the **County Hote**l and refurbished the building throughout. According to Mr. Bill Richards:

> The County Hotel enjoyed a great vogue during the last war, especially with servicemen. Everybody was certain of a warm welcome there and on Saturday nights in particular the place used to be literally packed to the doors. Rowdyism or bad behaviour of any sort was rare.

Charles Grey remained the proprietor of the County Hotel throughout the 1950s and it was later successfully managed by his two sons, Jim Grey and Douglas Grey – the latter a prominent local councillor. St. David's businessman David Lloyd then had a spell in charge, but the hotel went downhill in the early 1990s being placed in the hands of the receivers and becoming so dilapidated that one councillor was moved to describe it as 'a disgrace to the town'. The County enjoyed a brief renaissance under Rex Woodall but was boarded up again by 1995. Fortunately long-term salvation arrived in the form of local guest house owner William McBride who purchased the Grade II listed building and who has since made good his promise of turning it into a successful family hotel once again.

The **Ship Aground** was a seedy beer-shop near Salutation Square which was kept between 1850 and 1853 by William Williams. It was frequented by 'persons of bad repute' – prostitutes – for which Mr. Williams was fined and admonished by the local magistrates in 1853. (No doubt the building of the railway through Haverfordwest and the presence of scores of navvies had increased the presence of these ladies in the area). Also near here was the **Nelson** which was kept by Henry Lewis. Formerly of the rather more imposing Nelson in Milford Haven (which he was responsible for naming) Lewis was the landlord of its less successful Cartlett namesake in the 1820s.

Between Salutation Square and Bridgend Square was Cartlett Road, better known as 'The Track', on one side of which was the marshy bank of the Cleddau, later drained and landscaped as Jubilee Gardens but now the site of the Riverside shopping development. A row of lime kilns occupied the Prendergast side of The Track, above which ran Prospect Place. On the junction of Prospect Place and Cartlett Road, stood the **Plough and Harrow**, where landlord John Eynon took in lodgers and provided refreshments on behalf of the Blue faction during the 1831 elections and later presented an itemised bill for £318 12s. 5d. John Parry, possibly the former landlord of the Britannia in Dew Street, held the licence from 1835 to 1840 and William Richards was landlord from 1844 until he died 'awfully sudden' in 1849. Reported the local press:

'The Track' in Cartlett was the scene of this protest march opposing the disestablishment of the Church in Wales in 1914. In the background can be seen one of the limekilns on the left with the Plough and Harrow in the centre, partly obscured by the large banner.
(Picture courtesy of Mrs. Sybil Edwards)

A cavalry parade outside the Plough and Harrow in about 1912.
(Picture courtesy of Mr. Roger Worsley)

The deceased, who was a very corpulent man, was attacked by a fit of apoplexy at his own house and died instantly.

His widow Mary Richards held the licence in 1850 and Charles Davies from Llangwm kept the pub between 1851 and 1871, latterly with the help of a domestic servant named Martha Seabourne. Martha herself was landlady from 1874 to 1884, and apparently 'Martha the Plough' tipped the scales at twenty stone. Frank John was the landlord from 1891 to 1906; in 1897 he was fined five shillings for watering down his whisky. His widow Mrs. Martha Ellen John held the licence from 1909 to 1926 followed by Mary Ann John. Charles Earle was there in the 1930s, between stints at the Lamb and the Dragon, but the pub seems to have closed just before the last war and like so much in this area has been demolished.

There were several pubs dotted around here in the days of lime-burning, one of which was the **Three Lamps** which was run by Slebech-born John Prickett in 1851 and by John Davies between 1861 and 1869. Crimea veteran Thomas Phillips ran the **Ivorites' Arms** overlooking the kilns in Prospect Place from 1868 to 1876, having previously run a pub of the same name near the Old Bridge.

And further along, in Jubilee Row, was a pub which went by the name of the **Weary Traveller** when it was run by Joseph and Elizabeth Owen in the early 1840s. It later became the **Limeburners' Arms**, being run by Elizabeth Owen in 1851. She was described as a widow in that year's census, but either her husband must have come back to life or she married a second man of the same name and age, because Joseph and Elizabeth were both alive and well and living at the Limeburners' in 1861.

Described by W.D. Phillips as being 'under the lime kilns', the **Odd Fellows' Arms** beer-house was kept by William Harries between 1844 and 1854. And Phillips also thought that the **Green Dragon** was between the lime kilns and the Old Bridge. This may have been the beer-shop near Cartlett Kilns run by Philip Gibbon in 1865. It was fairly seedy and a regular haunt of prostitutes – or 'nymphs of the pave' as the local press was wont to describe them.

CHAPTER THREE

Haverfordwest

PRENDERGAST

Once a separate village or 'township', Prendergast is an ancient settlement, being the way into town from the north and from the Norman strongholds of Wiston, New Moat and Llawhaden. It has always seen itself as independent from the rest of Haverfordwest and was only incorporated within the Borough as recently as 1840. And while Haverfordwest regularly appointed a town mayor with all due civic pomp and ceremony, the people of Prendergast responded by choosing their own 'mock mayor'. Qualification for the office of Mayor of Prendergast was fairly straightforward. As the *Welshman* newspaper noted in 1911: 'It is said by the older generation that the most drunken man in the village was always elected'.

For much of the 19th century Prendergast was a place to be avoided by respectable citizens. John Brown observed:

> In the early part of the century .... no bailiffs or constables ventured to show their faces there armed with writ or warrant, so debtors and criminals found it a city of refuge.

It was worse after dark, as a newspaper in July 1847 reported:

> On Saturday night last Prendergast Hill was the scene of dreadful fighting from about half past eleven until after one o'clock on Sunday morning without any intermission.

Not only were there plenty of pubs in the area, there were shebeens as well. In 1848, John Thomas was fined for running an unlicensed pub in Prendergast. He only opened on Saturday nights, but the house was a notorious den of iniquity where drinking, fiddle-playing, dancing, card-playing and carousing continued until dawn on Sunday morning. Not surprisingly it was frequented by 'females of questionable character'. And all this occurred before the building of the railway in the early 1850s which saw gangs of navvies regularly descend on Prendergast from the cutting at nearby Shoal's Hook to spend the evening drinking and fighting. One night an unfortunate navvy ended up so drunk that on the return journey to the workers' camp he fell into the cutting and was killed.

Several early Prendergast pubs were short-lived affairs and cannot now be located. These included the **Pelican,** which was run by William Davies in 1805, the **Wheatsheaf** where Benjamin Lewis was landlord in 1819 and the **White Horse** which William Richards ran in 1820. John Myer opened the **Plumbers' Arms** in the early 1830s but it seems to have gone down the drain fairly rapidly, and John Williams ran the **Old Black Horse** between 1828 and 1830. David Morgans was landlord of the **Drovers' Arms** from 1823 to 1826, William Smith kept the **Butchers' Arms** in 1825 and Peter Beezard is recorded as a spirit merchant in Prendergast from 1823 to 1826 and as landlord of the **George** in 1827, after which there is no mention of either. Landlord and landlady of the **New King's Arms** in Prendergast from 1819 to 1830 were William and Mary Ormond, formerly of the Mill Inn. And Philip Roblin was landlord of the **New Inn**, Prendergast from 1805 to 1824.

Near the foot of Prendergast Hill was the **Wellington** where Thomas Rees was landlord from 1815 – the year of Waterloo – to 1819. John

The Wellington on Prendergast Hill, at the foot of Wellington Steps.

Phillips was the long-serving landlord between 1824 and his death in 1859 aged 75. This was one of the 'Blue' pubs during the drawn out election of 1831, and being opposite the polling stations (one for each 'hundred') was invariably filled with supporters of Greville. John Evans kept the pub from 1861 until 1875 followed by his widow Charlotte Evans who was still there in 1880. Thomas Williams, a carpenter from Castlebythe, was landlord for most of the 1880s followed by his son-in-law Charles Adams and then by Charles' widow Mrs. Margaret Adams who was the landlady from 1901 to 1909. William George Evans took over in 1910, but there was no application for a renewal of the licence in February 1911 and the building is now a private house at the foot of Wellington Steps.

Thomas John was landlord of the **Old Inn** in 1805, later running the **Fountain** from 1809 to 1817; it may have been the same place under a different sign. Elizabeth John was in charge from 1818 to 1830 and John Owen kept the Fountain from 1840 to 1844. The inn was the headquarters of a benefit society called the 'Fountain Club', but this ceased to operate in 1845 due to lack of support. The pub may also have closed for a few years, because nothing further is heard of the Fountain until William Morgans became landlord in about 1868. Formerly licensee of the Boot and Shoe on the Cardigan Road, Morgans was a notorious poacher and it took him several attempts to persuade the magistrates (whose rabbits he had probably been stealing) to allow him to run the pub. He was still there in 1881 followed by his daughter Martha J. Morgans in 1884.

James Davies was landlord by 1890, and his career at the pub was nothing if not eventful. He filed for bankruptcy in 1891,

The Fountain stood out from the rest of the street.

subsequently being found guilty of defrauding his creditors, but after completing his six weeks' imprisonment with hard labour he was allowed to resume running the pub. Subsequently the Fountain gained considerable notoriety as a place where Sunday drinkers gathered. The police were fully aware of what was going on but never managed to gather enough evidence to close the place down, despite the efforts of one enterprising sergeant who tried to spy on the comings and goings from the garden of the Chief Constable's house near the castle – with the aid of opera glasses! However in 1894 the Fountain finally lost its licence in bizarre fashion, it being reported to the town's magistrates that landlord Davies 'had been ill-used by members of his family and had left home stating that he was in danger of his life'. In the circumstances, it is hardly surprising that the bench decided not to renew the licence.

There was a second **Old Inn** somewhere in the parish, having been opened in 1827 by William Jenkins. It was taken over the following year by John Lewis but had closed by 1830 and cannot now be identified.

The **Barley Mow** was an ancient Prendergast pub run by the Davies family. David Davies appears to have been the long-serving licensee between 1784 and 1821 (unless it was a father and son of the same name). James Davies had taken over by 1822 and he remained the tenant for some years after the Barley Mow was sold by auction in February 1839. According to W.D. Phillips, writing in 1925:

> The Barley Mow [was] kept by John [sic] Davies and afterwards by Mrs. Jane Owen, the grandmother of Mr. J.O. Morgan, J.P., who was one of the magistrates who, I regret to say, recently voted at the sessions that licensed houses should be closed at the preposterous hour of half past nine!

Jane Owen was landlady of the Barley Mow from 1847 to 1850, but in 1856 there is a newspaper reference to 'the old Barley Mow house'. Unlike most of the pubs in Prendergast it was on the eastern side of the street, in 'Prendergast East'. Also on this side of the street was the house occupied by publican Henry Evans at the time of the 1841 census. Unfortunately the sign of this beer-house isn't recorded (they rarely were) and by 1851 his occupation was given as 'butcher'.

The **Horse and Jockey** in Prendergast was kept by David Owens from 1811 to 1826, and perhaps this later became the **Horse and Groom,** a long-lived pub at 68, Prendergast. The fact that at least four generations of the James family ran this pub was perhaps the reason why the Horse and Groom was always regarded as the least rowdy pub in Prendergast in the days when the area enjoyed its reputation for hard drinking and fighting. From 1835 to 1844 the landlord was Thomas James, followed in 1850 by his widow Elizabeth James. In 1855 she was found dead in her kitchen having expired

The Horse and Groom was regarded as the least rowdy pub in Prendergast.

at the age of 72 from a ruptured blood vessel. A tailor named George James took over, possibly from his mother, and he was still the landlord at the time of his death, aged 82, in 1894. His obituary report stated that apart from a three-month period in London in 1831, he had spent his entire life in the county town. Stonemason William James, son-in-law of the previous landlord, kept the pub from 1899 to 1906, John James was there from 1909 until his death in 1919 and Kate James was the landlady from 1923 to 1940. Since the war the licence changed hands fairly regularly, and among those who ran the pub were Mrs. Margaret Davies, Gilbert John, Benjamin Thomas, Bob Slimmon and Duggie Squirrell. The Horse and Groom closed a few years ago and there were fears for its future as a pub, but happily it was in the process of being reopened as this book was being prepared.

The **Bull**, 'the old village hotel, with good accommodation for man and beast', was for many years the Phillips family inn. The pub was first mentioned in 1825 when James Phillips was the landlord, and he remained there until his death in 1848. As a staunch member of the Loyal Hwlffordd Lodge of the United Ancient Order of Druids, Mr. Phillips was given a ceremonial send-off by his fellow Druids who bore the coffin to the local graveyard. James' widow Ann Phillips was the licensee from 1848 to 1861 and one of their sons – also James Phillips – was the landlord between

*Robert Brown was landlord of the Bull when this photo
was taken in the early 1920s.*
(Picture courtesy of Mr. David Griffiths)

1865 and 1875. (Another son was Crimea War hero Tom Phillips, later licensee of the Ivorites' Arms).

One of the sons of the latter James Phillips was journalist, innkeeper and local historian William D. Phillips, author of *Old Haverfordwest* and a much-quoted source in this book. But it was James' daughter Martha who succeeded her father as licensee of the Bull in 1876. She subsequently married clog-maker Joseph Holt who was landlord in 1880.

Frederick Dennis kept the Bull in 1884, James John was landlord in 1891 and Miss Sarah Griffiths was there at the turn of the century. Miss Mary John ran the pub in 1906 and she was followed by Miss Phoebe John who seems to have become Phoebe Jenkins by 1916. In the early 1920s the landlady was Mrs. Sarah Pyart and she was succeeded briefly by Robert Brown and then by David Davies who kept the Bull for nearly 30 years. At one time the pub boasted a feature unique among town pubs – its own boxing ring upstairs. Charles Burchell took over behind the bar in 1956 and left in 1963 to be succeeded by Ritchie Martin. Herbie John was in charge for about 20 years, followed in turn by his daughter Debbie and son Paul. The Bull is presently run by Grant and Rachel Young who have overseen a number of internal alterations to the old building made necessary by

The Bull in Prendergast as it looked in 2005.

recent licensing and access regulations. This has meant the end of the tiny 'snook' or snug to the right of the front door, but happily many other old features, including the flagstoned floor, have been retained.

A blacksmith named Thomas Lloyd kept a pub called the **Stag and Pheasant** in Prendergast in the early 1840s. It appears from the census that he lived at the 'top end' of the village, near where the road forks for Cardigan or Fishguard, Thomas Davies was the landlord of a Prendergast pub called the **Farmers' Arms** from 1820 to 1826. Jonah Thomas kept a pub of that name from 1850 to 1855, but it may not have been the same place. The 1851 census shows that Thomas lived at Colby Scott, a cluster of properties on the east of the Fishguard Road, just south of the junction with the old road to the Withybush Showground.

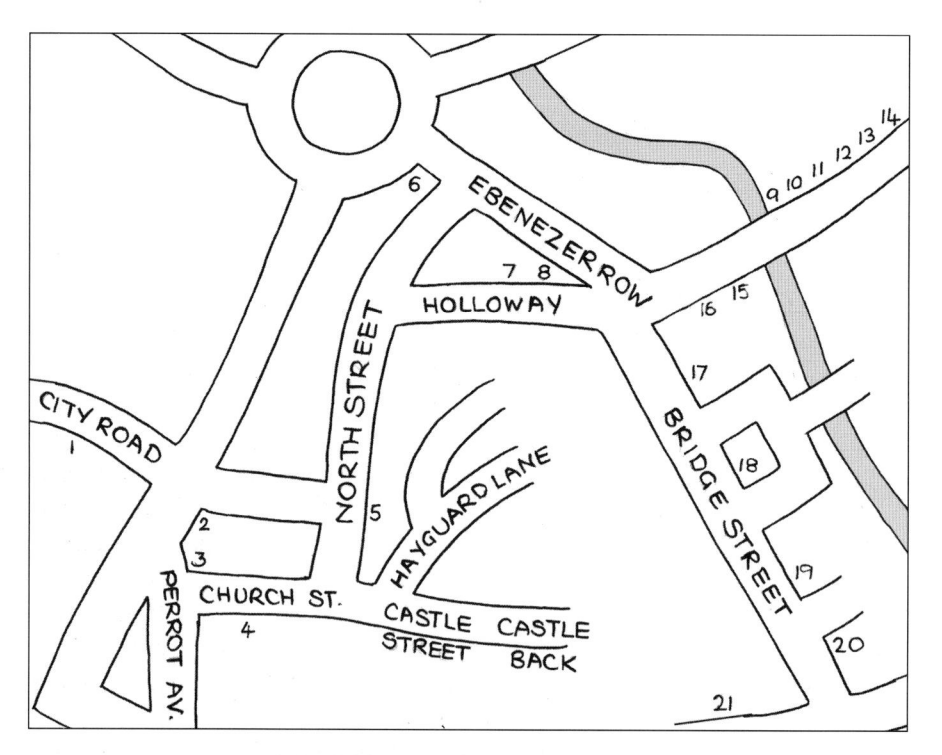

HAVERFORDWEST

OLD BRIDGE, CASTLETON & BRIDGE STREET
CHAPTERS 4, 5 & part 6

1	Turk's Head	12	Cambrian
2	Old St David's Arms	13	Stannard's Wine Vaults
3	Cromwell	14	Crown
4	Angel	15	Fishguard Arms
5	Falcon	16	New Inn
6	Rising Sun	17	Fishguard and Cardigan Arms
7	Farmers' Arms	18	Stag
8	Swan	19	Black Horse
9	Ivorites' Arms	20	Friars' Vaults
10	Commercial	21	Castle Inn
11	Plume and Feathers		

CHAPTER FOUR

Haverfordwest
BRIDGEND, OLD BRIDGE & SWAN SQUARE

Originally a ford at low water, and later the site of a crude wooden bridge, the Old Bridge was built in 1726. For a century it was the main access to the castle town and numerous inns and ale-houses were opened here as a result. It was expected that when the New Bridge was completed a few hundred yards downstream in the 1830s it would hit trade in the Old Bridge area. However the New Bridge was a toll bridge and the Old Bridge was free, so Pembrokeshire's canny farmers carried on crossing the river at the more northerly bridge for many years to come.

The building of the Old Bridge led to the creation of Bridge End Square at the foot of Prendergast Hill – an area largely obliterated by recent road schemes. One survivor, however, is the **Bridge End Inn**, mentioned in 1826 when Thomas James took out an ale-house licence for the inn (see map on page 18). He was still there in 1828, but Thomas Cornock kept the Bridge End during the 1830s. The landlord from 1840 to 1858 was George Davies, during whose time the local lodge of the Foresters' benefit society met at the pub, its members apparently willing to parade around town decked out in green sashes and carrying toy bows and arrows.

Even more bizarre were the members of a benefit society known as the Ancient Order of Druids. In 1844, a parade of these worthies emerged from the lodge room at the Bridge End inn, each of the men 'clothed in long dresses like bed-gowns, reaching down to their feet, with spectacles on their noses and collars round their necks' as the *Pembrokeshire Herald* reported gleefully. Each of the Druids also sported a ridiculous false beard made out of horse-hair. A raucous crowd lined Prendergast Hill, hooting with derision as the column of Druids shuffled solemnly by, two by two, marching to Prendergast Church for a special service.

When George Davies died he was succeeded by his daughter Ann Davies who was licensee from 1861 to 1867. From 1870 until his death in 1885 the licensee was William Milligan Phillips, the local inspector of weights and

The Bridge End Hotel on Bridgend Square in about 1903.
(Picture courtesy of the *Western Telegraph*)

measures, who had married Ann Davies' sister Harriet. (Attentive readers of this series of books will doubtless remember that it was W. Milligan Phillips who handed out bottles of champagne through the window of the Royal Edinburgh in Pembroke Dock at its reopening party in 1882). When Mr. Phillips died at the age of 41 his widow carried on for a few years, while a family named Edwards ran the pub for most of the 1890s.

The Bridge End has survived the devastating changes brought about by road developments.

By 1899 the Bridge End was owned and run by councillor – later alderman – Thomas Henry Thomas who was there until his death in 1931. The pub then changed hands for £1,210, being purchased by David John Griffiths of the Greyhound Hotel who moved to the Bridge End and was still there in 1939. At this time the Bridge End was always busy on mart days and when Haverfordwest AFC were playing on the nearby Bridge Meadow – a fact recognised by the magistrates who grudgingly allowed the pub to stay open longer on these occasions. By the 1950s the ownership of the pub had passed to brewers Hancocks of Cardiff and their tenants included Keri Williams and Dai Jones who took over in 1957 and was there for several years, followed by Bertha Jones. Rocky Thomas was in charge in the 1980s, while present licensee Burt Paterson has been involved with the Bridge End for nearly 20 years – long enough for it to have acquired the nickname 'Burt's Bar'.

There were a couple of other pubs in the Bridge End Square area at one time, about which little is known. The landlord of the **Duke of York** from 1826 to 1830 was a tallow chandler called Francis Lemon. (A chap of that name later kept the New Inn and subsequently ran the town's workhouse). Also hereabouts was the **Royal Oak** which was mentioned in the *Welshman* in 1834. It may well have been kept by William Dultry who is listed as a beer retailer at Bridge End in a trade directory of the time.

On the right-hand side between Bridgend Square and the Old Bridge stood a terrace of some 20 properties facing down the river. Moving along this terrace from the foot of Prendergast Hill, the first pub to be encountered was the **Crown** where Edward Rigards was the landlord from 1805 to 1830. George Rigards seems to have followed him in 1835 but Thomas Mathias kept this popular beer-shop from 1840 until his death in 1869. Known locally as the 'Bumbies and Flies', the Crown closed following Mathias' death, the premises later becoming part of Bland's motor works.

STANNARD'S
WINE & SPIRIT VAULTS
WHOLESALE AND RETAIL,
OLD BRIDGE, HAVERFORDWEST,
ESTABLISHED OVER A CENTURY.

T. E. WILLIAMS

BEGS to announce that he has taken over the above old-established Business, with th old Stock of WINES AND SPIRITS, and by selling the Best Articles hopes t obtain the support received by his predecessor.

AGENT FOR MAX GREGER'S GENUINE HUNGARIAN WINE.

T.E. Williams reopened Stannard's Wine Vaults in about 1890.

Thomas Thomas' name is emblazoned on what was once Stannard's Wine Vaults in about 1900.
(Picture courtesy of Mr. Roger Worsley)

Almost next door was the **Wine and Spirit Stores**, kept by Richard Phillips from the 1820s until his death in 1856. His widow Ann decided not to carry on with the business which was taken over by Alfred Stannard who had previously been in the wine trade in Bristol. It became **Stannard's Wine Vaults** and seems to have possessed an 'on' licence at this time. The building was unoccupied at the time of the 1881 census, Mr. Stannard having relocated to Picton Place, but T.E. Williams reopened the business in the late 1880s, once again as the Wine and Spirit Stores. Thomas Thomas took over in 1897, describing the business in an advert as being 'established over a century'; he was still there in 1902. The Spirit Stores closed in 1916, the local magistrates being informed that the licence had changed hands five times in the previous two years. It was a W.H. George's house by this time, the war making it difficult for the wine company to find a steady tenant.

It is hard to be certain, but it appears there was a corner pub either side of the lane leading to the Bridge Meadow. On the Bridgend Square side was the **Cambrian** run by Thomas 'Wymble' Smith who was there from 1871 until early 1892. Later that year the magistrates refused an application for the licence to be renewed in the name of Mr. C.H. Allen. They closed it down on the basis that it was 'not required and not structurally adapted for a public house'.

In 1856, Col. Robert Greville decided to sell several properties in Haverfordwest in order to raise money for various improvements to the town and docks at Milford Haven. This sale included most of Greville Place – the part of the terrace running from the Old Bridge to the Bridge Meadow lane – and among the lots which went under the hammer were the Plume and Feathers and the Newport Arms. The **Plume and Feathers** seems to have been the older of the two pubs, and William James held the licence in 1826 followed by Mary James who was there in the early 1830s. William Devereux kept the Feathers in the 1840s and Elizabeth Llewellin, who was there in the 1850s, seems to have been the last licensee. According to W.D. Phillips the pub stood on the opposite corner to the Cambrian at the end of Greville Place and later became Tom Phillips the tinman's shop.

John Roblin kept the **Newport Arms** beer-shop from about 1842 to 1851. It stood a few doors along from the Plume and Feathers and seems to have closed following the sale.

Mid-way between the Bridge Meadow entrance and the Old Bridge was the **Commercial** which was recorded in 1823. Thomas Davies was licensee from 1826 until his death in 1835, and he was followed by James and Mary Thomas. Thomas James was the licensee from 1850 until his death in 1861, initially as a tenant of the Greville estate and from the 1856 sale onwards as the freeholder. His widow Elizabeth James carried on until about 1874 with the help of her son Thomas, later to become an alderman of the town and licensee of the Bridge End Inn.

Levi Harries from Lampeter Velfrey kept the Commercial from 1876 to 1892, assisted by his wife Elizabeth and stepdaughter Jane Wilkinson who was barmaid. The inn also ran to an ostler and a coachman at this time and was noted for its

The Commercial in its latter years. The building now forms part of Wilkinson's store.

'clean and comfortable carriages, good horses and steady drivers'. In fact, in 1882 Harries provided the carriage and horses to convey the Duke of Edinburgh from Haverfordwest to St. David's, a fact which the canny landlord duly emblazoned on all his advertisements and business cards for years to come.

Harries then moved to take over the Salutation and Benjamin Davies was there in 1895. John Thomas from Freystrop was in charge in 1899 and his wife Mrs. Ada Thomas held the licence from 1902 to 1910. Tom Jeenes was behind the bar from 1911 to 1916 when the licence passed to a former colliery worker from Aberaman called Charles Perry. Mr. Perry was a lucky chap; having booked his passage from America on the *Lusitania*, he was delayed and narrowly missed the ill-fated liner's final departure from New York. Charles and Emily Hugman ran the pub in the early 1920s followed by Albert Devereaux. Following his departure in 1930 there was a regular turnover of licensees, the Commercial by this time being part of the clutch of pubs under the wing of Castle Square wine and spirit merchant L.H. Thomas. Following Mr. Thomas' death in 1938 the pub was acquired by James Williams of Narberth, and they eventually found a steady tenant in Evan Mathias who was mine host during the 1950s and '60s. Eddie Lucas was one of the last licensees, the pub surviving regular floodings but not the redevelopment of this part of town in the early 1980s. The pub façade has been preserved as part of Wilkinson's store.

Named after a Friendly Society, the **Ivorites' Arms** at the Old Bridge end of the terrace was mentioned in 1847 when William James was the landlord. Mary Owens kept the pub in 1852, while in 1854 the licence passed from Caleb Griffiths to William Jenkins. He died the following year and in October 1856 the pub changed hands again, from Evan Davies to carpenter Thomas Phillips, a member of the Phillips family of the Bull in Prendergast and an uncle of W.D. Phillips.

Reputed to be a 'crack shot', Tom Phillips had volunteered to serve in the Crimea with the Scots Fusiliers and was wounded going up the heights of Alma. He came home to a hero's welcome and was left with a permanent limp and a string of medals which he wore on every possible occasion. Despite his admirable service record, Mr. Phillips was a bit of a rogue; he was fined £1 and bound over to keep the peace in 1866 after admitting a string of offences including drunkenness, riotous conduct and refusing to allow a police officer to enter the pub. At the court hearing one of the Haverfordwest magistrates, Joseph Marychurch, felt moved to comment:

> I have no sympathy whatever with public houses. They are the root of all evil. Disorderly public houses which are kept open all night .... are the greatest evil of this town.

Phillips must have cleaned up his act, because he was still running the Ivorites' when the pub closed in 1868. The Ivorites' became a private house, while Phillips moved to a house above Cartlett Kilns for which he was granted a licence. This he also called the Ivorites' Arms and it is referred to in the chapter on Cartlett.

The **Square and Compass** was one of the main strongholds of the Blue party in the 1831 election, being on Col. Greville's land and handy for the polling stations at the foot of Prendergast Hill. It was described at the time as being 'on the Bridge', but no other information has come to light. Another inn which has proved difficult to pin down was the **Dungleddy** near the Old Bridge. Taken over by Henry Lewis in 1849 it soon disappeared – although there is a suspicion that the Dungleddy and the Ivorites' Arms were one and the same place.

Across the river, the sole survivor of the Old Bridge pubs is the **Fishguard Arms**. Jane Thomas was licensee from 1826 until her death in 1838. In 1834 she went to court to try to recover the cost of drink and lodgings supplied to supporters of the Blue party in the 1831 election – a sum approaching £600. There being some doubt as to whether she had ever been authorised by Greville's campaign managers to offer such free hospitality she lost her case. William Thomas – probably a son – continued running the pub until about 1850.

An early 20th-century view of the Fishguard Arms, with the New Inn to its right.

In 1846 Thomas started a stagecoach service from the inn to Milford Haven – much to the annoyance of local coach builder and operator John Gregory Partridge who already ran a service connecting the King's Arms in Dew Street with Milford Haven and Cardigan. So bitter did this rivalry become that one evening Partridge and his cronies hijacked the Fishguard Arms' coach and hid it in the stable yard of the King's Arms! In retaliation, Thomas together with a gang of friends and relations, lay in wait on the Cardigan Road for the arrival of Partridge's coach. After a furious scrap, the coach was captured and driven in triumph to the Fishguard Arms. 'Partridge's

A early 21st-century view of the Fishguard Arms.

feathers got dreadfully rumpled' reported the *Pembrokeshire Herald* cheerfully, adding that both coaches were eventually returned to their rightful owners.

The meeting place for many years of a benefit society called the Royal Union Club, the Fishguard Arms was extensively repaired and altered in 1849 when new stables were built alongside. Although William Thomas continued to live at the pub until at least 1857, he seems to have taken a back seat in later years, because James Evans and John Roberts are listed as licensees in the 1850s. A newspaper advertisement in 1857 looking for a new tenant stated that the premises were in good condition and that the position of the inn 'on one of the principal thoroughfares of the town' meant that it enjoyed a profitable trade. John Port seems to have answered the call, for he was there in 1858, while Abel Morris was licensee from 1861 to 1871. James Davies had taken over by 1874 and his widow, Mrs. Maria Davies, was landlady between 1880 and 1906. W.F. 'Fred' Rees was landlord from 1909 until his death in 1935 and Mrs. Mary Evans was licensee in the 1940s. Frederick Evans – 'Freddie the Fish' – was there in the 1950s and '60s, while Harry Knight, who was landlord in the 1980s, made a number of structural alterations and improvements to the pub. Other changes have followed in recent years including the addition of a restaurant and beer garden overlooking the river, turning the Fishguard Arms into a thriving town centre pub.

Next door to the Fishguard Arms was the **New Inn** where Richard Carter was the landlord between 1826 and his death in 1829. Mary Carter took over and held the licence until 1844. In 1847 an advert appeared in the *Pembrokeshire Herald* offering the tenancy of:

> The well-known hostelry or public house called the New Inn situate opposite the Swan Inn and on the South side of the Old Bridge.

Francis Lemon was the chap who took over, but only briefly because William Evans kept the pub in the early 1850s and Martha Lewis was in charge in 1858. John Evans ran the New Inn from 1861 until his death in 1867 when his widow Martha took over. The pub seems to have been the property of the trustees of the Perrot Charity and in 1872 it was partially demolished to allow the street to be widened, being rebuilt on a reduced scale. Martha Evans remained in charge until her death in 1894, being succeeded by her son Arthur Evans who was the landlord until 1906. Gilbert Thomas ran the pub from 1909 to 1924 in which year he was twice fined for serving on a Sunday and once for refusing to admit a police constable. Not surprisingly the magistrates referred the New Inn to the Redundancy and Compensation committee the following year.

The former Swan Inn, now sadly demolished.
(Picture courtesy of the Bisley H. Munt Collection)

The town's cattle mart stood across the road for many years until elbowed out by the new traffic scheme. In later years it had its own watering hole, the **Hammer and Gavel**, where auctioneer and estate agent Rowland Jones obtained an 'on' licence in 1969 so that farmers and cattle dealers could have somewhere to socialise following the closure of the Swan.

The **Swan** was a sturdy old coaching inn which faced down Bridge Street and its demolition in 1968 to be replaced by a depressingly featureless retail store was yet another blow inflicted on the town by planners and developers. The *West Wales Guardian* was still lamenting the decision in 1987:

> One of [Haverfordwest's] greatest losses is the Swan Hotel which stood for four centuries on the Swan Square. Built in 1536 it was a splendid old coach house with a busy trade, especially on mart days. It had deep cellars, spacious accommodation including a beautiful oak-panelled lounge, garages, outhouses and stabling. As late as the 1940s it employed not only the normal hotel staff but ostlers and stable boys to look after the horses and carts of farming customers.

Where the date '1536' came from is something of a mystery, but it was certainly a well-established hostelry by 1807 when the following advertisement appeared in the *Cambrian* newspaper:

> For sale.
> All that well-accustomed inn called and known by the name and sign of the Swan Inn, with the brewhouse, back kitchen, two stables, yard and garden, fronting Bridge Street in the parish of St Martin.

According to the notice, the Swan had been 'lately occupied by Mr. Thomas Moore, gardener', but was vacant at that time. Samuel Midgley ran the inn between 1826 and 1839, and shortly after he retired another advert offering the lease appeared stating that the Swan had 'lately been thoroughly new-built'. By now it possessed ten bedrooms, 'extensive stabling, coach-houses and corn-lofts', and was situated at the end of 'one of the greatest thoroughfares of the town'. Benjamin Fawke seems to have taken up the lease, but he soon left because John Gwyther was the 'universally respected' landlord between the 1840s and his death, aged 82, in 1862. During his time a stagecoach left the Swan three times a week, its destination being the Cameron Arms in Swansea, while the Dungleddy Lodge of Ivorites friendly society had a lodge room at the inn.

On Gwyther's death the licence passed to his daughter Miss Esther Gwyther. She was followed during the 1880s by her widowed sister, Mrs. Mary Emment. John Sime was proprietor from 1891 to 1895 followed by Mrs. Sime in 1899. According to W.D. Phillips:

> The Swan Hotel was the resort of the better class farmers, having prime stabling accommodation. The company in the smoke room was very select, being frequented by some of the best-class tradesmen in the town, each of whom had his favourite chair and place on the pipe rack for his church-warden. They were all of the old school and comprised maltsters, chemists, corn merchants, bankers and auctioneers – not forgetting 'The Crumb' – public interpreter and accountant.

Edwin Bowles – the town's former postmaster – took over the inn in 1905, but sadly the 'better class farmers' can't have been free-spending because he was declared bankrupt the following year. Mrs. Adelaide Rees became owner and licensee in about 1910, evidently becoming Mrs. Adelaide Davies in about 1913 and going on to run the Swan until her well-earned retirement in the early 1930s when she installed Emrys Voyle as tenant. The ownership of the inn eventually passed to William Hancock, the Cardiff brewer, and when Emrys Voyle died in 1945 his widow Florence took on the tenancy. The upper floors of the hotel were badly damaged by a fire in 1953 caused by sparks from a chimney igniting the roof timbers. Later that year the inn was taken over by an ex-Navy man by the name of J.F. Horrigan who had previously run the Royal Oak in Pembroke, but he soon shipped out to be followed by Cliff Woozley, Eric Bradley and then Raymond Llewellyn who took over in 1963 and was there for the Swan's swan-song.

CHAPTER FIVE

Haverfordwest

HOLLOWAY, NORTH STREET, QUEEN'S SQUARE & CHURCH STREET

This maze of narrow, ancient streets clusters below the castle and forms the area known as Castleton. Most of the streets wind their way up to Queen's Square which lies between St. Martin's Church and the castle and this may well have been the town's medieval market place. The area immediately around this square was once known as 'Castle Back', although the term seems to have meant different things to different people over the years, covering parts of Queen's Square, North Street and Church Street, thus making any pub described as being 'in Castle Back' difficult to pinpoint.

From Swan Square the main route to the castle was along Holloway, where the **Farmers' Arms** still stands near the foot of the hill. John Harries, who was landlord of the Farmers' in 1826, found himself in trouble with the authorities following the Portfield Fair of that year. According to an official report:

> Harries, Farmers' Arms ... ought to be admonished for aiding the horse dealers to conceal horses and colts sold in and purchased in the fair to evade the payment of tolls.

John Harries remained at the Farmers' until his death in 1860, being a noted horse-breeder and dealer and a hirer out of post horses. Henry Walters from Mathry kept the pub between 1867 and 1876 and his widow Mrs. Ann Walters was landlady from 1881 to 1901. David J. Griffiths held the licence from 1909 to 1914, in which year an application was made for the licence to be transferred to a bookmaker named George Ormond Thomas. He was only granted the licence on condition that he gave up his other occupation. 'I do not regard betting as an honest trade,' said Deputy Chief Constable James, darkly. John John was the landlord from 1916 until his death in 1928. W.D. Phillips, writing in 1925, had this to say about the Farmers':

The Farmers' Arms at the foot of Holloway.

The Farmers' Arms has always been a popular house with country people. It was run by Mrs. Walters for many years. It is now run on the same lines by the present landlord, Mr. Tom [*sic*] John who has a useful side-line in the production of good horse-flesh.

Elizabeth John ran the pub from 1928 to 1941, followed by Mary Ann John and then by Harold John – another good judge of horses – who was there from 1947 to 1962. He was succeeded by Herbert Fair who left in about 1970. At one time a James Williams house, the Farmers' is now part of the Celtic Inns empire.

There were a couple of other pubs in Holloway at one time. The **New Black Horse** was the cumbersome name given to a short-lived ale-house kept in 1844 by William Lloyd who had moved from the Black Horse in nearby Bridge

Street. And between 1826 and 1830 John Griffiths ran the **Fountain** in Gloucester Terrace.

North Street led up to the castle from the medieval North Gate and there was briefly a pub at the foot of the hill called the **North Gate Inn**, run by David Berry in 1814. This area was a centre of the town's lime-burning industry with four kilns in operation for many years. There were several pubs in this narrow lane to slake the thirst of the lime-burners, the longest established being the **Rising Sun** at the bottom of the street, opposite the entrance to Kiln Road. William James held the licence between 1826 and 1835 followed by David Morse in 1840. George Thomas was the landlord from 1850 to 1876 followed by Martha Thomas (either his wife

The former Rising Sun in North Street.

or daughter), while a stonemason called George Christmas was the long-serving innkeeper between 1881 and 1916; he also ran a livery stable alongside the inn. Albert James Devereux held the licence in the early 1920s followed by William Griffiths and then Thomas Raymond. One morning in 1930, the house-keeper at the inn made a shocking discovery when she arrived to do her cleaning duties. Hanging from a beam was the body of Mr. Raymond, a 60-year-old widower. A note found near the body read: 'This is done through slack trade this last two months and worries of different things'. George Ward took over, but the inn was closed and referred for compensation a couple of years later.

In August 1855 Thomas Evans was granted a licence 'for a house in North Street to be called the **Albion Inn**' and the pub was still open in 1858 according to a trade directory. Also in August 1855, Bridget Harries was granted a licence 'for a house in North Street to be called the **Waterford Inn**', but it was a short-lived venture.

Benjamin Lewis was landlord of the **Wheatsheaf** in St. Martin's in 1830, having run a pub of the same name in Prendergast a decade earlier. It may be that the Wheatsheaf was the same place as the **Wheatensheaf** in North Street where Amy Phillips was landlady in 1860. It was a rowdy sort of place when

Thomas Mortimer was behind the bar in the early 1860s, because Tom liked a pint and it wasn't unknown for the evening to end with the landlord scrapping with one or more customers. He lost his licence after one brush too many with the law in 1865 and by 1867 Louisa Lewis was in charge, after which no more is heard of this pub.

Richard Owen was landlord of the **Falcon** in North Street between 1830 and his death in 1833 when he was succeeded by Harriet Owen. It seems likely that the pub name was changed to **Jolly Seaman** by Stephen Sinnett who was a North Street licensee from about 1840 until his death in 1857. The pub then seems to have been closed for a number of years before being reopened in the 1880s as the Falcon by George Woolcock who had moved from the Old St. David's Arms in Tabernacle Row. He was the landlord from 1890 to 1895, being followed by Elizabeth Hughes and Thomas Bill. John Warlow was the landlord from 1903 to 1909 in which year the pub – which stood directly opposite the entrance to Chapel Lane – was closed under the redundancy ruling with £171 compensation going to the Swansea Old Brewery and £19 to the tenant. (It could be that the Wheatensheaf, the Falcon and the Jolly Seamen were three separate establishments; equally they could be three different names for the same pub – the evidence is too sketchy to be certain either way).

THE "FALCON INN" AND PREMISES,

Comprising Brew-house, Stables, and Carthouse, &c., now held by Mr Woolcock, as yearly tenant. Also TWO SMALL COTTAGES occupied by Mr J. Knight and Miss Codd, having a frontage to North Street, and extending to The Hayguard; the total yearly rents being £23 10s.

Sale particulars of the Falcon in 1890.
(Picture courtesy of Pembrokeshire Records Office)

Between 1817 and 1820 there was an ale-house in that vague locality known as Castle Back. This was the **Plaisterers' Arms**, run by James Rowlands. The **Star** was in the area of Castle Back and Queen's Square and Thomas Davies was landlord in the early 1830s. However James Rowlands – presumably the chap mentioned above – was licensee between 1835 and 1851. W.D. Phillips recalled:

> Mr. James Rowlands duplicated his abilities as a landlord with those of an architect, tax assessor and rate collector. By dress and appearance you would have taken him to be a gentleman of the cloth.

The last known landlord of the Star was Thomas Peters who was there in 1861.

The presence of St. Martin's Church must have inspired the local innkeepers to give their pubs religious names, because as well as the Star there was the

Angel in Church Street. Thomas Owens, who was landlord of the Angel from 1835 onwards, was also parish clerk of St. Martin's. Owens died of consumption in 1846, to be followed by his widow Sarah, while the licence passed from William Evans to Thomas Carter in 1851. The pub then changed hands fairly frequently, passing from Thomas Harries to William Lewis and on to Thomas Young, becoming less angelic with each new licensee. Henry Walters, who was there from 1862 to 1867, was once fined for selling beer out of hours on a Sunday, and on another occasion he was charged with 'permitting persons of notoriously bad character to assemble together in his house'. The landlady of the Angel from 1870 to 1881 was Margaret Thomas, an elderly widow from Brawdy, and she seems to have rescued the pub's reputation for a while.

Silvanus Williams was the strikingly-named landlord in 1884 and Henry Maidment was the licensee from 1891 to 1897, during which time he was charged with 'permitting the inn to be the resort of known prostitutes'. A policeman lurking behind a gravestone in St. Martin's churchyard opposite had spotted Milford fishermen 'consorting' with Cassie Summers, Annie Naden and Ellen Mathias, three notorious prostitutes, inside the inn.

From 1899 until his death in 1923 the pub was kept by James Drinning who also worked as a 'plain and ornamental plasterer'. He was the son-in-law of George Woolcock of the Falcon, having married George's daughter Jane, and during his time in charge the Angel was one of the most popular pubs in town. Like many town inns the Angel had stabling at the rear which could only be accessed by means of the front door and passageway beyond. In his book *Changing Face of Haverfordwest*, Bill Richards recalled that one of the Angel's regular customers came to town in a donkey cart and that the donkey always jibbed at entering the front door.

> A Herculean struggle invariably ensued and it usually ended with the farmer seizing the donkey by its front legs and virtually carrying it through the premises. This conflict of wills and display of strength was loudly applauded by the Angel regulars.

Jane Drinning took over from her late husband and ran the Angel until 1931, the inn by this time being owned by wine and spirit merchant Lewis Henry Thomas of Castle Square. Charles Harries was licensee in the 1930s but the death of L.H. Thomas in 1938 seems to have blighted the Angel's prospects and by 1944 it was listed as being vacant. The building was demolished, apparently in the 1950s, and a hulking telephone exchange built on the site.

As usual, a couple of other pubs in St. Martin's parish have defied all efforts to track them down. The **Smiths' Arms** was open between 1826 and 1835 with William Stephens as licensee, and Margaret Tasker was licensee of the **Vine** between 1826 and 1835.

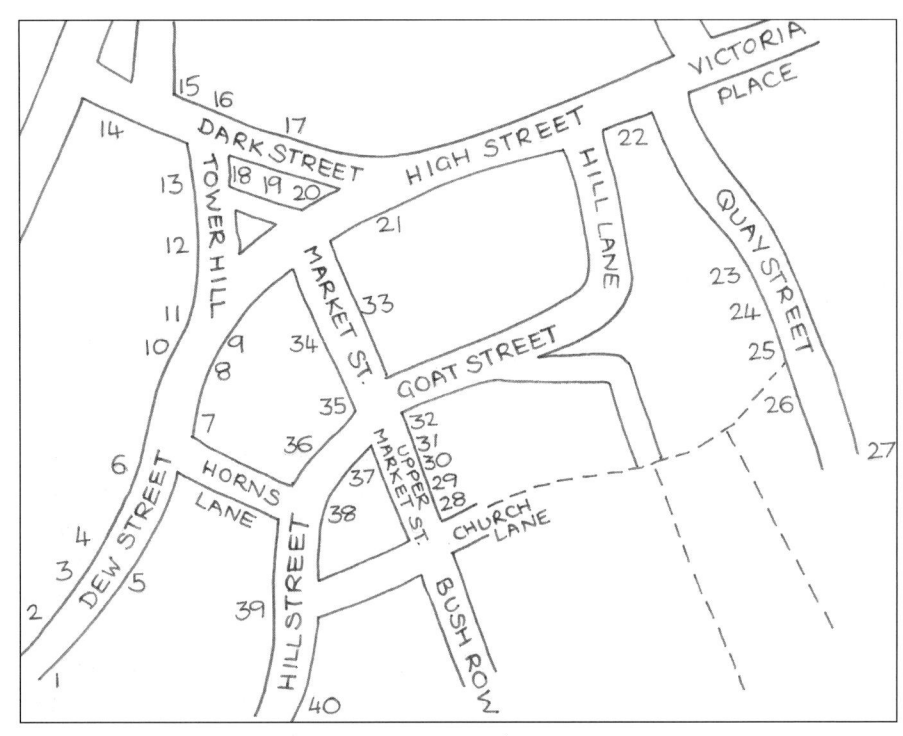

HAVERFORDWEST

HIGH STREET, MARKET STREET & QUAY STREET
CHAPTERS 6 (part) & 7

1	Lamb	22	Old Three Crowns
2	Plasterers' Arms	23	Seaman's Arms
3	Royal Oak	24	Old Seaman's Arms
4	Butchers' Arms	25	Waterman's Arms
5	Black Lion	26	Sailors' Arms
6	King's Arms	27	Bristol Trader
7	Carpenters' Arms	28	Bush
8	White Horse	29	Globe
9	White Lion	30	New Inn
10	Cat and Bagpipes	31	George and Dragon
11	Blue Boar	32	Bell
12	Six Bells	33	George's Inn
13	Three Tuns	34	Market Cellars
14	Hotel Mariners	35	Ivy Bush
15	Greyhound	36	Pembroke Yeoman
16	Gloster		(formerly Upper Three Crowns)
17	Liverpool Arms	37	Fox and Hounds
18	White Hart	38	White Hart
19	Dolphin	39	Ship
20	Coach and Horses	40	Dragon
21	Spirit Vaults		

CHAPTER SIX

Haverfordwest
BRIDGE STREET, CASTLE SQUARE & QUAY STREET

Now a pedestrianised shopping street, Bridge Street was the site of a Dominican friary in medieval times. The 'Black Friars' held all the land between the road and the river, with their monastic buildings being located at the Castle Square end of the lane. Following the dissolution of the monasteries in 1538 the friary was abandoned and its crumbling buildings were eventually demolished, some of the stone being used to build limekilns. The Haverfordwest property of the Black Friars was purchased by the Barlow family, who were becoming extensive landowners in Pembrokeshire, and the whole estate eventually passed to Sir William Hamilton on his marriage to Catherine Barlow. Sir William left the estate to his nephew Charles Greville – the founder of Milford Haven – whose own nephew Col. Robert Greville sold off his properties in Bridge Street in the 1850s and '60s to fund various improvements being planned in Milford.

Whether or not it was some memory of the former friary – monks being expert brewers – is impossible to say, but Bridge Street was for a long time the centre of the town's brewing industry. In 1830 the street boasted five maltsters, while between 1830 and 1840 three of the town's five breweries were here.

As far as pubs are concerned, Bridge Street had quite a few hostelries in the early part of the 19th century, but these gradually dwindled and the street was virtually 'dry' by the mid 1920s. Early pubs about which little is known include the **Ship** where James George was the landlord between 1826 and 1830. He later ran the **Boot and Shoe** in the street, possibly the place kept by Mary George in 1840-41. Mary Mathias was the licensee of the **White Lion** in Bridge Street between 1826 and her death, aged 81, in 1836. She was the oldest publican in the borough at the time. And William Davies ran the street's **Glaziers' Arms** between 1826 and 1830.

Benjamin Phillips held the licence of the **Royal Exchange** in 1826. This Bridge Street hostelry was yet another of the inns where Greville's supporters could enjoy themselves for free during the 1831 election; on 11 May the landlord provided beds for 40 voters and on 14 May he served 221 dinners and 107 breakfasts. One of the longer-lasting pubs in the street was the **Fishguard and Cardigan Arms** which was kept by William Thomas from 1851 to 1864 when maltster and brewer George Green applied for a warrant to have him ejected from the premises. Like most pubs in the street it was on the side nearer the river, in this case towards the Swan Square end.

Described as an inn, but really little more than a pot-house which offered simple lodgings, the **Stag** at 13 Bridge Street only had three bedrooms. Thomas Phillips was innkeeper from 1850 to 1856 in which year the pub was bought from the Greville estate by Mr. Henry Davies. Culm dealer Thomas Nash and his wife Margaret ran the pub from 1858 to 1861 and James Shankland from Laugharne, formerly of the Coach and Horses, kept the inn between 1862 and 1881, by which time he was a 63-year-old widower. Perhaps he married again, because Mrs. Elizabeth Shankland was landlady from 1891 to 1895. Mrs. Mary Davies was the licensee in 1897 before moving to the Royal in Broad Haven.

Sisters Emma and Alice Maybury were running the Stag at the turn of the century, and by 1903 it had had become notorious as a disorderly house. A police constable informed the

The former Stag in Bridge Street is now a shoe shop.

local magistrates that he had seen 'certain young women' in the pub and had called the landlady's attention to their character. He added:

> I went there one night and found there young men whose ages ranged from 16 to 30, and the house was so full that they were like sardines packed in a tin.

Horrified by the thought of all these young men enjoying themselves, the magistrates duly withheld the licence for a time. The pub eventually reopened and George and Florence Edwards were there at some stage before moving to the Hill Arms near Keeston, to be succeeded in turn by John Williams and

Tom Jeenes. By 1912 the Stag seems to have been on its last legs and the owners dropped heavy hints that they would be happy to see it closed under the redundancy ruling. However the authorities were too shrewd for this sort of thing. Realising that the pub was likely to close anyway they decided to avoid paying compensation by letting the Stag die of natural causes, which it did soon afterwards, becoming a grocery shop. It stood on the Old Bridge side of the Hole in the Wall 'drangway' and is now a shoe shop.

The **Black Horse** at 5, Bridge Street seems to have been built on the actual site of the friary of the Dominican Friars, and being the property of the Grevilles was another busy place during the election of 1831. Over the course of 19 days, Greville's supporters ran up a bill for £712 for food, drink and accommodation and also had to pay £14 5s. for breakages. The property extended from Bridge Street down to the Cleddau, and had its own wharf on the river. Mary Perkins held the licence in 1811, landlord William John died in 1825 and Richard English was in charge for the remainder of the 1820s. The Lloyd family then took over, with William Lloyd holding the licence between 1830 and 1842 when he moved to open the New Black Horse round the corner in Holloway.

James Lloyd took over, and in 1848 five hundredweight of contraband tobacco and a package of snuff were discovered concealed in a hay-loft at the inn. It was part of a large consignment of smuggled goods being transported from its landing place on the lonely north Pembrokeshire coast to the lucrative markets of Bristol. Landlord Lloyd naturally denied all knowledge of the smuggled goods, while the bootlegger made good his escape disguised as a hawker. Mr. Lloyd remained the licensee until 1850, while William Bean, George Charles, Elizabeth Lewis and George Phillips all took a turn at running the pub in the 1850s, at which time the property included warehouses, stables and stable-yard, a coach house and skittle alley. When a chunk of Greville's Haverfordwest estate was sold in 1861, Lot 1 was The Black Horse and the surrounding properties.

BLACK HORSE HOTEL,
BRIDGE STREET, HAVERFORDWEST.

JAMES DAVIES

Begs to return his sincere thanks to the Public for the kind patronage accorded to him since he commenced Business at the above old-established Inn. The Stabling Accommodation consists of STALLS, LOOSE BOXES, &c., with a good Yard adjoining Castle Square. HAY AND CORN OF THE BEST QUALITY KEPT.

Fine hay and corn were available at the Black Horse.

Licensee in the early 1870s was Jim Evans and lodging with him was his young nephew William Evans, an apprentice grocer from the Gwaun Valley. William later went on to earn fame and fortune in the Rhondda Valleys as one of the founders of the Thomas and Evans string of department stores and also as the man who launched the Corona soft drinks empire.

Mary Thomas ran the Black Horse from 1876 to 1880 and Seth Evans ran the pub in the 1880s, during which time he took out an advertisement in the local press in which he thanked his customers for the kind way in which they patronised his mowing machine and to advise them that he had now purchased 'an expensive reaping machine' which he was prepared to hire out during the forthcoming harvest. 'A ten acre field down in one day – distance no object', he declared.

There are glasses of a different sort at the Black Horse these days – part of the old pub is an optician's shop.

James Davies was in charge from 1895 to 1900, followed in turn by Charles Morris, Alfred Friend and Harry Griffiths. At this time the Black Horse was very popular with visiting farmers. It had nine rooms upstairs and six downstairs, one of which could accommodate 150 people. Stabling facilities were the largest in town and included 15 horse boxes where stallions would be housed during the siring season. Harry Griffiths was succeeded in 1912 by John and Mary Powell who still ran the pub in 1918 when it passed to Martin Alderwick who ran it for a couple of years before deciding not to renew the licence in 1921, apparently weary at having to fight to keep the pub open in the face of constant pressure from the authorities who wanted to reduce the number of pubs in the area. Now split into two, the building houses Specsavers and a charity shop, while an archway leads through to an arcade of shops where the sire horses were once stabled.

In May, 1751, a coasting vessel called the *Priscilla* sailed from Haverfordwest to Bristol, probably laden with Pembrokeshire coal. However the skipper of the vessel was also charged with making a number of special purchases for various customers in Haverfordwest – a linnet cage, oil of turpentine, scales for weighing gold. Among these special purchases it is recorded that the skipper was under instructions to buy 8lb. of tea for 'Mr. Davies of the **Ship and Castle**, Haverfordwest'. According to a mortgage document of 1758, which referred to a 'dwelling house, stables, yard and garden called the Ship and Castle Inn', it was in St. Martin's parish, so it may have been in the Bridge Street / Castle Square area.

James Jenkins 'Jimmy Thruppenny' established a business as a wine and spirit merchant on Castle Square in 1830. It was later run by his son John Jenkins and then, from 1876, by Mrs. M.B. Jenkins. By 1880 alderman Thomas James had taken over and he ran the business during the 1890s. He was succeeded by Lewis Henry Thomas, one of the leading freemasons in Wales, who ran the wine and spirits business at 5-7, Castle Square from 1899 until his death in January 1938, also overseeing a small string of licensed premises in the town. On his death the Castle Square business was taken over by Jean Thompson who gave it the name of **Friars' Vaults**. By 1955 the building had become part of the W.H. George empire and the firm

---

W. H. GEORGE & SON

~

DEALERS IN BEERS, WINES AND SPIRITS

~

BOTTLERS OF BASS AND WORTHINGTON ALES AND GUINNESS STOUT

~

5 Castle Square, HAVERFORDWEST

(Telephone 53) and

Park St., FISHGUARD

(Telephone 3221).

W.H. George made Castle Square its centre of operations.

later transferred most of its operations to Castle Square from the less convenient premises in Market Street.

When George's was sold to Allied Breweries the building – which seems to have held an on-licence at various times in the past – was converted into a smart and attractive town centre pub.

The **Castle Inn** on Castle Square is a well-established commercial and coaching inn which was for many years the watering hole of choice for the local gentry when they visited town. It is thought to date from the early 18th century and may have been built for the land-owning Barlow family of Slebech. In 1797 the inn played a role in the

The Friars Vaults was converted into an out-and-out pub when W.H. George was taken over.

episode known as 'the last invasion of Britain' when a motley force of Frenchmen landed near Fishguard. Plans to defeat the invaders were thrashed out at a hurriedly convened meeting at the Castle Inn, while the captured French officers were later confined at the inn overnight on their way to prison in Carmarthen. Landlord at the time was David Rees, famed as a breeder of prize Leicestershire rams. In July 1805, 'sensibly impressed with gratitude for the very liberal support he has experienced for a series of years from a generous public', Mr. Rees announced his retirement in the *Cambrian* newspaper. In the same issue, Lewis Pugh:

Castle Square showing the Castle Hotel before the right-hand part was demolished to make way for Woolworths.
(Picture courtesy of Sybil Edwards)

Begs leave to inform the Nobility, Gentry and Public that he has taken and entered on the above House and has purchased the whole of the Carriages, Stock of Excellent Old Wines and Spirits with every fixture and accommodation in that extensive concern which he has, and will still continue to improve.

In 1812 the inn was the venue for a gathering of the political supporters of John Owen of Orielton. 'A sumptuous dinner was afterwards served up in Mr. Pugh's usual style of elegant accommodation' stated the *Carmarthen Journal*. The Castle was also the meeting place of the town's freemasons in the early 19th century, while to celebrate the coronation of George IV in 1821, local member of parliament W.H. Scourfield dined at the Castle Inn with a number of notables and gentry. And to liven up the celebrations in the town he ordered several barrels of beer to be broached in Castle Square so that everyone could toast the new monarch.

Lewis Pugh remained landlord until his death, aged 74, in 1832. Sarah Pugh took over and ran the inn until her retirement in February 1837. Advertisements in the local press then appeared stating that Edward Pritchard of the Nelson in Milford Haven was pleased to announce that he had taken over the Castle as well; however a month later another advert appeared

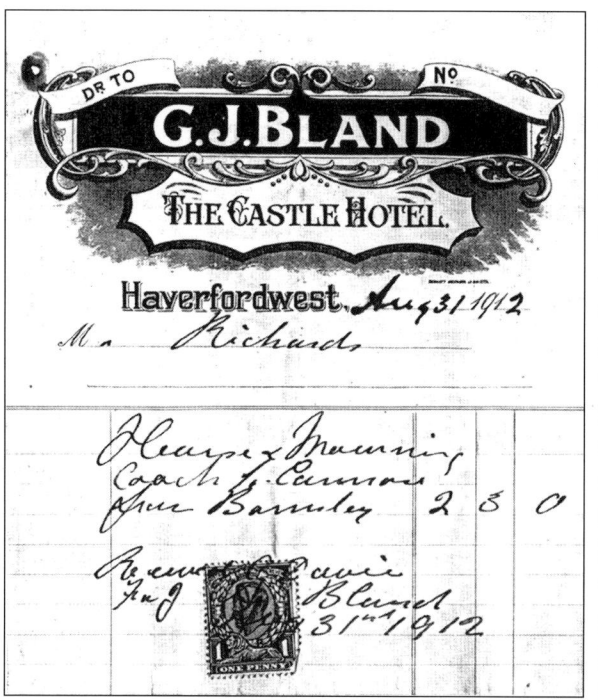

The Bland family were carriage operators as well as hotel proprietors – and they could even provide a horse-drawn hearse and a coach for the mourners.
(Picture courtesy of Mrs. Elfrida Jones)

stating that the deal had fallen through. Members of the Pugh family thus continued to run the inn for another ten years; the hotel boasted a 'Repository of Arts' at this time – evidently a kind of art gallery – and the mail coach departed at the rather uncivilised time of 3 am each day. When the Pughs finally left the Castle, it was purchased by Thomas Philpott who was licensee from 1849 until his death in 1855. Subsequently his widow Maria Philpott carried on running the Castle until 1875, for much of the time overseeing the Mariners' as well. Her habit of keeping half-a-dozen pigs in a sty at the back of the Castle Inn led to her falling foul of the local authorities in 1860 after neighbours complained about the smell.

Proprietors in 1881 were G.J. Bland and Sons while Elizabeth Ellis acted as hotel manageress. The staff at the time included 16-year-old Edward Morse who was employed as a billiards marker. George John Bland was an enterprising local businessman whose empire grew from running a fleet of waggons and carriages to becoming a contractor for the Great Western Railway, a carriage builder and hotel proprietor and later a pioneer of the motor trade. He seems to have run the hotel himself from 1884 to 1909, and his daughter Mrs. Louisa Hedley was the licensee from 1910 until her death in 1923 when Mrs. Rose Rees became the manageress, a position she held for the next ten years. The Bland family still owned the hotel at this time (and used part of it as a car showroom). Louise Anderson held the licence for a further ten years before moving to the Mariners' and Mrs. Lily Jenkins was in charge from 1944 to 1959.

At around this time there were fears that the whole building might be pulled down and replaced by a Woolworths store. Eventually a compromise was reached, with half the building remaining as an inn and half being turned into a shop. Licensee in the early 1960s was Frank Thomas, and when he left in 1965 a publican from Gowerton applied to the magistrates for a protection order. The police objected, however, since the applicant had picked up a couple of black marks against his name while running the Gowerton establishment. Describing the Castle Inn, Chief Inspector Jones explained:

> This is a public house which is frequented mostly by naval personnel. On Saturday nights it is absolutely lifting with sailors, and a certain type of female goes there as well. Unless we have a strong, firm licensee we will be courting trouble.

The magistrates took due note and refused the application, looking more favourably on a subsequent application by Eifion Morgan and he was there for a number of years before moving to the Broad Haven Hotel. For a period in the 1980s the Castle Hotel was the social headquarters of Haverfordwest Rugby Club which was in the process of moving grounds, after which it became part of the portfolio of pubs being assembled by Mr. Jasper Slater of Haverfordwest Coin Machines. His daughter Juliet Llewellyn has been the licensee since 1990.

In July 1758, Sir William Owen of

The half of the old Castle Inn that remains a hotel.

*The attractive jumble of old houses and warehouses
which once made up Quay Street.*
(Picture courtesy of Haverfordwest Reference Library)

Land-shipping who was 'His Majesty's Lieutenant for the County of Pembroke and the Town and County of Haverfordwest', gave notice of a meeting to be held at the **Angel Inn**, Haverfordwest, at '10 o'c. in the forenoon' of August 15 following. This meeting was open to all men 'qualified according to the several acts to serve in the Militia of the said County and Town, and willing to accept commissions for that purpose'. Three years later the inn was the venue for the auction of Pembrokeshire property belonging to Sir John Pakington and it was also a regular meeting place of the Society of Sea Serjeants.

The Angel was the victim of an 18th-century Haverfordwest wit and poet, sadly (though perhaps wisely) anonymous:

> Of the Popes I remember it said since a child,
> All Innocents cruel, all the Leos were mild,
> Which remark with two Houses in Ha'rford will suit,
> For the Bear is obliging, the Angel's a brute.

The names of the early, brutish licensees are unknown, although in 1823 the *Carmarthen Journal* reported the death of a Mrs. Davies, formerly of the Angel, Haverfordwest, aged 93. Sarah Roberts held the licence in 1826 and John Morgan kept the inn in 1830. Where the Angel stood is something of a mystery. A trade directory for 1830 says Bridge Street while a draft indenture dated 1849 refers to 'a messuage built on the site of the Angel Inn, situate in High Street'. Possibly it was at the junction of Bridge Street and High Street – Castle Square – and disappeared during the redevelopments of the early 1830s.

In 1826 Benjamin Lewis is recorded as being licensee of the **Rifleman** – not the much more recent pub on St. Thomas' Green. There is a suggestion that this was also in the area of Castle Square, a place where soldiers and militia regularly mustered.

Formerly known as Ship Street, Quay Street was once the 'sailortown' of Haverfordwest, a narrow, dimly-lit jumble of lodging houses, cottages, warehouses, beer-houses, and ships' stores. The arrival of the railway marked the beginning of the end for Haverfordwest as a port, and out of six pubs in the street in the 1830s, only one was still open in 1900. Even so, Quay Street remained a fairly insalubrious thoroughfare well into the last century; in 1910 it was reported that 'a house of ill-fame' had been discovered there, while according to one source: 'It was an area which the honest citizens visited with apprehension'. Since the 1930s Quay Street has undergone a gradual transformation, with many of the older buildings being removed and the street widened. Happily many of the old warehouses still stand, recalling the great days of the coasting trade.

Quay Street has always been divided into two parishes; from High Street to the flight of steps leading up to the Parade is within the boundary of St. Mary's, beyond that is St. Thomas'. On the right-hand side, moving along from High Street, were two pubs side by side. Carpenter Thomas Griffiths and his wife Frances were licensees of the **Seaman's Arms** from 1840 to 1861 and David Lewis kept the pub in 1867. In 1870 his widow Ann Lewis was granted permission for a licence in respect of the building which stood next door, on the Castle Square side. Having moved house, Mrs. Lewis was still in charge in 1876, but John and Sarah Ambrey were there in the early 1880s before moving to the Horse and Jockey in Portfield. Charles Taylor kept the pub from 1884 to 1892 and Sarah Taylor was there in 1893. In 1894 the pub's licence was not renewed following objections from Haverfordwest Temperance Association and the police who described the premises as 'defective'. An attempt to reopen the house the following year failed.

When Ann Lewis decamped from the original Seaman's Arms, the pub remained open as the **Old Seaman's Arms**. George and Eliza James were in charge in 1871 but he died the following year and it was the widowed Eliza – helped by her son Tom – who ran the pub for the next 20 years. In

1890 Mrs. James found herself before the town's magistrates charged with keeping her pub open on three consecutive Sundays. Police, watching from a warehouse opposite, counted 73 customers on the first Sunday, 59 on the second and 82 on the third. However, the magistrates were in lenient mood and fined her just £1 for each Sunday. The real hammer-blow fell the following year when they refused to renew Mrs. James' licence and the pub closed.

In 1843, Thomas Jenkins of the **Waterman's Arms** shot dead a dolphin, 11 feet in length, which had made the mistake of venturing upriver to Haverfordwest and had become trapped between the bridges. Mr. Jenkins had run this beer-shop in Quay Street since 1835, but by 1844 the Waterman's was being kept by George Hassell. Evan Davies took over in 1855, handing on the following year to David Lewis who was still there in 1861. The Waterman's appears to have stood about four doors along from the Old Seaman's Arms, close to the steps, and must have closed in the 1860s when landlord Lewis move to the Seaman's Arms. The terrace containing these three pubs has been demolished and the building housing Vaughan's Radio now occupies much of the site.

Just beyond the flight of steps leading up to the Parade, a few ruined stone walls are all that remain of the **Sailors' Arms**. This beer shop was run for many years by Peter Perkins, a master mariner from Trefin, and his wife Elizabeth. In fact 'Betty Perks' was often called upon to take charge while her husband ploughed the main. They were in charge from 1840 to 1867 and Henry Lewis was there until his death in 1872. According to W.D. Phillips (who mistakenly calls it 'Jolly Sailor'), the ale-house sold home-brewed for tuppence a pint – 'plenty for the money but quality not A1'. Popular at one time with lightermen, the pub seems to have closed in the 1870s.

The **Union Tavern** appears to have been right on the Quay. An account for over £550 was sent from this pub for refreshments and accommodation during the election in May 1831. The long-serving Thomas Richards held the licence between 1826 and 1851, while Martha Richards carried on for a few years following his death. She was described as 'retired victualler' in the census of 1861.

The **Bristol Trader** still stands on the Quay, a pleasant reminder of the old coastal trading days. Thomas Llewhellin was landlord in the 1820s followed by the remarkable Mary Llewhellin in about 1830. She ran the Trader right through to 1870, also carrying on a successful business as a coal merchant. In 1871 she finally handed over duties to William Skinner, staying on in the pub as a lodger until her death the following year at the age of 90. It was reported in the local press that she had been 'for 57 years

The Bristol Trader has a fine quayside setting.

landlady at the Bristol Trader', which would mean that the Llewhellins had been there since about 1815.

Skinner was subsequently granted a 30-year lease on the property by the Haverfordwest Corporation, which owned the building. He ran the pub until his death in 1905, being famed locally as a first-rate shot, a keen angler and noted dog-breeder. He was succeeded by his widow Jane.

Thomas Victor Davies was the landlord between 1914 and his death in 1930 when the licence passed to Margaret Davies who remained in charge for a further five years. The licence changed hands regularly during the next 15 years, before Hilda Thomas steadied the ship by taking the helm for most of the 1950s. In 1959 Mrs. Doris 'Monté' Manson arrived from running the Sailor's Safety in Dinas and set about smartening up the place. As a result the 'Trader' became the first pub in town to have carpet on the floor rather than sawdust and bare boards – a change which caused problems at first, since the cigarette-smoking regulars took a long time to get out of the habit of dropping their cigarette-ends on the floor and stubbing them out with a foot! More changes have taken place recently under licensee Brian Harries, including the opening of an attractive restaurant extension.

Of the other pubs in Quay Street or fronting the Quay itself little is known. The **Hope and Anchor** in Quay Street is recorded in 1799, while Benjamin Evans kept the **Crown** from 1826 until 1844. John Jenkins was in charge of **Porters' Hall** between 1826 and 1830, and George Eynon ran the **Red Lion** in 1844. There was also a pub called the **Golden Slipper** in Quay Street where William Pritchard was the landlord in 1830. It is hard to imagine grizzled wharf-rats sinking quarts of ale in a pot-house called the Golden Slipper, which may help to explain why the pub didn't last very long. (There is a suggestion that this pub changed its name to become the Sailors' Arms, but this has been impossible to confirm).

In recent years Quay Street has rather bucked the trend for pub closures in the town. Although the **Barking Shark** has been and gone, there are currently two new pubs in the street, **The Quay** and **Blayney's Irish Bar.**

CHAPTER SEVEN

Haverfordwest
HIGH STREET & DEW STREET

Before the building of the New Bridge in the 1830s, pedestrians were able to cross the river at this point by means of a rather rickety wooden drawbridge. To reach this bridge meant passing through a riverside slum area along a muddy track known as Drawbridge Lane. This lane had at least one pub, the **Sawyers' Arms** which flourished briefly in the late 1820s and '30s – when it appears to have been kept by John Thomas – but seems to have closed soon afterwards. No doubt it was pulled down during the major redevelopment of this part of town in the 1830s which included the building of the New Bridge and the impressive terraces of Victoria Place and Picton Place which combined to create a grand entry into the town's High Street.

Originally a residential thoroughfare, High Street has never been very well served with pubs, and until 150 years ago it had very few businesses either. In the early 1800s, according to one account:

> From the top of King Street [Hill Street] to the old Drawbridge was all private residences and town houses – there were no businesses at all.

One exception was the **Old Three Crowns** on the corner of Quay Street and what was originally one of the town 'Rows'. Before the redevelopment of the 1830s there was an island of houses in the middle of High Street at this point, with two narrow streets on either side called Front Short Row and Back Short Row. These inconveniently narrow 'drangways' vanished when the island houses were demolished and the elegant Shire Hall was built next door to the pub.

Jane Griffiths held the licence of the Old (or 'Lower') Three Crowns in 1826 followed by William Griffiths who died in 1830 and Thomas Griffith who was in charge between 1835 and 1852. A coal and hay merchant from Neath named Henry Evans was landlord from 1858 to 1885, while William Morgan was running the pub and the coal-yard in 1886. Robert Butler Thomas held the licence from 1891 to 1897 before moving to take over the

A recent view of the Old Three Crowns with the Shire Hall alongside.

Mill Inn in Cartlett, and Thomas H.B. James – son of Elizabeth James from the Old Seaman's Arms in Quay Street – was in charge from 1897 to 1909.

In 1911 Mrs. Phoebe Maurice took over the licence and ran the pub for a few years, while Francis Morris was the landlord from 1919 to 1933 followed by Mrs. May Morris. Subsequent licensees included Minnie Cecilia Thomas, F.J. Setterfield and David Jones, with Maurice Cooke – who took charge in

1957 – being the longest serving and by far the best remembered. The pub was a warren of small rooms in his day and was so popular with solicitors and court officials from the adjacent Shire Hall that it earned the nickname of 'Court Number Three'. This fine old town centre pub went through an unhappy patch in the late 1990s with a couple of changes of name and 'theme'– including a bizarre interlude as the American-styled **Times Square**. Fortunately it has since been attractively restored and the original name (although with an 'olde' affectation) is back on the sign.

Although it never appears to have held an 'on' licence, the business run by Carew-born George Palmer and Son at 36 High Street had a big influence on the town's licensed trade. Wine and brandy merchants from 1856 until after the First World War, the Palmers made their name as whisky blenders and liqueur importers, supplying the inns of the town and further afield. The company also built up a small portfolio of tied houses in the town, including the Upper Three Crowns and the Ivy Cottage.

The Spirit Vaults can be seen on the right of this old postcard view.

On the left-hand side, opposite the top of the steps leading to Dark Street, were the **Spirit Vaults**. John Gibbs was a wine and brandy merchant in Haverfordwest in 1811 and seems to have established a family dynasty because Charles Gibbs was both a saddler and spirit dealer in the 1830s and '40s. Initially he had business premises in Market Street and High Street, but eventually he made the latter his centre of operations and he was still in business in 1858. Elizabeth Gibbs – better known as Bridget – was in charge from

1861 to 1875, and as W.D. Phillips recorded, 'Gibbs' Gin Shop' was one of the social centres of the town.

> The bar was divided into two parts, one division of which was called 'The House of Lords' and the other 'The House of Commons'. Miss Gibbs catered for solids as well as liquids, and for a small sum you would be served with Crabb's Ship Biscuits and some prime Stilton cheese, with a variety of home-made pickle.

The Spirit Vaults seems to have been closed for a few years around 1880, but William Devonald Edwards was in charge from 1891 to 1895. R.H. Jones was there in 1909 and Mrs. Beatrice Jones held the licence in 1910. In 1911 a commercial traveller from Abertillery called Essex Thomas took over the licence but he didn't last long and neither did William John nor Robert Richards. The Spirit Vaults was referred for compensation in 1916, by which time the business was being managed by John King on behalf of Narberth wine merchants James Williams. They were finding it difficult to obtain tenants due to the war, although even before that the tenancy had changed with alarming regularity. The building was subsequently taken over by Octavius 'Ocky' White and became the launch-pad for the successful family business which still continues in Bridge Street.

Cleverly-named but short-lived, the **Yard of Ale** was set back from the High Street in a courtyard. It was open for a few years in the 1970s.

If the lower reaches of High Street were relatively bereft of watering holes, all that changed as one reached St. Mary's Church. This was where the town's twice-weekly market was held – one of the 'greatest and plentifullest' markets in Wales according to the Elizabethan writer George Owen. This open-air market must have been a chaotic affair, crowding the narrow streets around the church with stalls selling meat, fish, poultry, butter and woollen goods. The corn market was here; there was a meat shambles underneath the Guildhall (which stood at the junction of High Street and St. Mary's Street), while numerous butchers were to be found displaying and selling their wares in the churchyard itself. And as the market grew in stature over the years, so did the variety of goods available, with traders offering wine, spirits and salt offloaded at the Haverfordwest quays, along with bales of linen and locally-produced goods such as clothing, boots and shoes, gloves and saddles.

Also in this busy part of town could be found the town stocks which stood alongside the wall of St. Mary's Church in Pillory Street (now part of High Street). In 1845 a clogmaker and notorious drunkard named Enoch John was given six hours in the stocks. Reported the *Welshman*:

> Hundreds of persons visited the spot. The poor creature was almost insensible all the time. He sat with his arms folded and a dirty pipe in his mouth.

By the 1820s the market stalls and 'standings' in the streets were becoming a nuisance, especially as they tended to block the thoroughfare when the gentry in their carriages were trying to get past. It was therefore decided to build a covered meat and provision market half way up the steep street previously known as Shoemakers' Street but which later came to be called Market Street. A butter and fish market was subsequently built a little further up High Street, at the junction with Tower Hill.

And as with all market areas, this part of town was well served with hostelries of every kind. One of these was the **Fleece** which can be seen in the background of a drawing of the Guildhall probably made in 1822 by Thomas Ellis. The *Carmarthen Journal* of July 1820 reported the death of a Mrs. Summers, 'for many years the respectable landlady of the Fleece, Haverfordwest'. She was succeeded by Sarah Williams and in 1822, members of the Waterloo Club met at the Fleece to drink to the memory of their 'valourous and deeply-lamented countryman, Gen. Picton'. Sarah Williams left in 1824 to run the King's Arms in Dew Street and there are no further references to the Fleece in the records.

The sign of The Fleece is visible in the centre of this drawing of the Guildhall.
(Picture courtesy of Mr. John Warren)

Another pub which stood near here was the **Haverfordwest Arms**, described as 'opposite St. Mary's Church' in the *Carmarthen Journal* of November 1819. Landlord from 1819 to 1830 was Moses Phillips who advertised 'an ordinary every day at two-o-clock'. Two other pubs were recorded hereabouts in 1826, the **New Market** run by John Watts and the **Pelican** where John Allen was the landlord.

High Street becomes Dew Street above the junction with Tower Hill, the name perhaps deriving from Dewi, the Welsh patron saint. The upper part of the street – above the King's Arms – was once known as Shut Street, from the chute or conduit which carried water from the springs and reservoir in Fountains Row down to the properties in High Street. More than 20 pubs have been recorded in hard-drinking Dew Street, while to balance things slightly the anti-drink Rechabites also had their meeting room here. *The History of Haverfordwest and Some Pembrokeshire Parishes* painted a vivid picture of how the street might have appeared in mid-Victorian times:

> Almost all the house in this part are miserable thatched hovels, with manure heaps to front ... Our progress, as we keep to the line of houses, is constantly interrupted by a horse bench outside of every public house. These latter are very numerous, and from their doors stream forth an everlasting smell of new drink, for the inmates are constantly brewing. A publican, being asked concerning the age of the ale he was supplying to his customers, is said to have replied that it would be a fortnight old the following Thursday week ...

The lower part of Dew Street, near the top of Tower Hill, was once the site of the town's West Gate, but this area has been continually redeveloped over the years. The fishmarket has gone, while various schools – including the Grammar School which was built in the 1850s – have also disappeared, the County Library being built in their stead. A couple of notable hostelries have vanished in the course of the numerous changes, one of which was the **Blue Boar** which was mentioned in 1720 as part of a list of properties owned by Perrot's Charity. In 1752, a local wit set down the following verse in honour of the inn and its newly-painted sign:

> Our landlord here,
> And sign, I swear,
> Are very near akin;
> An ill-shaped Boar
> Hangs at the door,
> And a grumpish hog's within.

It is said that John Wesley once preached from the horse-block of the Blue Boar, 'his bible resting on the broad shoulders of a stalwart grazier'. Stephen George is known to have held the licence from 1799 to 1811; he may have been there longer because he died in 1821. He was sheriff of Haverfordwest in 1791 and one of his sons was Lieutenant John George of the Marines whose story is told by Mr. Dillwyn Miles in *The Journal of the Pembrokeshire Historical Society*, numbers 10 and 11.

Thomas Robbin was the licensee in 1826 followed by William Makin in 1830 and Griffith Davies who was there from 1835 to late 1840s followed briefly by his daughter Mary. The building was unoccupied in 1851 and in 1852, a sale notice appeared in the local press which described the Blue Boar as being 'situate in the fish market and opposite the north entrance to the meat market'. Added the notice:

> This old established inn has undergone a complete and thorough repair, with coach house, stabling, piggeries &c. entirely new. The house comprises brew-house, cellar, pantry, front and back parlours, bar, kitchen, handsome upstairs sitting room, six bedrooms and an attic.

Prospective tenants were invited to apply to the trustees of Lloyd's Charity, Haverfordwest. John Phillips seems to have become the new licensee, quickly followed by James Woollett. Evan Thomas was there from 1858 to 1870, followed by his widow Mary Ann Thomas between 1871 to 1874 and James Moses in 1876. The last recorded licensee was M. Jones in 1880 and according to W.D. Phillips the building later became a school.

Another pub to have disappeared was the **Cat and Bagpipes**. This name – unique in Pembrokeshire – is thought to have its origins in Scotland. The 'Caterans' were Highlanders who spent much of their time pillaging north and south of the border, no doubt to the soul-destroying wail of the pipes. Why anyone would want to name an ale-house after these kilted raiders is not known, but there is still an inn called Cat and Bagpipes in north Yorkshire. The pub in Dew Street had a sign outside on which were the rather puzzling words:

> The Cat and Bagpipes
> As you all well remember
> Was placed here on the tenth of December.
> Laugh not at my sign.
> 'Twas not my own choice.
> 'Twas placed here by the Magistrates' voice!

The landlord in 1830 was James Morgan and the licensee from 1840 to 1852 was Edward Peters, a butcher from Narberth. The pub is recorded in a trade directory of the 1860s, but this seems to be a mistake since it appears that the Cat and Bagpipes had become part of the new Grammar School long before this time.

Plasterer Henry Thomas ran the **Alma** hereabouts in 1861. Later that year the Alma tavern, coach house and stables were advertised as being for sale, which seems to have spelled the end of this short-lived hostelry.

Across the road was the **White Lion** – the more recent of two pubs of that name in Dew Street. A young woman named Mrs. Jane Butler ran the Lion in 1871 and by the 1880s the building had become the Lion Spirit House, or Lion Vaults, a wine and spirits enterprise with an 'on-licence' which was run as a sideline by local Poor Rate collector John Roch Phillips.

John Drummond Synge was the landlord by 1889, in which year an explosion outside the White Lion resulted in 20 of the pub's windows being blown in. The cause was a home-made firecracker which had been let off to celebrate the wedding of a Dew Street worthy. Unfortunately the merrymakers had misjudged the amount of dynamite to be used, with a result that they blew a crater a foot deep in the middle of Dew Street and smashed virtually every window in a 50-yard radius! Mrs. Synge took over the licence in 1911 and she was still in charge in 1916. The building appears to have been divided at some stage, with the right-hand side remaining as a pub.

The former White Lion in High Street, seen from Tower Hill.

In the early 1920s the owner and licensee was Mrs. Isabella Richards who sold the business to local wine merchants W.H. George. They awarded the tenancy to Sgt. Major Archie Phillips, while in 1927 Helen Lerway moved to the White Lion from another George's house, the Bellevue in Portfield. William Horan was licensee in the early 1930s before moving from the Lion to the Lamb, and Joseph Evans was in charge in the late 1930s. George Moody took over in about 1940 and held the licence until well into the 1960s. He was one of a family of boxers and publicans, Frank Moody running the Royal in Milford Haven and

Ben Moody running the Rifleman in Haverfordwest. Subsequent licensees included Violet James, Dorothy Drew and Emrys Stephens. In the early 20th century the White Lion became the vaguely hippyish **Ra Café Bar,** but that phase has passed and it is now a pub once more called simply **The Bar**.

Next door to the Lion, the **White Horse** at 16, Dew Street was a substantial pub with a chequered history – so much so that it almost appears to have been jinxed. An early landlady was Elizabeth Noot who married a Cardiganshire militiaman named Davies. Their daughter Anne subsequently married and moved to London. When her marriage broke up, Anne took to the streets as a prostitute in the St. Giles area of the capital. In May 1845 she became the victim of a murder which pre-figured the Jack the Ripper killings; she was discovered with her throat cut in a seedy back-street lodging house. A man named James Connor was later hanged for the crime.

Split personality – The old White Lion sign is still on the wall, but the pub had become the Ra Café Bar by the time this photo was taken in 2002.

William Price was landlord of the White Horse in 1835, later moving to the King's Arms. Joseph M. Jones, housebuilder, victualler, grocer, parish clerk and landlord of the White Horse Inn, Dew Street, was declared an insolvent debtor in 1843 – another victim of the jinx. He was followed between 1844 and 1850 by Joseph Jenkins and in 1851 by Thomas Thomas and his wife Emily.

*There is now nothing left of the White Horse Hotel on the right,
the fishmarket in the centre or the Grammar School on the left –
all have been demolished.*
(Picture courtesy of Mr. John Stevenson)

    Strange things took place at the White Horse during Mr. Thomas' tenancy – so strange that some people put them down to witchcraft. For night after night the pub was the target for volleys of stones which clattered on to the roof or smashed the windows. Sturdy members of the local constabulary concealed themselves in the garden and across the street in an effort to nab the culprits, but even though the windows continued to be broken – 18 in all – they could catch no-one in the act of throwing the stones. Landlord Thomas was one of several who were convinced that the whole thing was witchcraft and eventually it was determined that a servant girl at the inn, 19-year-old Jane Herbert, was using supernatural powers to cause the vandalism. She was brought before the local bench, but when the magistrates heard the 'evidence' they laughed the whole thing out of court.

    Thomas Thomas died in December 1856 and he was followed briefly by his widow, Mrs. Emily Thomas, who became Mrs. William Jones in 1858. Her husband, who became the licensee, seems to have been a gentleman with a very short fuse. In 1866 he assaulted a sergeant major in the Royal Pembrokeshire Artillery Militia, while in 1868 he was fined for his part in a fracas in Horn's Lane. A more serious charge followed in September 1871. A local auctioneer was having a quiet pint in the White Horse when for no apparent reason the landlord attacked him with a walking stick and gave him a thrashing. Jones gave no explanation for his behaviour to the magistrates who this time sent him to prison for one month with hard labour. Despite these weird aberrations Jones remained landlord until 1874 – though it is difficult to understand how he managed to attract any customers. Other licensees included James Baker from 1876 to 1895, George Herbert from 1899 to 1902, William Giles from 1906 to 1914 and Mrs. Margaret Lewis from 1920 to 1924.

The White Horse was described in 1921 as 'a very useful house which puts up a good many travellers and is largely used by trawlermen from Milford'. Unfortunately the language used by these sea-dogs was extremely salty, a fact which alarmed the authorities since the pub was directly opposite the classrooms of the Grammar School. Perhaps as a consequence the pub, which was owned by Haverfordwest Corporation, closed in 1924. It has since been demolished and the terrace redeveloped.

Four doors up from the White Horse was the **Carpenters' Arms** where the landlord between 1830 and 1835 was Thomas Griffiths. John Goodridge was licensee during the 1840s and his widow Jane kept this popular beer-house between 1850 and 1861. When the building came up for auction in 1857 the advertisement for the sale stated:

> The premises stand within a few yards of the west entrance of the Meat Market House and thus command a most desirable situation for business.

Stephen Davies took over as licensee in the early 1860s, remaining in charge until his death in 1867 after which his widow Ann Davies continued the business until 1881. David Harries held the licence in 1884, followed by cabinet-maker George John and butcher Horatio Lewis in the 1890s. Lambert Baillieux was licensee in 1901 before leaving to take charge of the town's Assembly Rooms, while Frank Thomas was landlord in 1906. The pub was owned by Harold James of the Spring Gardens Brewery by this time, and a regular turnover of tenants may be one reason the magistrates decided to close it in 1909 under the redundancy ruling. Mr. James pocketed £162 in compensation, while the tenant at the time, Sgt. Major Pearce, received £18. The Carpenters' became a private house and appears to have been demolished at the same time as the White Horse.

The **King's Head** was the next pub along, just below the junction with Horns Lane. John Jones was licensee from 1840 to 1852, followed briefly by Thomas Edwards. George Summers took over the running of the King's Head in 1855 but it closed soon afterwards.

The **Black Lion** was on the same side as the Carpenters', about half way between Horns Lane and the Lamb. Thomas Jenkins was landlord of the Black Lion from 1844 until his death in 1860. His dressmaker widow

Elizabeth took over, while Anne Watkins obtained a full licence in 1870, evidently upgrading from beer-house status. Sarah Richards was the landlady in 1875, while Thomas Davies, who was landlord from 1881 to 1895, had previously been coachman at Dale Castle. Mrs. Davies was there in 1899 after which the pub changed hands a couple of times fairly rapidly; it had closed by 1906.

Three doors further up was the **Lamb and Flag** run by Jane Evans in the early 1850s and by George Summers in 1861. And further along on the left was the **Boar's Head** where George Jones held the licence between 1826 and 1852 when he was 72.

Next door was the long-serving **Lamb** which stood at 60 Dew Street and seems to have been opened by William Evans who was there from 1835 to 1850. He was followed by Dick Davies and his French wife Anna who ran the Lamb from 1857 to 1869. Following her husband's death, Mrs. Davies continued as landlady until 1881. She was followed by the grandly-named Wellington William Pugh who was there in 1884. William Davies was landlord in 1891, succeeded in turn by John Jones, James Bowen, Jonas Lewis and William James who was there around the time of the First World War.

The Lamb in the 1960s.
(Picture courtesy of the *Western Telegraph*)

According to one account, written in the early 1970s:

The bar and smokeroom are separated by a narrow passageway whence, within memory, the fine shire horses were taken through for stabling. The cellar was used in the past for slaughtering purposes.

William Edward John from Narberth succeeded William James, being followed in turn by Charles Earle and by Mr. and Mrs. Reg Russell who were there during the 1930s. William Horan ran the Lamb before the last war, while after the war retired Royal Navy officer Leo Smith was advertising 'good beer in quiet, spotless surroundings'. By this time the stables at the rear of the building had been converted into 'a lounge bar of Old English effect' and the pub had become popular with personnel stationed at Brawdy. A West Country couple named Howard and Peggy Jennings were in charge from 1954 to 1970 and they were succeeded by Mr. and Mrs. Barry Knight and later by Ivor Squelch and Herbie John before he took over the Bull in Prendergast. The Lamb became well known in the town for hosting slightly off-beat sporting events, such as the annual conker match, marbles contests and even yo-yo competitions, but it closed in about 1999.

In February 1855, Margaret and William Lewis of the **Coburg** Inn, Shut Street, died on consecutive days; they had been ill for some time. The Coburg seems to have been three doors above the Lamb, probably where the garage was subsequently built. And eight doors up from the Lamb was the **Hibernia**, a short-live beer-house run by stonemason William Edwards in the early 1860s.

The King's Arms in 2002 still had a splendid pub sign, although it has since been replaced.

There were numerous pubs on the other side of the street, starting with the still-flourishing **King's Arms**. The first known reference to this fair-sized coaching inn occurs in 1813 when it was bought by Thomas Evans, while by 1820 this was the meeting place of the local freemasons who had their own lodge room on the premises. Sarah Williams took over the running of the

King's Arms in 1824, having arrived from the Fleece further down the hill. She used the inn as a stepping-stone, leaving in 1827 to run the rather more prestigious Mariners' in the town centre, and Thomas Evans was in charge again between 1830 and his death in 1833. His widow Hester put the place up for sale shortly afterwards, the advertisement listing two parlours, a bar, cellars, nine bedrooms, stables and a coach-house – the usual attributes of a successful coaching inn.

The advert stated: 'The premises have all been erected within a few years and are in good repair'. This wasn't entirely accurate, as the man who purchased the King's Arms, John Simlett, was obliged to spend a large sum on repairs and improvements. He ran the King's Arms in person for a few years, but was forced to look for a tenant in 1837 'due to a family affliction'. A neighbour called Richard John seems to have taken on the lease, and he was still the licensee in 1840. However by this time the unfortunate Simlett was declared insolvent and the King's Arms was sold again.

William Price, formerly of the White Horse, was the new owner/licensee, and he was there until 1847 when the inn changed hands again. Elizabeth Gibbon was tenant in 1848 when it was stated that the inn had been established 'above half a century', but she, too, became insolvent within a couple of years. Thomas Williams then became licensee and he made a more successful fist of running the place, remaining landlord until his death, aged 60, in 1863. These were the days when a horse-drawn omnibus would leave from outside the pub every day except Sunday, bound for the Commercial Inn, Milford Haven; indeed the King's Arms was known at the time as 'the principal resort for the respectable inhabitants of Milford and the hundred of Roose generally'. Thomas Williams was succeeded by his daughter Mary Ann Williams who married John Beynon in 1869. He became landlord, but died in March 1872 at the early age of 27.

Stephen Gwyther from Brawdy was landlord from 1875 to 1884, before moving to take over the Mariners' Hotel. He was replaced by John Canton Thomas, formerly of the Fox and Hounds in Hill Street. The new landlord offered home-brewed and other ales together with an ordinary on Saturdays and fair days, and also advertised: 'A brake will run to Little Haven every Sunday and Thursday throughout the summer'. He was still there in 1898 when Sam Evans took over. William Rowles was in charge by the turn of the century and Joseph Hussey was landlord from 1906 until 1909 when he was accidentally shot dead while partridge shooting near Hasguard. William Evans was there in the early part of 1912. However, he seems to have done a 'moonlight flit' in July of that year, and the new tenant approved by S. Allsopp and Sons of Wind Street, Swansea was John Morgans of Croesgoch. He kept the pub until 1930 when the licence passed to James Hurley who remained in charge until the end of the war. China merchant George Swift took over, and locals could still call in for a Swift pint in the early 1980s when Charlie Swift was in charge. The pub has changed hands a few times since the Swift family gave it up but is still going strong, having seen off nearly all its many rivals in the street.

Rats Island was the name given to an island of tiny, run-down houses in the middle of Dew Street, about where the King's Arms now stands. This block of dwellings, long since pulled down, once boasted its own inn – the unsavoury-sounding **Rats Island Tavern.** Joseph Davies was landlord in 1830.

The street's first **White Lion** was kept by shoe-maker William Codd from 1840 to 1844. It was two doors up from the King's Arms in what is now the Spice Box, but had closed long before the other pub of the same name appeared on the scene.

Next door to the White Lion was the **Jolly Sailor**, an ale-house run by boot and shoe-maker Thomas Martin and his wife Anne between 1841 and 1858. Blacksmith Thomas Walters was there in 1861, but by 1868 it had become the **Butchers' Arms** and the publican between then and 1892 was John Bowen who was helped by his wife Elizabeth to run the pub and also the grocery shop attached to it. Their daughter Sarah Bowen subsequently took over, finding herself in repeated trouble for serving out of hours; she was fined £1 for serving on a Sunday in 1897.

By 1910 the Butchers' was owned by Mr. Charles Mathias who also held the licence. However he lived next door and delegated the running of the pub to a Mrs. Williams without bothering to go through the formality of transferring the licence to her. This annoyed the local magistrates and the following year they decided that the Butchers' was surplus to requirements, quashed the licence and called time on the pub. Mr. Mathias received £300 in compensation; Mrs. Williams, by now the official licensee, received just £30. The building now houses the Pet Centre.

A couple of doors further up the street was the **Royal Oak** which was kept by stonemason John Rogers from 1835 to 1868. John Owen was the licensee from 1871 to 1884, but from 1891 to 1895 it was his widow Mrs. Mary Owen, who was pouring the pints. Their daughter, Mrs. Mary Ann Roberts held the licence in 1899 and her husband, butcher John Roberts, was licensee in 1902. The pub seems to have closed by 1906.

A little further along, the **Plasterers' Arms** has recently undergone a name change. Plasterer James Pugh moved from Portfield in the late 1840s to open the pub, which he ran with the help of his wife Martha (when she could spare the time from bringing up the couple's eight children, several of whom went on to run pubs). James died in the 1860s, but his widow Martha soldiered on until at least 1892. From 1895 to 1924 the Plasterers' was under the 'genial management' of Charles Griffiths, and the licence seems to have been held by Mary Griffiths from 1925 until her death in 1958. William Griffiths took over, followed by Jack and Edie Griffiths. Burt Paterson had two lengthy spells in charge between the early 1980s and 2000, also having an interest in running the Bridge End, the Railway in Johnston and the town's Market Hall. The Plasterers' became the **Haverfordwest Tavern** in 2005 but was temporarily closed at the time of going to press, apparently due to a dispute involving rear access rights.

There were a few other pubs in Dew Street, but their whereabouts cannot now be traced with any accuracy. John Robson was the landlord of the **Albion** in 1826 followed by Richard Rogers in 1830. Joseph Jenkins held the licence of the **Britannia Arms** in 1826 and John Parry kept the pub in 1830. And James Devereux ran the **Masons' Arms** in 1844.

No prizes for guessing the trade of the gentleman who opened the Plasterers' Arms.

The **Bunch of Grapes** and the **Kensington Arms** in Dew Street both supplied refreshments and accommodation to the Blue party during the election of May 1831. The Bunch of Grapes had six beds and a landlord called Price, while Daniel Denness ran the Kensington Arms from 1826 to 1831. Nothing else is known about these two hostelries.

CHAPTER EIGHT

Haverfordwest

MARINERS' SQUARE, DARK STREET,
ST. MARY'S STREET & TOWER HILL

St. Martin's Place is the name of the street running from the much-altered junction of City Road and Barn Street to Mariners' Square. Although relatively short, this was a busy little thoroughfare in its day and boasted its quota of pubs. One of these was the **Nag's Head** which occupied a corner position near the entrance to what is now the Castle Lake car-park. Benjamin Davies kept the pub in 1826 and Elizabeth Davies was licensee from 1830 until her death in 1848. Elizabeth Owen appears to have been the last to run the pub which closed in the 1850s.

Still going strong in St. Martin's Place, where it once stood alongside a row of almshouses, is the **Greyhound**, at one time a popular meeting-place for farmers on mart days. There is a reference in an old tradesman's book, dated about 1710, to 'John Jones of the Greyhound', although whether this is the same place isn't known. However we do know that Stephen Bowen kept the pub from 1826 until his death in 1830, followed by Martha Bowen who was there until 1849. She retired in that year, handing over to her daughter Ann and son-in-law Thomas Lewis.

Lewis was leading light in the Hwlfordd Lodge of the Order of Druids and hosted several dinners of the brethren. He was also a staff sergeant in the Pembrokeshire Militia which may account for the fact that he gave up the licence for some years during and after the Crimea War. Martha Bowen took over the licence again in 1854 but died the following year and the acting landlord from 1858 to 1862 was Robert Pockett who was followed by Thomas Lewis' son Wyndham. He obviously didn't enjoy the trade because he stepped down soon afterwards to be followed by a succession of short-lived licensees. By 1869, Thomas Lewis felt able to take up the leash of the Greyhound once more and he remained in charge until at least 1874.

There is a story about the Greyhound which tells how one licensee engaged a local artist to paint an appropriate sign for the pub. This the artist did, much to everyone's admiration, only for the publican to refuse to pay for the work. In revenge the artist crept back to the pub in the dead of night, armed with paints and brush, and when the landlord stepped out next morning to admire the sign he was horrified to discover that it now depicted an animal with the head and body of a greyhound but the legs of a fox terrier!

Robert Nicholson was landlord in the late 1870s, while from 1881 to 1884 James Davies, formerly of Roch, ran the pub with the help of his wife Jane. James Griffiths, who was behind the counter from from 1886 to 1910, concentrated on building up the livery and posting side of the business. He described himself as a 'job master' – a livery stable keeper who 'jobbed out' horses and carriages.

The Greyhound on Mariners' Square, probably photographed in the days when James Griffiths was licensee.
(Picture courtesy of Mr. David Griffiths)

A brother of Richard Griffiths who ran the Upper Three Crowns, he later ran a motor bus company from the City Road Garage.

More recent licensees included David Griffiths who was there throughout the 1920s before moving to the Bridge End inn, and John Brace who held the licence in the 1930s and early '40s. Bert Harries was the licensee from 1944 to 1965, and he was succeeded by David Peace and later by Mrs. A.M. Cuffe. There were fears for the future of the pub when it closed for a while around 2000, but happily it has been reopened by Carmarthen pub owner Mr. Steve Adams, ensuring there is life in the 'Old Dog' yet.

A more recent view of the Greyhound.

There were two pubs across the street, in the row which once stood to the rear of Bethesda Baptist Chapel. Thomas Williams was the landlord of the **Coach and Horses** in 1849 when it was described as being next to the chapel. In 1854, James Shankland of Laugharne, landlord of the Coach and Horses, was fined ten shillings for allowing gambling with cards to take place in the pub. He was still there in 1861 and may have been succeeded for a short time by his son George.

A new licence was granted in 1854 to John Bailey for 'the house to be known as the **Weary Traveller**' in Haverfordwest. The new pub was opposite the Greyhound Inn, according to the *Pembrokeshire Herald*, and it was also described as 'opposite the almshouses'. John Bailey was still there in 1863, while between 1867 and 1874 the landlady was Ann Bailey. It had closed by 1880.

Mariners' Square takes its name from the inn which has dominated it for many years. A sign on the wall of the **Hotel Mariners** claims that it dates from 1625, which – if true – would make it one of the oldest surviving coaching inns in the county; however the present building seems to date from the middle to late 18th century. It supposedly began life as the **Three Mariners'** inn, the name reflecting the importance of Haverfordwest as a port in former times, and with its large stable yard surrounded by coach houses and stabling, the Mariners' vied with the Castle Inn for the title of the town's most important coaching inn.

By the end of the 18th century the Mariners' had become the unofficial headquarters of the county's hunting fraternity. It was once said:

> In all of Pembrokeshire there can have been no more sporting crowd than the hard-riding squires, gentlemen farmers and huntsmen who gathered in the bar-parlour of the ancient Mariners' Inn. Every one of them loved sport for sport's own sake; every one of them loved a good horse; every one of them loved a good dog.

Given this reputation, it was ironic that in December 1807 a remarkable incident occurred at the Mariners' involving the pack of hounds hunted by H.W. Bowen Esq. The hounds chased a fox from Camrose for five miles right into the heart of Haverfordwest where the 'varmint' disappeared among the town gardens, only to reappear on the ridge of the roof of the Mariners', having reached that precarious point by way of various outbuildings. For fully half an hour the fox gazed down on his pursuers in the square below, but when he attempted to move off from his precarious perch he slipped on the slates and fell to his death – surely the strangest 'kill' in the annals of Pembrokeshire hunting. An engraving of this remarkable scene was published in 1808, said to show Squire Bowen of Camrose on a grey horse pointing with his whip at the daredevil fox.

The famous image of the fox on the roof of the Mariners'.

The names of the early licensees of the Mariners' are difficult to discover, but maltster and brewer Stephen Crunn conveyed the property to William Crunn in 1803. William Crunn remained landlord until his death in 1821, after which it was taken over by the oddly-named Lettice Crunn – presumably his widow.

The Mariners' was always a thriving establishment, but really came to life at election times when it was the headquarters of the Whig, or 'Blue' faction. At the bitterly fought election of 1831, Blue candidate Col. Robert Fulke Greville ran up a bill of £1,878 in providing hospitality at the inn for potential voters, which included £443 for food and £982 for drink. According to David Williams in *The Welsh History Review*:

> This particular item covered an astonishing quantity of drink. Forty-two barrels of beer, 67 gallons of brandy, 59 gallons of rum, 1,068 bottles of port and 780 bottles of sherry, as well as other more exotic drinks, all consumed in two weeks.

Sarah Williams was the licensee who would have benefited from Greville's ultimately unsuccessful attempts to buy votes – assuming he paid his bills. Formerly of the King's Arms in Dew Street, she had taken over the Mariners' in 1827 promising 'wines of the best quality, neat post-chaises, good horses and careful drivers'. Hunt Week 'ordinaries' were also a feature of the Mariners' at this time – an ordinary being a set meal at a fixed price – while the Sons of the Clergy held their annual dinner at the Mariners'; charge for the dinner was 5s. 6d. which included a pint of wine. Sarah Williams left in 1837 to open the newly-built Royal Hotel at Hobbs Point near Pembroke Dock and was replaced by D.M. Lloyd who was a son-in-law of the late Mrs. Crunn.

A widow named Charlotte Winsor was the licensee between 1841 and 1857, and her 'well-earned fame as a public caterer' was evident at the function at the Mariners' which followed a cricket match between Haverfordwest and Tenby in the summer of 1843. The local freemasons also met here in the 1840s to do their thing, while in 1845 the African entertainer Roscius performed to a packed assembly room at the Mariners'. After declaiming speeches from Othello and other notable works, Roscius finished his act with a popular song of the day entitled 'Oppossum up a Gum Tree'. In 1849 Mrs. Winsor introduced a new novelty to the hotel – hot and cold water baths.

In 1857, Mrs. Winsor assigned for £1,050 'the good will, business and furniture of the Royal Mariners Hotel' to Eliza Thomas of Haverfordwest, but she didn't stay for long and in 1859 the Mariners' was taken over by Mrs. Maria Philpott who already ran the Castle Hotel in the town. She remained in charge of both historic premises for a number of years, the old

> **MARINERS' HOTEL, HAVERFORDWEST.**
>
> # DAVID LAMB
>
> Begs to state that he has contracted with the Postmaster General for the conveyance of the Mails to and fro between Haverfordwest and St. David's, and that his contract authorises him to carry Passengers, Fares to and fro 7s 6d, Single fares 5s.
>
> **WINES & SPIRITS OF SUPERIOR QUALITY.**
>
> **BILLIARDS.**
>
> D. L's Posting Establishment is replete with every convenience.

The Mariners' was replete with every convenience in the days of David Lamb.
(Picture courtesy of Mrs. Elfrida Jones)

political rivalries having apparently been forgotten. David Lamb, formerly butler at Picton Castle, took over in 1870 and ran the inn for about seven years before moving to the New Inn in Upper Market Street; Henry Davies succeeded him, and interestingly the press notices announcing his arrival proclaimed that the Mariners' had been 'established a century', casting some doubt on the 1625 date.

There was a regular omnibus service from the inn to St. David's and Solva by this time, the coach departing from the stable yard of the Mariners' and terminating at The Grove in St. David's. Mrs. Elizabeth Hughes from Ambleston kept the Mariners' from 1881 until 1884, the census describing her as a 32-year-old sailor's wife and hotel keeper.

From 1884 and through the 1890s mine host was Stephen Gwyther; like Sarah Williams he had previously run the King's Arms. He renovated the Mariners', changed the name from 'inn' to 'hotel', and fitted it out 'with every modern improvement adapted to the requirements of a first-class house'. He seems to have been the chap who added the portico over the front door, and for many years this was emblazoned with the name 'Gwyther'. The Misses Gwyther were proprietors in 1899 and Howard Gwyther was the landlord by 1908 when he welcomed a visit from Mrs. Emily Pankhurst and a group of suffragettes. They used the hotel as their base for several days, travelling to address crowds all over the county. And a photograph taken at the time of the 1910 general election shows Liberal candidate Walter Roch standing on the portico of the hotel addressing a sea of supporters in the square below.

Successful candidate Walter Roch addresses the crowd from the portico of the Mariners' at the General Election of 1910.
(Picture courtesy of Sybil Edwards)

From 1914 to 1935 the landlord was William Mortimer Thomas. It was during his ownership that the name was changed from Mariners' Hotel to Hotel Mariners, the distinctive AA and RAC crests being added to the front of the building at the same time. Like the huntsmen who gathered at the inn a century before, Mr. Thomas 'loved a good dog', in his case the dog in question being the Sealyham – the hardy Pembrokeshire-bred terrier. He was a noted judge and breeder, and during his time at the inn it became the headquarters of the Sealyham Terrier Club. Next to take charge was Harold Hedley, previously of the Castle Inn. He kept up the Mariners' historic links with field sports, being a keen follower of the Pembrokeshire Hunt. Licensee from 1944 to 1958 was Miss Louise Anderson.

By 1960 the hotel was being run by David Green, but in the late '60s he sold the business to Allied Breweries who ran it as part of their Ind Coope Hotels Group, later Embassy Hotels. Soon afterwards a new manageress arrived to run the hotel. Mrs. Anne Cromwell was one of only two female hotel managers in the whole of the Ind Coope chain, but she was no stranger to Pembrokeshire. Her mother, Mrs. Doris Manson (always known as Monté) had run the Sailor's Safety in Dinas for several years before taking over the Bristol Trader on Haverfordwest Quay.

Like many coaching inns, the Mariners' was well able to cater for the motoring age.

During the 1970s there were a number of changes at the Mariners, including the acquisition by Allied Breweries of the adjacent James Williams-owned Spring Gardens storage depot and off-licence. Originally intended to be the site of a motel, this area is now an attractively landscaped car-park. The neighbouring Haverfordwest Little Theatre was also demolished in the 1970s. This building belonged to the Mariners and was connected to it by a door leading into the hotel's function room or 'Long Room' – formerly a stable block. Whenever there was a play in the theatre, the Long Room had to be kept clear as this was the main fire exit from the playhouse. The National Eisteddfod in Haverfordwest in 1972 briefly evoked the excesses of election days 140 years earlier. Mrs. Cromwell has described it as the wildest week of her time at the hotel, as vast crowds of drinkers spilled out of the Mariners, the Gloster and the Greyhound each evening to sing (in Welsh) and carouse in the square outside.

In 1981, Mrs. Cromwell purchased the hotel from Allied Breweries; she remains the joint owner with her son Andrew who now handles the day-to-day running of the hotel. They have made a number of changes and improvements to the inn in recent years. The two small bars have been converted into one large lounge bar, while extra bedrooms have been added and others modernised, so that there are now 28 en-suite rooms. The Cromwells have catered for any number of notable guests in their time. Prince Charles and

Margaret Thatcher have both dropped in for lunch (although not together), while the actor Jack Hawkins, broadcasters Alun Williams and Wynford Vaughan Thomas, and *How Green Was My Valley* author Richard Llewellyn have all stayed at the hotel – the latter locking himself in his room to write, much to the understandable annoyance of the cleaning staff.

T. JAMES,
SPRING GARDENS' BREWERY,
HAVERFORDWEST.
Pianofortes, Harmoniums, & American Organs, for Sale or Hire, and on the one two or three year's System.
GOOD ALES, WINES & SPIRITS.

Thomas James had a sideline in musical instruments when he ran the Spring Gardens Brewery.
(Picture courtesy of Mrs. Elfrida Jones)

The **Spring Gardens Brewery** mentioned above was at one time one of the largest malting and brewing businesses in the county and like the neighbouring Mariners' it was once in the hands of the Crunn family, notably Stephen Crunn and William Crunn. Thomas Skone, a magistrate and noted rider to hounds, ran the brewery in the 1840s while Matthew Whittow was in charge from about 1850 to 1870, his 'fourpence a quart' ale enjoying good sales. The brewery was later run by Messrs. Edmonds and Rees, but had ceased brewing by the end of the 1870s as more and more Burton beer began to arrive by rail. Maltster and wine merchant Thomas James took over the premises in about 1880 and ran the Spring Gardens Brewery as a bottling and distribution depot for many years, acquiring a number of pubs in the district at the same time, after which Harold James ran the business up until the First World War. Later still, James Williams acquired the site, using it as a retail and wholesale wine, spirits and ale stores. The brewery had a 'tap' at some stage and W.D. Phillips records that a Police Supt. Lewis, 'after his retirement, kept the bar at the Spring Gardens Brewery for a short time'. Miss Emma Hallett ran the 'tap' in 1910 but when it closed isn't clear from the records.

Somewhere in the area was the **Butchers' Arms**. William Griffiths kept the Butchers' from 1826 to 1830 and Mary Griffiths was there from 1831 to 1844. W.D. Phillips places it 'opposite the Spring Gardens Brewery Office' while trade directories have it both in St. Mary's Street and Dark Street, so it may have moved at some stage. This was yet another 'Blue' pub during the election of May 1831.

In May of 1866, a widow named Lewis was granted a licence to sell 'beer etc.' at her house in Mariners' Square. This appears to have been the **Gloster Arms**, because the death of a Mrs. Lewis, landlady of the 'Gloucester' Arms, is recorded just five months later. David Lewis was the licensee in 1867 and William Miller was there in 1871. William Burton was the licensee in 1875 followed by Slebech-born Francis John and then by Jesse Warren. Morgan Harries kept the pub from 1893 to 1906, while from 1909 to 1940 Mrs. Lydia Maud Thomas held the licence of what was by now a James Williams house. 'The Gloster Arms has a nice little trade and is well conducted by Mrs. Thomas,' was how the pub was described in the 1920s. Catherine Griffiths – 'Kitty the Gloster'– was there in the 1950s and '60s followed for some years by William 'Nobby' Pryor, a former C.P.O. at Brawdy. At the time of going to press the Gloster was firmly closed and boarded up – a sad sight.

The Gloster Arms was still open in 2002 when this photograph was taken.

Three ancient and narrow thoroughfares connect Mariners' Square with High Street, all of them overshadowed by St, Mary's Church. The first of these streets on the left, leaving the square and passing the Gloster, is the aptly-named Dark Street which seems only to have supported two pubs despite its proximity to the market area. One of these was the **Pembroke Arms**. In 1855 the licence passed from Mary Bevan to James Griffiths but the pub closed a couple of years later.

The **Liverpool Arms** at 5, Dark Street was literally in the shadow of the Temperance Hall and from 1867 to 1871 the publican was William Burton, later of the Gloster Arms. The landlord in 1874 was John James while James Davies – a smith by trade – held the licence from 1881 until 1884. He was followed by Thomas Martin Jones, Mrs. Mary Bartlett held the licence from 1891 to 1895 and George John was there from 1902 until 1909. The pub suffered a serious fire that year and before it could recover it was finished off by the magistrates who voted to close it under the redundancy ruling. The Liverpool Arms was owned by Harold James of the Spring Gardens Brewery who pocketed £475 in compensation. In 2006 the building housed the offices of a company called Buzinetsolutions.

The former Liverpool Arms in Dark Street.

Two pubs have appeared in Dark Street in recent years, the **Royal Cellar Bar** located – ironically enough – in the cellar of the old Temperance Hall and, across the road, **Bar Charlie**.

Running parallel to and a little higher than Dark Street is St. Mary's Street. Despite being short and narrow this was once a street of some importance, leading from the Guildhall to the 17th-century Council Chamber – a gaunt building perched on top of the north porch of the church. It was one of the main market streets of the town and it also boasted three early coaching inns. As *The History of Haverfordwest* revealed:

> The Talbot, the Fleece, the Tuns, the Coach and Horses and the Dolphin are all upon the spot and full of customers. Little but home-brewed is consumed.

A third pub, not mentioned in this list, was the **White Hart** which is believed to have stood at the Tower Hill end of St. Mary's Street and which was demolished at some stage to clear the way for the erection of the town's Assembly Rooms. Tradition has it that this was the town's principal coaching inn in the 18th century and that it was a stopping point for the first mail coaches running between London and Hakin Point.

In October 1889 a new Temperance Hall was opened in St. Mary's Street, capable of seating 650 people. And to make things even more satis-

A poster advertising the sale of the sometime Dolphin in 1887.

fying for the hundreds of temperance supporters gathered to watch Lady Kensington perform the opening ceremony, the hall was built on the site of a former pub – the **Dolphin**. The pub is mentioned in 1805 when it was reported that the owner of the Dolphin – John Warlow – had been made bankrupt; John Griffiths, a hairdresser by trade, held a lease for life on the Dolphin at the time. Licensee of the Dolphin from 1821 until 1835 was William Walters. In 1834 he pursued a court action in a fruitless attempt to be

The Temperance Hall was built on the site of the Dolphin. The former Coach and Horses was on the right of the picture.

reimbursed for the hospitality he lavished on the supporters of Greville during the 1831 election. The sale that followed Mr. Walters' death the following year listed the brewing equipment that a typical inn of the day must have possessed:

> A very valuable copper boiler, large oak kive, small ditto, two coolers, casks, tubs, buckets, pails, troughs, lead pipes, hop press etc.

Next to run the Dolphin was Mr. J. Williams during whose tenancy the pub was a meeting place for a benefit society known as the Royal Victoria Club – named in honour of the young queen. Thomas Herbert was in charge by 1840, but three years later he appeared in court as an insolvent debtor and that seems to have been the end of the Dolphin since it is not heard of again.

Next door along towards High Street was the street's third inn, the **Coach and Horses** where the landlord from 1817 to 1835 was Richard Parsell whose bill in 1831 for being 'Open for the Blues' was a relatively modest £398. The inn seems to have closed in the late 1830s and by 1866 it was in a dangerous condition, half the roof having fallen in. Arguments over the ownership of the building meant that it stayed in this state for some time, and there was a suggestion that the premises be demolished and replaced with a flight of steps 'so as to connect St. Mary's Street with Dark Street'. Eventually new Council Chambers were built on the site – just across the road from the earlier Guildhall.

Both St. Mary's Street and Dark Street connect High Street with Tower Hill, a precipitous lane leading from Mariners' Square to the bottom of Dew Street. This street was too steep to be of much use to the market traders who otherwise packed the lanes around the church – in wet weather the rainwater swept down in torrents – but it did boast several pubs and the town's police station.

Near the bottom of Tower Hill was the **Three Tuns**, variously called the Old Tuns and the Three Tuns and Thistle. A benefit society called the True Union Britons Society was founded here in 1812 and continued to meet at the Three Tuns until it folded in 1845. The 50 remaining members held a valedictory dinner at the inn and shared out the money left in the kitty; they received £2 17s. each. Richard Gibbon held the licence from 1826 until his death in 1838; he was also a wharfinger – someone who looked after the wharves on the river – and the pub was one of the busiest in town during the 1831 election, the Blue party supporters running up a bill for £947. He was followed in 1840 by Lettice Gibbon who presided over the last fling of the True Union Britons and was still in charge in 1846. James Stone kept the pub in 1850, while James Harries from Camrose, who was there between 1852 and 1867, was rapped over the knuckles for refusing to accommodate soldiers from the Royal Artillery who had been billeted on the inn during the Crimea War. The Tuns had closed by 1870.

The name of the **Six Bells** could have nautical connotations, but is much more likely to refer to the nearby bell-tower of St. Mary's Church. George Evans was landlord from 1844 to 1846, followed by William Rogers who was there in the 1850s, after which no more is heard of the Bells.

The death was reported in the *Cambrian* in 1806 of Mr. George Griffiths 'who for many years had kept the **Black Bear**, Haverfordwest'. Dinah Davies held the licence in 1826 but John Howell was landlord between 1830 and 1840. His widow Martha Howell was in charge from 1844 to 1852, while John Bowen kept the pub from 1858 to 1862. Like the Six Bells this was a popular tavern with the town's bell-ringers, but it changed hands regularly in the 1860s, passing from Margaret Phillips to Joseph Freeman and then to William Morgan, and like the rest of the pubs on the hill it had closed by 1870.

An inn called the **Swan** is thought to have existed at the top of Tower Hill at some stage, although it could have been around the corner in Dew Street. So many changes have taken place at this junction over the centuries that it is impossible to place 'lost' pubs with any accuracy, especially poorly documented ones like the Swan.

CHAPTER NINE

Haverfordwest
MARKET STREET & HILL STREET

Once known as Shoemakers' Street, the hilly thoroughfare of Market Street originally led from St Mary's Church to the medieval South Gate which stood near the junction with Goat Street. The lower part of the street became a focus of the town's open air market trade which spilled into the lanes around the church – hence the name – and this connection was underlined in the early 19th century with the building of a dedicated meat and provisions market half way along the street, with a corn market further up. And, as always, the presence of these markets led to the opening of numerous hostelries to provide refreshment not only for traders and shoppers, but also for their horses and donkeys.

In June 1805 the Temple Druid estate was sold by auction at the **Plough** in Market Street. The Plough itself was up for auction in 1808 according to a somewhat curious notice in the *Cambrian* which offered:

> All that commodious and well-situated public house formerly called the Plough but now the **Bear** or **Champion** situate in the market place land near the town hall in Haverfordwest, together with stable and scite [*sic*] of old walls, curtilages and gardens now in the possession of the widow of George Griffiths.

Whoever the purchaser was he must have closed the inn, because of the Plough (or Bear or Champion) no more is heard.

According to tradition, there was once a hostelry known as the **Feathers** at the lower end of Market Street in one of the three buildings which were demolished in the 1860s to make way for the impressive Commerce House. However no record has come to light of this establishment. Equally there is no sign of the **Rat Tavern** in any of the records, even though W.D. Phillips names Edward Ellis and Billy Williams as licensees and places this unlikely-sounding establishment opposite Commerce House.

Moving up the right-hand side of the street, the **Market Cellars** was the place where market traders and porters did their drinking; Elizabeth Gibbon

A early postcard view of Market Street.

was the licensee in 1830 while James Griffiths was in charge five years later. According to W.D. Phillips:

> The original Market Cellars was just above the steps of the Market House beneath the house now occupied by Mrs. Biddlecomb and which, externally, has the appearance of an underground cellar.

It seems as though the ale-house was shunted around the market complex several times during its lifetime and by 1844 it was recorded as being near the Dew Street entrance, with Alexander Price as licensee. It was apparently back in Market Street by the 1850s with John Owen, later of the Ship in Hill Street, pouring the pints – although records for this period are sketchy. In 1869 carpenter and innkeeper Thomas Lloyd obtained a full licence for the Market Cellars in Market Street, one door up from Kent House, and he was still there in 1871 when the building was badly damaged by fire. From 1881 to 1884 the innkeeper was Mr. Robert Nuttycombe from Somerset. The inn appears to have been acquired by Harold James of Spring Gardens Brewery at some stage, and tenants included Philip Thomas, yeomanry drill instructor John Beet and Herbert Morgan from Barry. In 1906 the landlord was Thomas Adams. He was still there in 1914 but the licence was not renewed the following year.

Across the road, the **George's Inn** bears the legend 'Established in 1803' – the date that James Brown set up in business as a brandy merchant in the town. He was still a spirit merchant in Market Street in 1830, the business being carried on by Martha Brown who was a spirit and beer dealer in the 1840s and '50s and also did a thriving bar trade which was apparently conducted under the sign of the **Three Horseshoes.**

This business was continued by John Brown, a notable character who – as has been mentioned elsewhere – penned an interesting book called *Haverfordwest and its Story*. John Brown died in 1890 and the business was taken over by William Henry George, a 36-year-old businessman who had been born at Nash Farm, Llangwm. W.H. George had spent a number of years in London, employed in the licensed trade and working with a large firm of distillers, before returning to make his mark on Pembrokeshire. He built up the Market Street business to such an extent that within six years he was able to sell up and retire, concentrating his energies on other matters. He was mayor of Haverfordwest in 1901 before moving to Guildford in Surrey and becoming mayor there in 1906. He then moved in Brighton for a number of years before eventually returning to Haverfordwest where he died in 1930.

In 1897 W.H. George sold his business to Thomas Ford of Swansea, but it was reacquired in 1905 by his son Ernest George who later lived at Foley House in Goat Street. Trading as W.H. George and Son, the company continued to thrive and expand, importing, bottling and distributing wines, spirits, beer and stout and building up an empire of about 30 public houses in the town and beyond. The company was later managed by Tom George and

For many years The George's housed a wine and spirits enterprise.

in 1954 it moved most of its business operations to the Friar's Vaults in Castle Square. W.H. George and Son was eventually acquired by Allied Breweries in about 1969, but the company name was later revived by another member of the family dynasty, Peter George, who set up as an independent brewery wholesaler in 1983.

When the Market Street premises were vacated in 1954, the building became an out-and-out pub, the George's Inn, with Arthur Griffiths as manager from 1955 to 1958. Elsie Griffiths is remembered as being licensee for many years; her splendid parrot is equally well recalled. The George's was particularly lively in the late '60s and early '70s when the Market Hall was one of the county's top night-spots, attracting some of the big name bands of the time. Since the closure of the market and the redevelopment of the hall site in the 1990s the George's has reinvented itself and has become more of a restaurant than a pub, catering mainly for the lunchtime and early evening trade.

Just up from the provision market, on the corner of Hill Street, was the **Ivy Bush**. Richard and Maria Morse kept this pub in the early 1840s, followed by their daughter Frances and her husband, a clerk named David James. Mr. James died in 1856 but Frances carried on running the pub until at least 1867. Wine merchant Ebenezer Phillips was there from 1870 to 1874 when John Williams from Castlemartin took over the licence. He remained until 1892 and Thomas John was the landlord from 1894 to 1912. This large but apparently unremarkable pub was owned by the Haverfordwest Corporation which made no application for a renewal of the licence in 1913.

Above the site of the medieval South Gate is Upper Market Street. Known at St. Thomas Street at one time, it had a high concentration of pubs and out of a dozen properties on the side of the street opposite the corn market – Cleveland Row – five were licensed at various times.

In the *Carmarthen Journal* in 1826 there appeared an advertisement for the sale of the freehold of the **Bell** 'opposite the Corn Market'. The sale was precipitated by the collapse of Nathaniel

This building was once the Ivy Bush inn.

108

There were once four pubs in this row of houses. The corner property used to be a warehouse, after which came the Bell, the George and Dragon, the New Inn and the Globe.

Phillips' Haverfordwest Bank. John Lewis was landlord at that time but by 1830 William Morris was behind the bar. He handed over to William Phillips in 1846 but the pub closed some time in the 1850s.

Next door was the **George and Dragon** which was also offered for sale in 1826. It was occupied at the time by William Golding, and he was still around in 1844, having billed the Blue party for £423 following the 1831 election. A professor of music from London named James Ribbon was the next licensee and he ran the pub until the mid 1850s when he seems to have given up selling beer to concentrate on teaching music.

Next door along was the **New Inn**, a popular haunt of Haverfordwest traders and businessmen in the days of the affable John Robbin who held the licence from 1826 to 1858. On a single day during the election of 1831 he supplied visiting voters with 52 breakfasts, 99 dinners, 36 suppers, 11 gallons of cider, two and a half gallons of whisky, one and a half barrels of ale and one and a half gallons of gin; he also provided ten lunches and teas 'for the band'.

'Here a coterie nightly met in the private smoke room,' recalled W.D. Phillips. 'Each member of the company had a particular chair and a church-warden pipe'. John Robbin's widow Mary took over from her husband and 'always insisted on proper decorum and quietness in her bar'. In 1865 she catered for 60 tenant farmers who were treated to dinner at the inn by their landlord, J.H. Scourfield M.P. of Moat, and she was still there in 1871. Charles Thomas held the licence of the New Inn in 1875 followed in fairly rapid succession by William Paddon, Thomas Lloyd and a Scotsman named David Lamb, formerly of the Mariners'. The pub, with its three-stall stable and loose box, seems to have gone into decline and it closed in 1886, being converted into a lodging house.

The fourth pub in this boozy row was the **Globe**. A butcher named William Thomas held the licence between 1826 and the early 1840s, followed by his widow Mary Thomas who was still in charge in 1851. Richard Thomas was licensee in 1861, while by 1867 the tenant of the pub was his wife or widow Elizabeth Thomas. She attempted to do a 'moonlight flit' that year but got no further than the station, the fact that she was trying to make off with three feather beds rather hindering her progress. David Narbett was the licensee in 1870, followed in turn by Benjamin Thomas, Maria Dimond and Mrs. Ann Davies who held the licence at her death in 1886. Charles Pugh was the landlord between 1891 and 1909 when the licensing authorities closed the Globe under the redundancy ruling. Mr. Pugh, a son of the James Pugh who launched the Plasterers' in Dew Street, was awarded £10 compensation; his widow later ran the Rifleman.

At the end of the terrace, on the corner of Church Lane, was the **Bush** which appears to have been opened in the mid 1850s by Jimmy Jacks who perhaps spotted a gap in the market caused by the closure of the two pubs further down. Jacks remained landlord until 1866, surviving a fire which damaged the building in 1864. William Collins took over and he was still there in 1874. The Bush then changed hands fairly regularly over the next 15 years, the licensees including William Nisbett, George Barzey, John Rees and Thomas Williams. It seems to have closed in the 1890s.

Hill Street was once known as King Street and – especially in its upper reaches – was one of the more fashionable streets of the town. Many of the county's gentry families kept town houses in Hill Street, to which they would repair during the 'season' of balls and dinner parties, steeplechases and hunt meets. In the 1820s it became the first street in town to be paved and duly became a popular place for the young men and women of the town to promenade on fine evenings. It was a mainly residential street, and many well-to-do townsfolk chose to live in the elegant three-storey houses which graced the upper part of the street.

The lower part of Hill Street, being in close proximity to the town's main fairs and markets, was a less desirable neighbourhood and this was where

Charles and Martha Davies outside the Fox and Hounds in the early 1900s.
(Picture courtesy of Mr. Charles Davies, Haverfordwest Town Museum)

most of the hostelries were to be found. Going up the street, away from the Market Street junction, the first property on the left past the cinema (the old corn market) was the **Fox and Hounds**. Thomas Reynolds kept the pub from 1826 to 1852 and in the 1831 election he entertained voters on behalf of the Orange party; three years later he was still trying to get his money back. His widow Mrs. Jenny Reynolds was the popular landlady from 1858 to 1876 and John Thomas from Freystrop was landlord from 1878 to 1884 when he took over the King's Arms in Dew Street. At this time the pub was noted for its home-brewed harvest ale, which farmers – unable or unwilling to brew for themselves – could purchase for a shilling a gallon to supply to the haymakers in the field. Charles Sutton Davies was the landlord between 1891 and 1911 before moving across the road to the Upper Three Crowns. The Fox and Hounds seems to have gone steadily downhill afterwards as local wine merchant Harold James struggled to find a steady tenant and it appears to have closed in early 1915.

Next door was the **White Hart** which was recorded in 1822 as being leased by Thomas Tucker who held a 99-year lease dating from 1765. He in turn sub-let the pub to John Llewhellin who was still the landlord in 1830. The pub seems to have been closed for a few years in the 1840s but was in full swing between 1850 and 1871 when the licensee was grocer John James. He was notorious for his 'profane cursing' and 'violent conduct' when drunk – after which he would go round town apologising to the people he had offended!

On one occasion he was fined ten shillings for allowing drunkenness and disorderly conduct in the house. Labourers and colliers had been drinking steadily since 4.30 one afternoon and 'in the course of the evening a fiddler was introduced and dancing commenced'. Naturally the evening ended with a massive free-for-all and the police had to be called to break up the brawl. Following his death his second wife, Mrs. Mary James, kept the pub from 1875 to 1892 and also ran the grocery business. Thomas Phillips was there from 1895 to 1899, William John ran the pub from 1901 to 1906 and Fred Rogers held the licence from 1911 to 1914. It was reported in 1920 that the White Hart – which was owned by St. Thomas' Church – still held a licence, but that it had ceased trading. Although it was subsequently reopened by wine merchants W.H. George, with Charles Joseph Davies as licensee, the pub was axed in 1924 by the magistrates with £116 being paid in compensation.

The **Pembroke Yeoman** opposite was for many years called the **Upper Three Crowns**. Matthew Walters was landlord from at least 1826 until his

Splendid sign-writing on the Upper Three Crowns in the days when Charles Davies was licensee.
(Picture courtesy of Mr. David Griffiths)

death, aged 71, in 1835. His widow then continued the business until Michaelmas 1837 when she retired due to ill health. This prompted an advertisement in the press advertising the freehold of: 'That newly-built and well-established Public House called the Three Crowns, situate in King Street near the Corn Market'. The property included a parlour, tap-room, bar, brewhouse, dining room, five bedrooms and stables. Henry Watts was landlord of the Three Crowns from 1840 until his death in 1846 after which it was run by his widow Sarah until 1850.

Richard Phillips, formerly of The Grove, took over and remained there until 1873 when he died aged 66 and weighing 22 stone. His widow Mary Phillips carried on for a few years followed by David Phillips, while William Davies from Lampeter Velfrey held the licence from 1881 to 1884. Richard Griffiths was landlord from 1890 to 1902; he was a brother of James Griffiths of the Greyhound, and like his brother he fathered a family of 11 children.

The pub was owned by Palmer's wine merchants by 1910; their tenants came and went fairly rapidly – too rapidly for the liking of the local magistrates who thought this indicated that 'the trade of the inn was gone' and debated closing it down. Fortunately Charles Sutton Davies, formerly of the Fox and Hounds across the road, revived the fortunes of the inn, being mine host from 1914 to 1931. Even so he was given a severe ticking-off by the justices for serving late one night during the First World War; they fined him

The Upper Three Crowns is now the Pembroke Yeoman.

£10 and threatened to call in the Board of Liquor Control if he reoffended. William E. Nutt was the landlord of the Upper Three Crowns from 1935 to 1944 followed by Basil Davies and William Evans who took charge in 1955.

It was Bill Thurston in the late 1960s who changed the name of the pub, renovating and modernising it from what had previously been something of a 'spit and sawdust' local. The new name reflects that fact that the Yeomanry had their headquarters nearby for many years. The present licensee, Nigel Brock, arrived from running The Glen in 1984 and by 2006 was the longest-serving publican in the town.

The **Plough** seems to have been virtually next door to the Three Crowns and may have opened when the Market Street Plough closed. James Allen was licensee in 1811 followed in 1812 by his widow Elizabeth. In that year the Plough was advertised for sale, together with brewhouse, dairy and three-stall stable. A Mr. Davies was the landlord in 1820, Thomas Evans kept the pub in 1826, Mary Francis held the licence in 1830 and John Woolcock was there in 1835. In 1838, Richard Robinson of Hill Street, described as a cordwainer and leather cutter, took out a 60-year lease on the Plough. Isaac Williams was the licensee from 1841 to 1852, followed by George Hughes who was there from 1858 to 1861. Tradition has it that the pub closed at about this time and that the licence was transferred to a house in Shipman's Lane.

John Owen from Letterston obtained a full licence for the **Ship** in 1870, having run it as a beer-house with his wife Martha since about 1858. He was a Trafalgar veteran who lost his leg in the battle and the

At one time this was the Ship Inn, run by Trafalgar hero John Owen.

114

building was later named Trafalgar House in his honour. The pub stood next door to Hill House College and appears to have closed in the 1870s when Mr. Owen died. It was demolished along with the college in 1964.

In December 1836 the **Grove** inn at the top of Hill Street was transferred from James Murphy to William Phillips who advertised the fact in the local press.

> The house, stables and coach house have recently undergone extensive improvements and are well calculated to suit the comfort and convenience of all classes of visitors, the situation being a most healthy part of town as well as in the immediate neighbourhood of markets and fairs and, in particular, persons coming from the towns of Milford and Pembroke.

William Phillips was still there in 1840 while Richard Phillips was the landlord between 1844 and about 1850. The Grove closed around that time and seems to have become the home of attorney Henry Mathias before being incorporated with neighbouring properties to form the town's Baptist College in 1864. The glassed-in coach arch in the centre of the former college – now a guest house – suggests that this was the building which once housed the Grove Inn.

Across the road, Bongo's Rhythm Shack was for a century and a half the **Dragon** inn. At one time the elegant town house of one of the local gentry families, the building was allegedly the birth-place of Waterloo hero General Sir Thomas Picton; tradition states that his mother was attending a ball in the town when she went into labour. Richard Phillips seems to have turned the house into an inn when he left the Grove in 1850; certainly he was the landlord in 1851 when he handed over to Martha Allen and moved

The Dragon in its final days as an inn.

down the road to run the Upper Three Crowns. Robert Gregson took over from Daniel Jones in 1855 but died in 1862 at the early age of 35 and Martha Evans was in charge by 1867. She left to run the New Inn on the Old Bridge and Charles Thomas took over.

Probably the most successful landlord of the Dragon, and certainly the longest-serving, was John Mathias from Ambleston, a leading light in the local lodge of Odd Fellows – the Loyal Cleddy – who was in charge from 1874 to 1912. 'The glories of the Dragon were at their zenith on Portfield fair days,' recalled W.D. Phillips. 'It was difficult to get served, so great was the crush.' In 1912 the licence passed to John Mathias' widow Lettice. Sergeant Major George Black and his wife Lily subsequently took over. A former staff-instructor to the Pembrokeshire Yeomanry who served with the Welsh Horse in the First World War, Sgt. Major Black became the manager of the Palace Theatre in the years after the war and it was his wife who then held the licence of the Dragon. The couple left in 1926 to become stewards of the Riverside Conservative Club in Cardiff, being succeeded in turn by Jane Thomas, Mrs. Annie Roch and John Rice who was there between 1932 and 1938. Charles and Sarah Earle were in charge in the 1940s, followed by Thomas Rowlands in the 1950s and Grace Daniels who kept the Dragon from the 1950s through to the 1970s. Billy Flynn then had charge for a number of years followed by Tom Haswell in the early 1980s. The inn subsequently changed hands several times – always a bad sign – and in December 2003 it was reported in the local press that a planning application had been received to convert the Dragon from a pub to a 'non-residential institution'; by 2005 it had become Bongo Clive's 'Rhythm Shack'.

There were a couple of other pubs in the street at one time. Thomas Price ran the **Bush** in King Street in the 1820s and John Lloyd was landlord of the **Pembroke Arms** in 1830. An account was sent from this pub for refreshments and accommodation during the election in May 1831 when the landlord's surname was Thomas. And a much more recent arrival on the scene is the subterranean **Hideaway Bar**, previously known as the **Tudor Cellar Bar**.

CHAPTER TEN

Haverfordwest
ST. THOMAS' SQUARE, MERLIN'S HILL & SHIPMAN'S LANE

Now a sprawling car park, St. Thomas' Green was once a true 'village green', well grassed and the site of May Day revels around a maypole. After the Portfield Enclosure Act of 1838 it became the town's fair ground, being the venue for the annual hiring fair in October and also the monthly livestock fairs. The first three County Agricultural Shows were also held on the Green in the 1840s before moving to a dedicated showground at the top of Barn Street. The livestock fairs were tremendously busy occasions, with cattle and sheep penned on both sides of the Green and right up Merlin's Hill to the junction with Milford Road, where the horse-fair took place. The following is a description of an early 19th-century fair on the Green:

> Black cattle and horses were the chief objects of the meeting, which had scarcely any diversions; no shows, nor any jugglers, except a recruiting party and two or three cattle jobbers or middle men. ... But we had some rural sports; a party of rustics were dancing on the green to the notes of a miserable scraper. ... Close by a game of see-saw seemed to create much diversion among the by-standers.

For some reason there were fewer pubs on the Green than might be expected, given its role as a fair ground. One pub was the **Rifleman**, the name recalling the regular use of the Green as a parade ground for the local militia. Collector of rates Thomas Martin and his wife Ann were in charge from 1861 to 1884, but they had given way to Sergeant Major Isaac Johnston, bandmaster of the militia, by 1891. The property, which was then owned by the Picton Castle Estate, boasted stables for 20 horses and a coach house. Sergeant Major Johnston was declared bankrupt in 1894 and Miss Harriet Griffiths was the landlady from 1899 to about 1908. From 1910 to 1925 Mrs. Mary Pugh 'ably conducted' the Rifleman; she was the widow of Charles Pugh, evidently another of the Portfield dynasty

The Rifleman no longer stands, although the alleyway to the right is still called Rifleman Lane.
(Picture courtesy of the Bisley H. Munt Collection)

of publicans, who must have died soon after arriving at the Rifleman from the nearby Globe.

Mrs. Pugh was followed by George Evans who was there from 1925 until the 1930s. Stan and Julia Hurford were at the Rifleman during the war and Timothy Horgan was licensee in the early 1950s. In 1957 Ben Moody, another member of the well-known boxing family, took over and ran the pub for a dozen years, while the last licensees were Ray Llewellyn and his wife Beryl. They were at the Rifleman in 1983 when it was announced that this Ansells house was to be closed and demolished. Remarkably the Llewellyns already had experience of a Haverfordwest pub being shot from underneath them, having been licensees of the Swan when it closed. Their farewell party at the Rifleman included members of the Showmen's Guild who had built up a strong relationship with the pub over many years of attending St. Thomas' Fair. The pub was demolished in 1984 and a surgery and pharmacy built on the site.

Flying the flag for Wales – The Oak in 2001.

The **Oak** is a terraced cottage pub in Grove Row, still open for business. It was recorded in 1835 when Henry Southwell was the landlord, and he was still there in 1855. In August 1845, a bare-knuckle fight was staged outside the Oak involving a local cobbler known as 'The Baron' and a blacksmith who went by the nom-de-guerre of 'Smiler'. The fight was reported in the *Carmarthen Journal* in colourful style.

> The Baron led off the ball by a terrific blow on Smiler's mug, flooring him and drawing a profusion of claret. Smiler came up groggy but not dismayed, and rushing to his antagonist caught him on the left ogle, putting it in mourning and dropping him like a hot potato.

Thus the fight progressed for four five-minute rounds until a 'beak' appeared and put an end to the entertainment. The Baron and his friends headed for the Oak, where they could be heard singing 'Give me the girl that's true to me, when I goes rolling home'. Later that night the Baron announced his retirement from the bare-knuckle ring; he was, after all, nearly 60.

Henry Southwell was followed by his widow Mary Southwell who was there from 1855 to 1861, and then briefly by their son James Southwell who died in 1862. James Jones held the licence in 1867; he had problems with his wife Elizabeth who would occasionally become 'mad drunk'. It was partly because of this failing that Jones lost his licence later that year, the pub passing to Reuben Thomas who remained the landlord until 1881.

The pub was a popular meeting place during the horse-fairs and cattle-fairs on the Green, and inevitably attracted the attention of pickpockets; a farmer named Bushell who went into the pub to conclude a cattle sale in 1885 was relieved of gold and notes to the value of £26 by a 'dip'. James Pugh, son of James Pugh of the Plasterers', held the licence from 1884 to 1916, by which time he was 60, and Mrs. Pugh was there in 1920. William Giles was landlord from 1922 until his death in 1948 and David Davies – 'Dai the Oak' – took over in 1950 and remained the popular licensee for many years; since his day the licence has changed hands on several occasions.

At the Merlin's Hill end of this terrace was the **Barley Mow** kept in the 1860s and '70s by coachman Henry Owen, usually known by the nickname 'Harry Blazes'. Also at the southern end of the Green was the **Red Cow.** This pub seems to have been named with a certain amount of gallows humour, since it was originally linked to a slaughterhouse where beasts sold in the cattle fairs met a bloody end. William Adams kept the Red Cow between 1826 and 1835 and it was occupied by James Sinnett in the 1840s. W.D. Phillips recalled a licensee named Tom Lee, while the census records show that William Lee lived there from 1851 to 1871. When it stopped being a pub isn't known.

Shipman's Lane had a pub at one time, although the evidence is sketchy. It was apparently called the **Plough** and George Hughes was the landlord in the late 1850s / early 1860s having moved from a pub of the same name in Hill Street. There is also a reference to him running the **Court House** pub in Shipman's Lane, but again the information is vague. The 1871 census shows George Hughes, carter, living in Shipman's Lane, and there is a local tradition that the house tucked away behind the present-day garage was once a pub. Another unconfirmed tradition is that there was a pub called the **Vine** on Merlin's Hill, close to the junction with Shipman's Lane.

In the 1860s, John Phillips Jones – formerly a gamekeeper on the Butterhill estate near St. Ishmael's – ran the **Gamekeeper's Arms** on Merlin's Hill. Unfortunately Jones, 'a fine, powerfully-built man', unaccountably dropped dead in the middle of Tower Hill in March 1872 at the age of 67. Consequently an advert appeared in the press a month or so afterwards offering the freehold of:

That fully-licensed public inn called the Gamekeeper's Arms situate in St. Thomas' Green with excellent garden and out offices thereto, now in the occupation of Mr. Thomas Williams.

The Gamekeeper's Arms on Merlin's Hill, still with its coach arch alongside.

Thomas Williams remained licensee until 1880 when James and Elizabeth Thomas took over. They kept the inn for some 30 years and James Thomas was the owner and licensee in 1911 when the licensing magistrates decided that the Gamekeeper's Arms was surplus to requirements and suppressed the licence. Thomas received £300 in compensation for the loss of his livelihood. Although now a private house, the former pub at 19, Merlin's Hill still has its coach arch which would once have led to the stable yard beyond.

Butcher Thomas Adams and his wife Sarah ran the **Ivy Cottage** on Merlin's Hill in the 1850s, but when Thomas died in 1858 the licence passed to James Roch who was licensee from 1859 to 1867. Scotsman George Reid ran the pub in 1870, but decided to take a back seat two years later and advertised for a tenant; the advert stated that the pub 'has been a licensed house for a long period and a good trade is being transacted in connection with the fairs'. Thomas Gould was the man who took over the pub, but it didn't work out and Reid was soon back in charge, remaining the licensee until at least 1884.

In 1891 the landlord was Thomas James, Miss Annie Morris was in charge in 1895, while tailor and innkeeper William James kept the pub from 1898 to 1909 followed by James Skone of Milford Haven. Sarah Davies was

The old Ivy Cottage, with the fire station watchtower looming over it.

landlady during the war and in 1915 she was fined 20 shillings for selling bottled beer on a Sunday – 'a very serious offence' according to the magistrates. She must have left immediately afterwards because local wine merchants George Palmer and Son were soon advertising for a tenant for the Ivy Cottage, pointing out its 'prominent position on the Fair ground' and 'good garden'.

The pub had passed into the hands of wine merchants James Williams by the early 1920s, with Thomas Adams holding the tenancy – the second person of that name to hold the licence of the Ivy Cottage. It was reported in 1921 that 'half the time the licensee was without anything for people to drink and the house was closed during those periods'. William Palmer from Llangwm took over later that year, but his somewhat cavalier approach to the licensing hours led to the closure of the pub by the magistrates in 1923. The house still stands close to the fire station looking every inch a former pub, although boarded up in 2006 and awaiting conversion into offices.

Still a popular local, the **Stonemasons' Arms** at the top of Merlin's Hill was once the Jones family pub and benefited from the fact that the town's horse fair was held outside. As W.D. Phillips recorded:

> In the days when horses were in demand, the horse fair at the top of Merlin's Hill was worth going to see, nearly all classes of horse-flesh being well represented. Dealers came from far and near. Many a deal has been effected in the Stonemasons' Arms.

Thomas Jones – a stonemason, naturally enough – kept the pub from 1850 to 1874, followed by his widow, Mrs. Martha Jones, who held the licence until about 1892. James Rowland Jones was there from 1895 to 1905 when the property passed to Mary Edwards. She seems to have installed various tenants including John Mathias to run the pub. By the early 1920s it had become a James Williams house, with Martha Roberts holding the

The Stonemasons' Arms once overlooked the town's horse fair.

tenancy. David Williams – 'Dai the Stone' – took over in 1925 but he was employed at Hook Colliery so it was his wife, Jane Williams, who held the licence from 1927 to about 1944. Their daughter Sylvia 'Rosie' Faulkner took over as licensee, becoming Rosie Hughes when she married Jimmy Hughes. They later divorced, Jimmy Hughes moving down the hill to the Prince of Wales, but Rosie carried on running the Stonemasons' until she retired in 1986, latterly with the help of her son David Faulkner.

Remembered fondly as 'a lady you didn't argue with', Rosie catered for so many off-duty personnel from the nearby police, fire and ambulance stations that the Stonemasons' earned the nickname of 'HQ'. On one occasion an over-zealous copper raided the pub late one night and discovered a group of after-hours drinkers supping quietly in the dimly-lit bar. Just as he was about to throw the book at them, he discovered to his dismay that they were all high-ranking police officers, including the Chief Constable of the county! Following Rosie's retirement the pub was run for a few years by her son Billy. When he departed it ended the family's long association with the pub which has since changed hands fairly regularly.

CHAPTER ELEVEN

Haverfordwest
BARN STREET, CITY ROAD, PORTFIELD & PORTFIELD GATE

The area between the top of Dew Street and the top of Barn Street was open fields before 1843 when Shut Lane was built to connect the two streets. This was later renamed Albert Street and for nearly 40 years the Pembrokeshire Agricultural Society held its annual show on land bounded by Dew Street, Barn Street and Albert Street, eventually outgrowing the showground in 1884. According to G.D. James (who lived in Albert Street) the **Agricultural Arms** once stood in this street. No pub of this name has come to light; however in 1846, Thomas Williams – for many years a waiter at the Castle Hotel – opened the **Greyhound and Agricultural Inn** somewhere in the town, and this could well be the same place. Williams' housewarming dinner was attended by 40 gentlemen who paid 7s. 6d. each for dinner – served at 5pm – and a pint of wine, but despite this auspicious start the enterprise soon folded.

In 1859 a property developer and postmaster named Richard Francis built a number of houses near the top of Barn Street, just below Fountains Row. One of these became the **Four-in-Hand** which was opened in the 1860s by Richard's son Caleb Francis. He was still the innkeeper in 1874, but George Griffiths held the licence in 1880. Mrs. Charlotte Thomas had taken over by 1884 and Miss Elizabeth Griffiths kept the pub in 1891 followed by Maria Harries who was fined half a crown for being drunk behind the bar in 1892 and then by David John who was still there in 1909. Arthur H. Lloyd was landlord in 1914 followed by Mary and Alfred Holloway who were fined five shillings each in 1916 for serving after time. Mrs. Elizabeth Staley took over in 1917, her husband being at the Front, and in 1919 the pub was reportedly doing a very good trade, shifting 60 barrels of beer a year and 430 dozen bottles.

Mrs. Staley – a daughter of James and Sarah Ambrey of the Bellevue – was fined £1 in 1920 for serving out of hours. A second minor conviction followed soon afterwards, prompting the town magistrates to decide somewhat harshly in March 1921 that the licence should be revoked because of the 'disorderly manner' in which the pub had been conducted. An appeal against this controversial decision failed and the building is now a private house, still called Four-in-Hand.

The Four in Hand in Barn Street closed in the 1920s, since when it has been a private house.

There was a beer-house called the **New Put Up** at the top of Barn Street occupied in the early 1860s by Adam and Mary Roch. W.D. Phillips described it as being 'near the corner, turning for the Havens, but now demolished'. Phillips also mentioned an otherwise elusive pub called the **Crown** in Kensington Gardens, kept by one Jacob Botha.

The junction of Church Street and Barn Street is still known as Cromwell Corner, the tradition being that Oliver Cromwell stayed at a house at the bottom of Barn Street when he passed through the town in 1648. When a pub was opened on the junction 200 years later it honoured this tradition by taking the name of **Cromwell Arms**. Unfortunately it proved to be one of Haverfordwest's more disreputable beer-houses, being involved in numerous court cases throughout its brief career and once being described as 'a haunt of drunkenness and vice'. It was stated that men and boys 'of the very worst classes' tended to gather outside the pub on a Sunday evening, so that any woman making her way to one of the many places of worship in the area would be subjected to 'all sorts of ridicule and annoyance from this lawless assembly'.

The pub was involved in a particularly sordid murder case in the summer of 1850. The trouble began when a widow from Rosemarket by the name of Elizabeth Barnett was chucked out of the pub for being too drunk even by the lax standards of the Cromwell. In the street outside she became involved in a drunken argument with a passer-by, a 23-year-old prostitute named Jane Evans. Later that night Barnett was found seriously injured in a ditch below

Pigs Parade; she died two days later without regaining consciousness. A reward of £50 was offered for information leading to the capture of the murderer, and a week later Evans, the prostitute, and a youth named Thomas Thomas were charged with the murder. They were committed to the next assizes where both were acquitted due to a lack of any real evidence. Margaret Francis was the landlady of the pub at the time.

Early in 1852, Evan Thomas obtained a transfer licence of the Cromwell and immediately re-named it the **Railway Inn**, even though it was a long way from the projected station. Mary Lewis took over in 1853 but it remained a fairly rowdy establishment even after the name change, being regularly mentioned in court cases throughout the 1850s. It seems to have closed by 1860 and by 1901 the building, still called Cromwell House, was being occupied by coachbuilder William Reynish. It stood at the Church Street end of Tabernacle Row.

The **Old St. David's Arms** also stood in Tabernacle Row, facing up City Road, but most of the properties in this area were demolished as part of a road improvement scheme at the Barn Street / City Road junction. William Lloyd held the licence in 1826 while the biblically-named Meshach Owen was there between 1830 and 1835. During the election of May 1831 he entertained the voters who entered town along City Road from Dewsland Hundred and later presented the Blue party with a bill for £255. Jane Thomas was in charge between 1839 and 1844 while David Thomas – presumably a son – was the licensee between 1850 and 1861. John Evans ran the pub from 1867 to 1871 while his widow Martha Evans remained the landlady until 1880. Pembroke-born George Woolcock was in charge in the early 1880s before moving to the Falcon in North Street, at which point the pub seems to have closed.

The **Turk's Head** occupied one of the first houses on the left going up City Road. John Sambrook was the landlord in 1835 followed by Elizabeth Sambrook who ran the pub in 1844 and John Lewis who was landlord from 1849 until 1858 (apart for the 12 months that he spent in jail for beating his wife). Martha Beynon was the landlady between 1861 and 1876, while Essex Rees Harries was the landlord from 1879 to 1895. The Turk's Head became so notorious for its flouting of the Sunday closure law that in 1897 two policemen spent the day hiding in the back of Tabernacle Sunday School from where they could spy on the comings and goings at the back door of the pub. A regular stream of callers beat a path to the rear of the Turk's Head – many of them from a nearby garden where an all-day drinking session was taking place. It was, said Supt Francis, the worst case he had met with in connection with Sunday drinking 'and showed the manner in which some persons spent their Sundays'. Landlord William Roberts was fortunate not to lose his licence, being hit with a 40 shilling fine instead, but the pub seems to have closed a couple of years later. The Turk's Head no longer stands, having been demolished to make way for a new house called Sunnydale.

There were a couple of other pubs in City Road, and the **Golden Ball** was said to be the first house after passing City Road Terrace; it was later a shop. In 1851 a chap by the name of John Lewis kept a pub in Elm Place, which seems to have been at the top of City Road, near the junction with Hawthorn Rise. An old hand-written list of pubs in Haverfordwest refers to a house in City Road called either the **Fiddlers' Arms** or the **Peddlars' Arms**; possibly this was John Lewis' pub.

The Bellevue as it looked in about 1950.
(Picture courtesy of Haverfordwest Reference Library)

The Portfield area of town was named after the De la Poer family who gave the town the Common on which the racecourse was situated. Organised racing took place on the Common as long ago as 1727, so it comes as no surprise to learn that the **Bellevue** on the junction of the Dale Road and the Haven Road was formerly the **Horse and Jockey**. The landlord from 1852 to 1861 was plasterer James Pugh, a member of a dynasty of licensees and evidently related to the Pughs who ran the town's Castle Inn and also the Rutzen Arms in Narberth. His eldest son James opened the Plasterers' in Dew Street, while another son, Lewis, succeeded his father at the Horse and Jockey. In 1866 Lewis was fined £5 for beating up one of his customers. However the customer had the last, bitter laugh, because the landlord – who was in his early 30s – collapsed and died a few months later. Various members of the Pugh family continued to run the pub for the next ten years, but John Williams from Llysyfran and his wife Ann were there in the early 1880s.

By about 1885 the licensee was Mrs. Sarah Ambrey who had previously kept the Seaman's Arms in Quay Street and she soon changed the name from the Horse and Jockey to the more genteel-sounding Bellevue. However, she must have left for a time, because ten years later the tenant was Thomas Phillips. An 1895 advert for the sale of the freehold stated that the premises had recently undergone complete restoration and added that there was a coach house and stable with loft over facing the Dale road. By 1901 Mrs. Ambrey was back in charge of this W.H. George house and she was still there in 1913.

Thomas Leigh was landlord in 1914 while William Phipps, the next licensee, was forever getting into trouble with the magistrates who were delighted to see the licence being transferred in 1916 to Miss Helen Lerway, formerly of the Landsdowne Hotel, Cardiff, and she remained at the 'Belle' until about 1927. Thomas Marchant held the licence from 1928 to 1936 when William Ambrey took over the tenancy – a case of homecoming for him since he was the son of Sarah and was born at the Bellevue. A butcher by trade, he ran the pub for 15 years.

A recent view of the Bellevue.

At this time the Bellevue comprised a smoke-room, a bar and a tiny 'jug and bottle' room with a counter for off sales. The landlord enforced a strict 'men only' rule in the public bars – ladies with the temerity to call in would be ushered behind the scenes into the family's private dining room and served their drink there. The pub stayed in the Ambrey family until the mid 1950s, Miss Marjorie Ambrey having succeeded her father William in about 1950. John and Gladys Peebles ran the pub in the late 1950s and early '60s, with Mrs. Peebles running it on her own after 1962. She was followed by Ieuan and Phyllis Morgan in the late '60s and Wilf Ryder in the early '70s. Jack Kirkby was there from 1982 to 1992 as a tenant of Ansells before moving to the Penry Arms for six years, during which time the Bellevue was run by a succession of managers employed by the brewery and later by Sycamore Taverns. By 1998 the Bellevue had closed, but Mr. and Mrs. Kirkby returned, bought the pub and made it a thriving concern once again.

A couple of references exist to a **New Inn** in Portfield (evidently not the one out at Portfield Gate). Mrs. E. Williams was the landlady in 1875 and Arthur Williams was landlord in 1884, but frustratingly neither appears on the 1881 census.

Portfield Common was where the annual October hiring fair was held until the Portfield Enclosure Act of 1838. Thereafter it was switched to St. Thomas' Green where it survives as the annual funfair still known as Portfield Fair. A booklet published in the 1870s and entitled *Haverfordwest Charities, with Numerous Interesting Local and Historical Notes and Useful Information* had much to say about the old Portfield hiring fair – a day 'of unbounded enjoyment and mirth'.

> Buxom, ruddy-faced servant lads and lasses – the latter tricked out in rare finery and flaunting ribbons – were there in hundreds and hundreds, while our townsfolk of 'Honey Harfat' swelled the thousands who thronged to the place. And who will not remember mine host of that old country inn – The Whale – who in those days had far more custom than himself and his many assistants could attend to, while the refreshment booths, the shows, swings, knock-em-downs and other similar places were so largely patronised that their proprietors reaped a golden harvest and the gooseberry, ginger-beer braggat and treacle tart vendors, and the nuts, cakes, gingerbread and other stalls transacted such roaring business that few, even if any, of our other country fairs could stand a comparison with it.

The **Whale** was run by John Jenkins from 1818 to 1822, becoming the **New Inn** in 1823. (A note on the recognisance of 1823 describes the pub as 'New Inn [late Whale] Poorfield Gate'). Jenkins continued as landlord until at least 1828, Richard Tuder was the landlord in 1851, James Harries had charge in 1861 and John Hughes was there in 1871. Francis Lewis, who was

The former New Inn at Portfield Gate, now known as Tafarn Newydd.

the landlord from 1881 to 1898, also ran a tailoring business in the house next door. Walter John was mine host from 1901 to 1906 while Thomas Stanford took over in 1910. When he died in 1915 his widow Elizabeth took on the tenancy of what was by now a Palmer's Brewery house.

From 1923 to 1926 William Thomas kept the pub, which was a popular 'stopping-off' point for day-trippers from Haverfordwest to the Havens. Howell Waters was the licensee from 1926 to 1950, followed by Mrs. Lettice Jones, who was still there when the pub – which had become rather run-down by this time – became one of the last victims of the redundancy ruling in 1957. An inspector who visited the New Inn stated that it was little used and reported:

> It is not kept clean and presents a very untidy appearance. When inspected recently the room called a cellar contained a bucket of kitchen refuse and on the floor of the lounge was a sack of poultry food.

Arguing in court against the closure, solicitor Ivor Rees made a plea in support of the humble cottage pub.

> Our ancestors in their wisdom thought it proper that in little communities people should have some place where they could congregate. Are you going to bring the chopper down on this old custom?

The answer was 'Yes' and the licensee received compensation of £265. Much renovated, the building still stands and is now called Tafarn Newydd.

The Penry family were Carmarthenshire landowners who lived at Cwrt-y-Ceidrim near Pontarddulais (the wonderfully-named Henry Penry was High Sheriff of that county in 1756). A branch of the Penrys also seems to have acquired land at Portfield Gate near Haverfordwest, and John Penry-Jones is recorded as living at Sutton Lodge in 1870, around the time that the pub name **Penry Arms** first appears in the local trade directories. James Harries was the landlord from 1871 to 1892 and Edward Pearce was in charge from 1901 to 1906. The ground landlords, W.H. George and Son, seem to

The interior of the Penry Arms in the 1970s.

Last orders for the Penry Arms were called in 2000.

have struggled to find a steady tenant up to and during the First World War, their tenants including Margaret Hughes, Francis Morris (later of the Old Three Crowns), John John and James Pegram. D. Absalom kept the pub in 1923 followed by Edward O' Connell and Rupert Stanley Devote who was there in the early 1930s. Elizabeth Bulman was licensee from 1936 to 1939 followed by Gladys John who was still in charge in 1954 when she became Mrs. Raymond.

After going through a sticky patch in the late 1950s (there were five different licensees between 1955 and 1959) the Penry was renovated and extended in the 1960s after which it gained a reputation as one of the first and best 'food pubs' in the county, especially under the management of Vic and Betty Price. Subsequent licensees included Bob Bottrill, Ron Groves and Jack Kirkby on a sabbatical from the Bellevue. The Penry Arms was bought in 1997 by Mr. Mark Falzon, but by this time the pub was only busy during the summer months and trade fell away dramatically during the winter. Finding the business unsustainable, he ceased trading in October 2000 and planning permission was given in February 2001 for the Penry to be converted into two houses.

CHAPTER TWELVE

Slebech & Uzmaston

At one time the main route into Haverfordwest from Carmarthen wound through the Norman strongholds of Llawhaden and Wiston, but in later years this route was superseded by the turnpike road which crosses the Cleddau at Canaston Bridge and then passes through the parishes of Slebech and Uzmaston – the route of the present A40 trunk road.

These days there are no roadside pubs to be found between Canaston Bridge and Haverfordwest, reputedly the result of an edict by a local squire with Temperance leanings. However there were several inns along the road at one time and James Matthias was the landlord of the **Green Dragon**, Slebech, from 1805 to 1824. The **Royal Oak**, also in Slebech parish, was opened in 1826 by John Prickett, with Stephen Prickett running the place in 1828. 'Prickett's Wood' is the name given to a small woodland to the south of the lay-by at the top of Toch Hill, so presumably this was the location of the Royal Oak.

One of the few ale-houses located off the main roadway was at Midcounty, between Slebech and Wiston, where John James was in charge in 1784; the sign of this ale-house isn't recorded. Back on the turnpike road, the **Square and Compass** was probably the ale-house kept by William Lewis in 1795 and by Martha Lewis from 1805 to 1810. Isaac John was the landlord from 1811 to 1828, and this was at the farm now known as 'Square' on the left hand side of the road going down Arnolds Hill.

John Page opened an ale-house at the very bottom of the hill in 1811, over the parish border at Deep Lake in Uzmaston, and he was still there in 1815, being succeeded by William Roblin. The licensing records for Michaelmas 1819 state that this farmhouse inn was called 'Home Bound', probably short for **Homeward Bound**, a sign calculated to appeal to weary countryfolk on their way home from Haverfordwest market and faced with a steep pull up Arnold's Hill.

But if the sign offered a welcome, the landlord very often did not. William Roblin seems to have been a disagreeable sort of chap, and he could become ill-tempered and violent after a few drinks. One of his farm workers was William Davies from Uzmaston who became so disgusted at his employer's 'bad habits' that he left the farm and found employment with Thomas Thomas of Boulston. On a summer's evening in 1820, Davies and Thomas were passing the Homeward Bound when they encountered Roblin, who – as usual – had been drinking heavily. He began ranting at Davies, and, as the *Cambrian* newspaper reported:

> A violent quarrel arose betwixt and which continued some time and at length terminated in the former procuring a pistol from his own house with which he shot Davies through the head.

Somehow the 23-year-old Davies survived, though in a critical condition, and he was taken to Haverfordwest for his wounds to be treated. Meanwhile the search started for Roblin, who had fled immediately after firing the shot, and various special constables were sworn in to help with the hunt. They also had to search for Roblin's wife Margaret who had mysteriously vanished from Deep Lake – but whether she was an accessory, a second murder victim or simply scared of her husband no-one could say.

Margaret, who was 50, turned up after a few days and was detained in Haverfordwest gaol while the hunt for her husband continued. William Roblin was on the run for over a fortnight before he was tracked to a cottage called Tyborn on the other side of the river, not far from the present-day Canaston Bowl. He was arrested on Monday, 4 September and charged with battery; this became a charge of wilful murder on the following Saturday when the unfortunate Davies succumbed to his injuries and died. At the spring Great Sessions in Haverfordwest, the two Roblins were tried in connection with the murder. There being little evidence against Margaret she was found not guilty, but the jury wasted little time in returning a guilty verdict against her husband. He was sentenced to hang the following Monday.

On the morning of 23 April 1821, Roblin made the short journey from his cell in Haverfordwest gaol to the nearby gallows. After receiving the sacrament from the Rev. James Thomas of St. Mary's, Roblin mounted the platform, shaking hands with a number of people as he did so. As the noose was placed around his neck he was asked if he had anything to say; he was reported to have replied: 'No. Lord Jesus receive my soul. Save me, a miserable sinner'. With that, the trapdoor beneath his feet opened and Roblin was 'launched into eternity' – and also into the history books as the last man to be hanged in Pembrokeshire. After his body had been cut down, it was sent to a local surgeon to be 'anatomised' before the remains were buried in the castle grounds. But that wasn't the end of the story. According to one account, Roblin's remains were exhumed some 40 years later and sold to a retired sailor for 1s. 6d.!

Not surprisingly, perhaps, the Homeward Bound seems to have closed after this incident, and the next we hear of a pub at the foot of Arnold's Hill is in 1841 when Thomas Thorne ran an unidentified ale-house in one of the six properties that comprised the hamlet of Deep Lake. Ten years later, carpenter and publican William Lewis was running an ale-house at Deep Lake which he called, naturally enough, the **Carpenters' Arms**.

Several accounts of the story of William Roblin refer to his ale-house as the 'New Inn', the mistake arising from the fact that there was a **New Inn** at Deep Lake farm some 40 years after the murder. William and Elizabeth Harries opened this ale-house in the 1850s and in 1866 John Harries of New Inn, Deep Lake, was fined five shillings for serving beer during prohibited hours on a Sunday. It may have been this crime which brought about the closure of the pub.

An ale-house not on the main road was the **Plough**, kept by Thomas Jones between 1851 and 1854. This seems to have been on the lane between Have-a-Care Bridge and Creamson (although it is difficult to be certain) and it had closed by 1860.

The **Hermit** was kept by Mary Phillips in 1844 and according to W.D. Phillips the pub was notable for its signboard on which was the verse:

> A hermit of old,
> Drank water when cold.
> His form was fast fading away.
> But the hermit found out
> That good brown ale and stout
> Was the thing to moisten his clay.

William Phillips, 64-year-old clogmaker, lived at the Hermit in 1861 and the inn seems to have stood between Good Hook and Little Clarboro'.

Three properties appear under the entry for Green Plain in the 1851 census, one of which was the **Farmers' Arms** kept by farm labourer Thomas John. No other reference to this pub has come to light.

The following report appeared in the *Welshman*, April 1836:

John Evans, in the employ of Mr. Wilson, Cresswell Quay, was driving a cart laden with millstone and drawn by bullocks, from Haverfordwest. When it arrived near the **Shepherd's Arms** on the Narberth Road he attempted to get into the cart but unfortunately falling over the pole the wheel went over his body and crushed him so severely that he died in a few minutes.

But where was the Shepherd's Arms? Assuming the unfortunate Evans had dismounted to ease the burden going uphill, it may be that the Shepherd's Arms was a cottage inn on Arnold's Downs where the road levels out near the present golf club.

CHAPTER THIRTEEN

Merlin's Bridge

Merlin's Bridge has nothing to do with the wizard of Arthurian legend. The name of the village is thought to be a corruption of Maudlen, there having been a Magdalen Chapel and leper hospice here in medieval times, a safe distance outside the town walls of Haverfordwest. The bridge carried the important turnpike road to Pembroke Ferry over Merlin's Brook, which in turn powered a mill and later served a tannery.

It wasn't until the 1920s that Merlin's Bridge began to develop from a rather dispersed village into one of the largest suburbs of Haverfordwest, and the *Pembrokeshire Herald* observed in 1924:

> Great improvements have been made lately at the Merlin's Bridge. New styles of houses and bungalows have been built there. Electric light has been installed at some of the houses for private use and attempts are now being made for the reception of wireless broadcast there by a young enthusiast.

As was noted at Cartlett, tremendous changes have taken place in Merlin's Bridge in recent years, prompted by the demand for more roads and wider. No longer is the ancient turnpike to Pembroke Ferry the main thoroughfare; nowadays the traffic sweeps along the town bypass, around the new roundabout with its inevitable burger bar, along the Merlin's Bridge by-pass and up Dredgman's Hill towards Milford Haven and its refineries. Parts of the original village have disappeared in the face of this road building frenzy, with several old properties having to be demolished.

One victim of the various road widening and road building schemes was the **Prince of Wale**s, once part of Quarry Row near the foot of Merlin's Hill. The Prince was kept by Thomas Waters from 1850 to 1852, while Thomas Davies was the publican between 1861 and 1880. He was followed between 1881 and 1887 by his son Henry Davies who died that year aged 38. Arthur Jones held the licence in 1891 and Sam Evans was there in 1896. Mrs. Minnie Elizabeth Creber was landlady from 1899 to 1906, Miss Margaret Jenkins kept the pub from 1909 until her death in 1927 and John Thomas was mine host from 1929 to 1932.

Owned by the Glen estate and leased by W.H. George, the Prince was kept by Edward O'Connell in the 1930s, followed by William Hire in the 1940s and then by Jimmy Hughes. His sister Alice Damant was the last licensee of the Prince, the pub closing on 9 December 1961 when the licence was transferred up the hill to The Glen itself. Mrs. Damant applied for an extension of hours from 3pm to 6pm on the pub's final day, in order that people from Merlin's Bridge could give the Prince a worthy send-off. Churlishly the magistrates refused this last request and a few years later the building was demolished.

The Prince of Wales on the right advertised 'Good stabling' at the turn of the 20th century.
(Picture courtesy of Mr. John Stevenson)

The conversion of **The Glen** from a gabled country house on the outskirts of the town into a pub-cum-hotel was carried out by W.H. George who acquired the building and grounds following the death of Haverfordwest businessman and sometime mayor Herbert Dickenson who was the last to live there. It was

A view of the Glen in about 1995.

George's flagship hostelry, and the first to run it was Richard Barklie Long from Sully, followed by William Hunter. Mr. and Mrs. Jack Parkin held the licence in the early 1970s before moving to the Roch Gate Motel, and they were followed by Ken Mynatt and then Nigel Brock who was at The Glen for six years before moving to the Pembroke Yeoman in 1984. He was succeeded by Bob Bottrill. For the past few years The Glen has been owned by Mr. Jasper Slater of Haverfordwest Coin Machines, with various managers taking charge of the hotel.

Across the old bridge, on the Burton road, the **Commercial** once faced an important junction. All traffic heading south from Haverfordwest would have passed this way, some carrying straight on for Pembroke Ferry and some turning right to take either the Steynton road or what is still called the Old Hakin Road. The Commercial was a substantial hostelry, three storeys tall, and John Davies was the landlord in 1880. James Rees held the licence in 1884, Sam Evans kept the pub in 1891 followed by John Devereux in 1895 and Mrs. E. Miller. William Phelps from Johnston was the landlord from 1899 to 1906, followed by Richard Griffiths (it seems to have been a pub where no-one stayed for very long). In 1911 licensee William Jenkins was fined 20 shillings for selling liquor on a Sunday, W.H. John was landlord by 1914 and Mrs. Minnie Bamkin held the licence in 1923. In 1927 the Commercial was forced to shut when the Redundancy Committee decided to close it down, with £400 in compensation being awarded. In 1955 Mr.

The Commercial Inn on the left now houses Merlin's Bridge post office.
(Picture courtesy of Mr. Roger Davies)

Herbert Dickenson received planning permission to create a shop and flat out of the old Commercial Inn and it is now the local post office.

There were numerous other pubs in the Merlin's Bridge area, but information about them is extremely sketchy. John Mathias opened the **New Inn** in 1816 but had closed it by 1819, while William Jones was licensee of the **Lion** from 1826 to 1830. Another Merlin's Bridge pub was the **Jolly Sailor** where Elizabeth Mathias was landlady in 1844, followed by John Mathias in the early 1850s and John James in 1858. The **Victoria** or Royal Victoria was near the junction of the Pembroke Road and Haylett Lane and was run by Job Noott in the early 1850s, perhaps as a short-term venture to serve the navvies building the railway line to Neyland.

The long-serving landlord of the **Three Horseshoes** between 1853 and 1901 was a carpenter from Steynton called John Merchant. He initially ran the pub with the help of his wife Martha and was still in charge at the age of 86. The pub seems to have been somewhere near the junction of the original Steynton Road and the Old Hakin Road. Meanwhile the **New Inn** was near the old bridge itself. The landlord here in 1871 was John Phillips and in 1875 it was William George. (There is a possibility that this pub later became the Commercial).

Further down Merlin's Brook, near where it enters the Cleddau, is Haroldston Bridge. This bridge gave access to a large area of farmland and the lane past Fern Hill was also the shortest route from Haverfordwest to the coal-mines at Little Milford and Hook. This lane was evidently well used, because George Lewis and William John both found it worth their while to run ale-houses here in the early 1800s. Another early ale-house near Haroldston Bridge was the **Anchor** which was kept by Benjamin Phelps between about 1813 and 1815.

The *Carmarthen Journal* of June 1843 recounted an incident which happened at an ale-house called the **Bridge End** Inn at Haroldston Bridge. Late one night three men armed with sticks appeared outside the inn, the implication being that they were 'Daughters of Rebecca' straggling home after a midnight attack on one of the despised tollgates. This strenuous activity having given them a thirst, they hammered on the door of the inn demanding to be given a drink. When this failed to rouse the household the three men took to smashing the front windows of the inn. This had the desired effect of bringing the landlord to the door, but what followed was not what the Rebeccaites had in mind at all. Evidently the landlord was a burly fellow, and having wrested a stick from one of the men outside, he proceeded to give the three of them what the *Journal* gleefully described as 'a sound thrashing'. According to a trade directory of 1844 the landlord of the Bridge End Inn was called John Phillips.

CHAPTER FOURTEEN

South of Haverfordwest
FREYSTROP, HOOK, LLANGWM, BURTON & ROSEMARKET

The Pevsner *Guide to the Buildings of Pembrokeshire* dismisses Freystrop as: 'Barely a village at all, just a scattering of houses along the road'. However, it must have seen plenty of passing traffic in the days when the road in question was the main turnpike from Haverfordwest to the horse-ferry at Burton, and this is reflected in the fact that there were three ale-houses here in 1784 run by William Morgan, William Cousins and John Thomas. The village is also on the Pembrokeshire coalfield and anthracite was mined locally until about 1907. Coal pits were scattered all over the area between Freystrop and Hook, and each seems to have had its own local ale-house which thrived or struggled according to the fortunes of the pit, sometimes surviving for just a couple of years.

In the early days, before a rail link was built to Johnston, coal from the various workings around Freystrop was transported downriver on shallow-draught vessels which tied up at Little Milford quay. Naturally there was an ale-house here to serve the men carting and loading the coal, and Martha Evans is known to have kept a pub at Little Milford in 1795 followed by John Evans between 1805 and 1821. This was the **Anchor**, and it was later kept from 1824 to 1828 by David Griffiths. There is a local tradition that a pub called the **Bumble Bee** existed at Little Milford at one time, but this may simply have been a nickname for the Anchor in order to differentiate it from another pub of the same name at Hook quay.

In 1811, Lord Milford of Picton Castle granted a lease for three lives to David Canton, a collier of Freystrop parish. It was for the **Rule and Compass**, the rent being £4 annually. Otherwise the records simply show the names of early Freystrop licensees, without the sign of their ale-house. These were: John Thomas (1805 to 1809), Hannah Thomas (1810), John Bennett (1808), Thomas Phillips (1811), John Barrah (1815) and Thomas Lloyd (1813 to 1814) whose pub was at Black Hill/Holwell Back. Perhaps one of these people kept the **Pelican** which, tradition has it, was near Cardmakers Pool.

Thomas Jenkins opened a pub in 'Low Freystrop' in 1811 and ran it for a couple of years. It was called the **New Inn**, and the landlady from 1813 to 1827 was Martha Cozens; the address was sometimes given as 'Mutton Hall'. Joseph Phillips took over, but nothing more is known about this pub. It appears that when she left the New Inn, Martha Cozens opened the **Lamb and Flag** nearby and she carried on running this wayside inn until 1841. Coalminer Owen Jenkins was landlord from 1851 to 1861 and James Yeo was in charge in 1867. The pub, which was in Lower Freystrop near the junction with the lane to Little Milford, was converted into a grocery shop shortly afterwards. It may have been the building now much modernised and called 'The Old Manse'.

The closure of the Lamb and Flag left a gap in the market which was filled by the **Travellers' Rest** at the foot of the hill; quite possibly the licence was transferred. This pub was up and running by 1869 when it was kept by William Gwilliam, a mariner, and his wife Martha. However she died that year, aged 26, and coal miner and publican Absalom James ran the Weary Traveller (*sic*) in 1871 – presumably an error in the census. George Russell was landlord of the Travellers' Rest in 1874 and John Russell was in charge

A group of workmen outside the Travellers' Rest, Freystrop, in about 1900.
(Picture courtesy of Beryl Davies)

in 1880. George Morgan held the licence from 1891 to 1917 when the pub was better known as 'the Tiddley', which it still is – perhaps a throwback to the days when beerhouses were known as 'Kiddleywinks'.

George Morgan was followed by William Cousins and his wife Sarah who were there for 40 years – he was always known as 'Billy the Tiddley'. Thomas Maxted was landlord in the early 1960s followed by Freddie Holder who later ran the New Anchor in Hook. Former navy man Ron Pitt, who was there in the 1970s, played host to the pub's most famous visitor when Prince Charles dropped in for a drink one evening with a few naval officers while he was staying at Brawdy. The Pitts were succeeded by Neville and Jane Lewis, and when they left to run the Cottage Inn at Llangwm the 'Tiddley' was taken over by Brian James. John Fry and Adrian Price both had periods in charge before present licensee Angela Jarvis took over in 2001.

Licensee Sarah Cousins at the door of the Travellers' Rest, Freystrop, in 1930.
(Picture courtesy of Beryl Davies)

The Rising Sun was on Maddocks Moor, at Summerhill. It was kept by William Harries, innkeeper and colliery labourer, in 1851. And the **Ship and Line** at Freystrop Mountain was kept in 1861 by Philip Philps who described himself as 'collier, farmer of six acres and innkeeper'.

The **Cross Inn** was run by John Griffiths from 1795 to 1813. This may have closed for a while, to be reopened as the **Colliers' Arms** at Freystrop Cross where Sarah Rees held the licence in 1826 and John Barrow was

Known to locals as 'The Tiddley', the Travellers' Rest is still going strong.

providing refreshment for the miners in 1827-28. There is no trace of the pub for a number of years thereafter, not until William Bennett is recorded as keeping the Colliers' Arms on Freystrop Cross from 1861 to 1880. A coal-miner by trade, Bennett was once charged with serving beer on a Sunday 'and attempting to bribe PC 46 with a pipe of tobacco'. Tradition has it that the pub closed under pressure from the local chapel minister; whatever the reason, it had become Bennett's Corner Shop by 1895. The building was demolished as part of a scheme to improve the junction in the 1950s.

Like Freystrop, Hook was an important centre of the local coal industry, and for a century and a half anthracite was shipped downriver from a wharf known as Hook Quay. The original stone quay is thought to have been built in the 1790s, and shortly afterwards William Eynon opened a pub called the **Anchor** nearby – no doubt causing some confusion, since there was another Anchor just up the river at Little Milford. He was still there in 1827, but his son – another William Eynon – had taken over by 1841. He ran the pub until the 1870s when he handed over the reins to his son, William the third.

The former Anchor at Hook Quay.

This William died at an early age, leaving his wife Elizabeth to run the pub. She remarried, and her second husband Thomas Reid was landlord for some 15 years. Benjamin Hitchins kept the pub in 1906, Austin Jenkins was in charge in 1910 and Thomas Jenkins was landlord in 1914, after which the pub closed for a couple of years during the war. It reopened in 1919 as the coasting trade picked up once more, and the landlord from then until 1942 was a local collier named Stanley Morgan. Sarah Morgan took over in 1942, but handed over to William Locke the following year. In August 1945, with the coal shipping trade coming to an end, he moved the pub licence to a building in Cleddau View, naming it the **New Anchor**. Locke remained the licensee until 1968 after which the pub was taken over by James Williams of Narberth who gave the interior their usual 1960s' make-over and installed

The New Anchor at Hook in 2002. It has since become a private house, leaving the village without a pub.

Freddie Holder, previously of the Travellers' Rest, as licensee. Richard Coulson was in charge in the early 1980s, followed by Victor Baddeley and Anne Lukeman. The New Anchor closed in about 2003, leaving the village without a pub for the first time in two centuries.

'Middle Hook' is the name given to the outlying part of the village near Sprinkle Pill. In the early 19th century this area was dotted with coal-pits, and a tramway took the anthracite down to a wooden quay on the edge of the tidal Pill. John Brock ran the **Colliers' Arms** at Middle Hook in 1826, but since everyone seems to have called it the **Pill Inn**, he eventually changed the name to suit. Rachel Brock kept the inn from 1841 to 1861, when she was helped by a lodger named Sarah Childs. By 1871 Sarah was running the pub with her husband Thomas, but it seems to have closed during the 1870s.

The outlying pits gradually closed as the seams ran out, and the main Hook Colliery itself was shut in March 1948 because of the danger of an inrush of water from old workings – although the reserves of coal were pretty much exhausted in any case. As a result of the closure 88 miners lost their jobs.

Llangwm village in the early part of the 20th century.

Llangwm is a former fishing village on an unspoilt reach of the Cleddau river. There were substantial oyster-beds here at one time, and herring were netted from traditional black-tarred boats. Llangwm fisherwomen in their distinctive costume were once a familiar sight on the county's roads, carrying their fish and shellfish in panniers to sell in the streets and markets. To the people of Haverfordwest, the women of Llangwm were a race apart, and the Rev. Thomas Watts declared in 1861:

> I have lived among a heathen people, but I solemnly declare that I have never heard even among an ignorant negro population language which could for vileness and indecency be at all compared with that used by the women of Llangwm.

The Llangwms also liked a drink, and in 1784 there were six ale-houses in the village, plus another at Black Tar kept by Lettice Howell. In 1856 a visitor to the village complained:

> Some of the inhabitants of a riper age, I regret to state, are to be seen rolling from one end of the village to the other in a state of beastly intoxication.

He was dismayed to discover that the village came under the jurisdiction of the Little Haven police officer who (unsurprisingly) was never seen in Llangwm, and that the village constable was himself a publican.

Members of the Skyrme family were ale-house keepers, both in Llangwm and across the river in Coedcanlas where they kept the Ferryside pub and operated the ferry across the Cleddau (See *The Pubs of Narberth, Saundersfoot and South-East Pembrokeshire*). William Scurm (*sic*) ran an ale-house in Llangwm in 1784, as did Mary Skyrme in 1795, and the family were in charge of two village pubs in the early 19th century. One of these was the **Fisherman's Arms** where James Skyrme was the landlord from 1810 to 1816, and the other was the much more durable **Three Horseshoes** on the village green. John Skyrme held the licence in 1805, while Elizabeth Skyrme was the landlady from 1808 to 1851 when she was a 74-year-old widow. An inquest was held here in January 1864 into the death of a local man who had celebrated Christmas rather too well at the pub. Reeling home late at night he tripped, fell, and bashed his head so severely that he never regained consciousness.

Grocer and innkeeper Ann Skyrme was the licensee at the time, having taken over some time during the 1850s, and she was still there in 1881. The Llangwm Good Samaritan Friendly Benefit Society used the pub as its registered office in the 1880s, by which time James Powell was the licensee. He seems to have been a surly sort of chap and on one occasion was charged with wounding one of his customers in an argument over payment for a drink. Perhaps this hastened the demise of the pub because it appears to have closed soon afterwards.

Also near the village green was a beer-house called the **Ship and Castle** which was kept by Walter Wilkins and his wife Sarah between 1851 and 1875. On a Sunday in November 1865 P.C. George James was called away from evensong at Llangwm church to sort out a disturbance at Wilkins' pub which stood nearby. Here he found oyster fishermen William Palmer and Thomas Harbit both roaring drunk and singing 'Slap, bang, here we are again' at the top of their voices. With difficulty the constable ejected the two choristers from the pub; both were fined at Haverfordwest Petty Sessions later that week. Walter Wilkins' wife, or widow, Sarah Wilkins kept the Ship and Castle in 1875.

The **Jolly Sailor** in Llangwm dated back to at least 1784 when Robert Randall was the ale-house keeper. He was followed in 1809 by Jane Randall and then by William James. The pub seems to have been closed for a few years before being reopened by Thomas Llewellin who was landlord throughout the 1820s. In 1856 the death occurred 'awfully sudden' of Mrs. Anne Llewellin, landlady of the Jolly Sailor. (She was 98, so it couldn't have been too unexpected). Fisherman Thomas Llewellin, aged 60, was in charge in 1863.

The location of this pub isn't known, nor do we know very much about two other short-lived Llangwm pubs. Thomas Childs was the landlord of the **New Inn** in 1875, presumably having moved from the Pill Inn at Hook, while publican and egg merchant Hester Esmond kept the **Church Inn** near the Rectory in 1861.

Probably the best remembered pub in the village was the **Black Horse**, now known as Knowle Cottage. This inn was at the 'top' of Llangwm near where a footpath to Port Lion met the roads to Hook and Johnston. In her unpublished *A Short History of Llangwm*, Miss E. Morgan noted:

The erstwhile Black Horse, home of Maria Shrubsall who was said to be 'occult'.

> This was the house where the fishermen of old used to gather on Saturday evenings to discuss their luck – or lack of it – and everything concerning their work. There was no drunkenness here – it was run by a lady of high repute.

This was Maria Shrubsall, described by Miss Morgan as 'a fluent conversationalist and masterful when the necessity arose'. A native of Llangwm, she was baptised Maria Thomas and seems to have been the sister of Charles Thomas who ran the Dragon in Haverfordwest at one stage. Maria ran a grocery shop in the village and seemed set for a life of spinsterhood when, at

148

the age of 41, she became pregnant and married James Shropshell or Shrubsall, a 28-year-old travelling agent for an oyster company who sometimes lodged with Maria's family.

Mr. W. Grenville Thomas, in one of his *Llangwm Essays and Sketches*, recounted the tragic events of the next few months. Just four weeks after the wedding, Maria's husband died suddenly. A month later she gave birth to a son, duly christened James, but the child was sickly from birth and followed his father into the grave after only a few weeks.

How this tragic chain of events affected Maria can only be imagined. But life had to go on, and in about 1869 she converted part of the grocery shop into a pub – the Black Horse. She continued to run the pub for over 30 years and by all accounts was a striking figure with a reputation for being 'occult'. She fought a constant battle with the temperance brigade who were determined to close the pub down, and she also had the occasional set-to with the authorities. In 1892 she was charged with using false weights on her weighing scales. Her defence was that she had been using the same weights for 27 years and that they had probably worn down!

A remarkable tale is told of the occasion the Duke of Edinburgh – Alfred, the 'sailor son' of Queen Victoria – visited Milford Haven in his ship. Apparently Mrs. Shrubsall wrote to the Duke and offered him the present of a beautiful black cat. Not only did the Duke accept, he sent a pinnace up the river to collect Mrs. Shrubsall and the cat from the beach at Port Lion. Having taken tea with the Duke on board the ship, Mrs. Shrubsall then invited the Duke's daughter and two grand-daughters to accompany her back to Llangwm. After travelling up river in the pinnace, the royal party had tea at the Black Horse where Mrs. Shrubsall read the young ladies' fortunes in the tea leaves. Or so the story goes. ...

In 1913 the *Pembrokeshire Herald* declared of Llangwm: 'There is not a public house in the village. The last publican died in Haverfordwest workhouse'. And sadly that appears to have been the fate of the feisty Maria Shrubsall.

Llangwm remained without a pub for 50 years before the **Cottage Inn** opened. This was a bakery and shop before becoming a private members club in the 1950s known as 'Rock House and Cottage Club'. In 1962 John Leite successfully applied to convert the premises into a public house and in 1964 Ros and Gerry Bolt took over as licensees, running the pub into the 1970s. Various members of the Halpin family were in charge during the 1980s and Neville Lewis has been licensee for the past 15 years.

There was a **New Inn** at Nash Mountain between Trooper's Inn and Llangwm and B.G. Charles has noted its appearance as 'New Inne' as far back as 1641. There is a record of Mary Phillips keeping a pub at Nash from 1808 to 1811, while John Williams ran the New Inn at Nash Mountain from

The Cottage Inn at Llangwm.

1819 to 1822, but that appears to have been its last flowering as a pub and for the past 150 years or so it has been a private house named 'Tallyho'.

B.G. Charles has also discovered a 1678 reference to the place name 'Troopers Inn', and another to 'Troopers End' in 1704, but where the name originated is a mystery. In 1803 George Venables took out a lease on a house and field at **Trooper's Inn** and he was still the landlord of this crossroads ale-house in the 1840s. Farmer and innkeeper William Young was the landlord from 1861 to 1875 followed by Jane Young who brewed and sold her own beer in 1881. A widow named Sarah Yeo was the last known innkeeper at Trooper's Inn in 1891.

Rosemarket was once a settlement of some importance, standing near the head of a long arm of Milford Haven, and in Norman times 'Rhos marche' was the commercial centre and market place for a wide area. However its early importance had long faded by the time a Victorian writer felt moved to describe the village as 'mean and miserable enough'. There was a pub in the village in 1784 run by George Venables, while

How Troopers' Inn got its name is a mystery.

150

from 1795 to 1819 Anne Kintley ran the **Old Rosemarket Tavern**. John Jones took over and was still there in 1828.

Opposite the entrance to what is now Lucy Walters Close is a modern house called Barley Sheaf. This stands on the site of one, or perhaps two, cottage pubs, the history of which is confusing in the extreme. There is a reference in 1844 to a pub called the **Barley Sheaf** kept by Elizabeth Thomas with the help of her sister Mary Jones. By 1850 it was being run by Thomas Burns, but when he died in January 1860 his widow Mary took over, Before the year was out she had remarried, her husband being a soldier named Henry Llewellin.

The confusion arises from the appearance of the name **Barley Mow** in the records at about this time, the licensees being the aforesaid Henry and Mary Llewellin. This could just be a simple – if pointless – change of name. However it is thought that the 'Mow' was next door to the 'Sheaf' and that the Llewellins moved at some stage. The issue is clouded further by the fact that William Rogers, Henry's stepson, held the licence of the 'Mow' in 1863. However, when Henry died in 1870 it was his widow Mary who kept the pub going until at least 1881, by which time she was 75.

There is a reference to the **New Inn** in 1847 when a tithe assessment meeting was held here. The pub hit the headlines, such as they were, in 1851 when it was the focus of a manslaughter trial at the Haverfordwest summer assizes. On trial was a Rosemarket man named William Jones, a 'dissolute and quarrelsome man' according to press reports. Late one April night, in the courtyard of the New Inn, the inebriated Jones struck an elderly and equally inebriated farmer named Thomas Stephens. The old man died and a coroner's jury returned a verdict of wilful murder. However the jury at the assizes took a more lenient view after hearing that the drunken farmer had prodded Jones with a stick – apparently after mistaking him for a horse in the darkness. Not unnaturally Jones had struck out at Stephens who fell back and hit his head on the courtyard wall, killing him. By a grim coincidence the inn featured briefly in another manslaughter case less than two years later. A fight between navvies on the new railway line being built near the village ended with the death of one of them. His body was brought to the New Inn and the inquest was held there the following day.

David Rees held the licence in 1851, helped by his daughter Hesther. She subsequently married a farmer named Stephen Morris who was landlord from 1861 to 1871. In 1869 he appeared in court to apply for his licence to be renewed, but unfortunately he was so drunk that the magistrates sent him away. He returned the following week, full of contrition, and was granted a renewal. Something of a rogue, Morris was forever in trouble with the law for minor infringements – allowing pigs to stray on the highway or not

George Venables was landlord of the New Inn, Rosemarket, when this picture was taken in about 1906.
(Picture courtesy of Mr. Roger Davies)

keeping his malting records up to date – and he seems to have been quite a character.

Landlord in 1875 was Henry Nash while Blanche Morris, 19, was the manageress of the New Inn in 1881, occupying the property with her sister Elizabeth and brother-in-law George Venables. It is thought that the inn was

The Huntsman is on the left with the former New Inn on the right.

originally a cottage ale-house and that it was rebuilt and enlarged in 1886 by the owners, the Lawrenny Estate. According to a local tradition the pub stopped serving beer at this time, even though the licence was kept up. That story, however, seems to be untrue, since a photograph taken around the turn of the 20th century shows what is obviously a thriving ale-house, with a pub sign on the wall and an advert for Burton beer in the window. Landlord from 1891 to 1906 was George Venables.

The Huntsman at Rosemarket.   Top: The inn pictured in 2002.
Bottom: The interior in the 1970s.
(Picture courtesy of the *Western Telegraph*)

The village was without a pub for 60 years before the **Huntsman** was opened in a stone-built house known as 'The Winch' almost opposite the New Inn. It was opened in 1967 by Alice Slater who remained in charge until 1990. The pub remains in the same family, being owned by Mr. Jasper Slater of Haverfordwest Coin Machines, and the licensee for the past few years has been local cricketer Neil Adams.

The Stable Inn - a relatively recent addition to the Pembrokeshire pub scene.

In 1860, thirty-six people signed the pledge in Burton chapel after hearing a lecture on the temptations that young men from the country faced when going into large towns. Whether this had any effect on the local pub, the **Butchers' Arms** at Hill Mountain, isn't known. John Bowling and his wife Anne are mentioned as keeping the Butchers' in 1838, and they ran the pub for so long that the bend in the road here is still called Bowlings' Corner. Anne Bowling was in charge from 1864 to 1871 when she was a widow of 74. The licensee in 1875 was George Gwilliam and from 1881 to 1896 his widow Mrs. Mary Ann Gwilliam was in charge. In that year the owner of the property, local landowner Sir Owen Scourfield, objected to the renewal of the licence, partly on the grounds that the two-room cottage was unsuitable for a pub and partly because the landlady 'by reason of bodily infirmity' was unable to run the business properly. The magistrates agreed and withdrew the licence.

There was a pub in Houghton at one time, run by Sarah Hodge between 1841 and 1851 when she was 80. It stood on the left-hand side of the road going towards Burton Ferry, but the pub sign isn't known. In Burton itself is the **Stable Inn**, a relatively recent addition to the Pembrokeshire pub scene, which opened in 1976 in converted outbuildings attached to a farmhouse in the centre of the village. It was known from the outset for its food and these days is very much a pub-cum-restaurant.

For centuries the chief ferry crossing in Pembrokeshire was the one between Pembroke Ferry and Burton Ferry, linking the north and south of the county. The Hussey family had a long involvement both with the ferry trade and the licensing trade and Hugh Hussey kept a pub at Burton Ferry in 1784, as did John Hussey in 1795 – although there must have been an ale-house here from a much earlier date.

The Dean family of Burton Ferry also combined maritime matters with running pubs. They were an enterprising clan of ship-builders and ship-

The original Jolly Sailor can still be discerned behind the flat roof extensions of the 1960s. This picture dates from about 1971.
(Picture courtesy of the *Western Telegraph*)

Extensions on the extension – This is how the Jolly Sailor looked in 2002.

owners, sailors and publicans, the Dean brothers working in the family boatyard on the shore or skippering the ships while the womenfolk brewed and served the beer in the nearby **Jolly Sailor**. The first reference to a pub of that name is in 1809 when Thomas Dean became licensee, and the Dean family remained involved in running the pub for over a century.

During the early part of that time the Deans built and launched a series of beautiful smacks and schooners on the shore at Burton Ferry, each launch being duly celebrated at the Jolly Sailor. It is recorded that following the launch of the smack *Emlyn* from the yard in 1848, master shipwright Thomas Dean regaled his men 'with plenty of the essence of John Barleycorn'. Many of the vessels built in the yard stayed in the family, including the aptly named coasting smack *Brothers* which was built for the Bristol Channel trade and was captained by William Dean, and the 57-ton schooner *Sisters* which was skippered by James Dean. However the family fortunes suffered a series of setbacks in the late 1850s, with the loss at sea of both the *Brothers* and the *Sisters*, while further financial problems led to the closure of the shipyard in the 1860s.

However the Jolly Sailor survived these storms and remained in the family, continuing to be well patronised by workmen from the nearby Trinity House depot, which was open from 1850 until it moved to Swansea in 1926, and by passengers waiting for the pulling/sailing ferry across the Haven. Thomas Dean seems to have retired to a nearby 14-acre farm and the licensee of the pub in 1861 was Martha Thomas, possibly a niece. Thomas Dean's youngest brother William and his wife Ann were in charge by 1871 and Ann

Dean continued as licensee until 1901 when she was a widow of 70. Her son-in-law William Prout was the landlord in 1906 followed by Mrs. Mary Prout from 1910 to 1913.

Mrs. Esther Picton was the landlady from 1918 until her death in 1939 and John Henry White was there from 1940 to 1955. Haydn Francis was licensee in the early 1960s, while the Jolly Sailor had been extended and transformed into a 'gourmet's paradise commended by many of the country's leading good food guides' by the time John Wathes was in charge during the late 1960s and '70s. Now owned by Punch Taverns, the Jolly Sailor remains popular with diners, having been extended still further to take full advantage of the pub's enviable position overlooking the Cleddau. The Bosun's Bar has an interesting collection of nautical memorabilia.

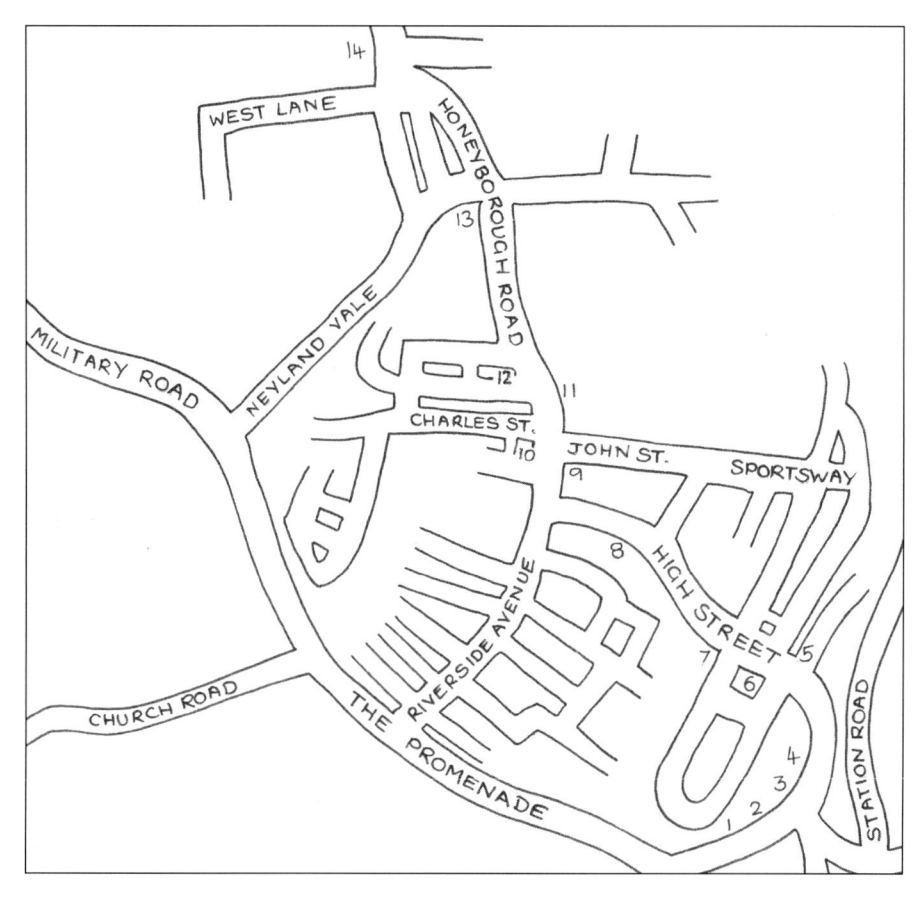

NEYLAND

(CHAPTER 15)

1	Mariners	9	Forresters' Arms
2	Picton Castle	10	Prmbroke
3	London Coffee House	11	Globe
4	South Wales Hotel	12	Admiral Benbow
5	Lawrenny Castle		(formerly Commercial)
6	Great Eastern	13	Rose and Willow
7	Gunnings Bar (formerly New Inn)		(formerly Odd Fellows' Arms)
8	Coburg	14	Farmers' Arms

CHAPTER FIFTEEN

Neyland
HONEYBOROUGH, LLANSTADWELL & WATERSTON

The history of Neyland falls into two periods – before and after Brunel. Before the 1850s, when the great engineer decided to make it the Welsh terminus of the Great Western Railway and a steamer port, 'Nailand' had been a small fishing village in the parish of Llanstadwell, with a modest ship-building and ship repair industry on the sheltered shore of Westfield Pill. All this changed when the GWR descended with devastating effect and the village was reinvented as a brash new railway town – briefly renamed New Milford – with rows of terraces overlooking the harbour.

Little is known about the pubs which predated the railway age, some of which would have been swept away in the building of the marshalling yard, workshops, engine sheds and harbour facilities. These included the **Royal William** which was kept by Elizabeth Field in 1850 and which was demolished in 1855.

Other ale-houses had vanished long before. Mary Morgan kept an ale-house somewhere in the parish from 1784 to 1795, and this was possibly the **Angel**, a pub which was run by Anne Morgan in 1822 and by William Morgan in 1827. Another early ale-house was the **Square and Compass** run by Thomas Williams in 1811, while the **Ship** was run by John James in the 1820s.

The opening of the naval dockyard across the Haven at Paterchurch in 1814 provided a shot in the arm for the parish of Llanstadwell, as numerous men from the surrounding villages found work at the new yard. They either rowed themselves across the Haven from the Neyland shore or were ferried in small boats, and one of the first ferrymen was Charles Child. According to Desmond Davies in *The End of the Line*:

> Mr. Child owned three passenger boats and one horse boat and lived near his ferry in Chapel Row in the original village of Neyland.

Like so many ferrymen he also ran a pub as a sideline and he held a licence for the **Ferry House** from 1815 to 1820.

A general view of Neyland from the waterway in the early 20th century.

According to George Mason in his *Historical Sketches of Pembroke Dock*, the **Shipwrights' Arms** stood near Neyland Point. It was run by the Scurlock family who also operated a shipbuilding yard nearby – hence the pub name. Joseph Scurlock was the landlord from 1805 to 1818, after which there is no sign of the pub in the licensing records – although Mason suggests that the licensee in 1834 was a Mrs. Margaret John. At some stage the Scurlocks moved their shipwright operations to Church Lakes, and shipbuilder and ship owner Peter Scurlock – presumably a son of Joseph – kept a pub at nearby Mount Pleasant in 1841.

John Rogers opened the **Roebuck** in 'Nailand' in 1817, having moved from a pub of the same name in Steynton, and he remained licensee for many years. However, by the time he died in 1852 at the age of 96, he was running the **Stag** inn – although whether this was simply a change of name for the old Roebuck is impossible to tell. The pub evidently closed when the landlord died.

Four years later the first train arrived in Neyland and shortly afterwards it was noted in the local press:

> Steps are being taken by a company (supposedly the Paddington Hotel Company) for the erection of an hotel in Neyland immediately.

These steps included the purchase of the vacant Stag inn and surrounding land, on which was built the **South Wales Hotel**. This was a substantial three-storey building, designed by the prominent Haverfordwest architect William Owen – with, it is said, some input from Brunel himself. It had numerous bedrooms, hot and cold baths, commercial and sitting rooms and a billiards room where a local lad was employed to act as billiards marker. Although most of the hotel guests arrived and departed by train or packet steamer, it was still thought necessary to build a large stable block nearby, while an attractive feature was the formal garden laid out behind railings between the front of the hotel and the Haven.

The imposing creeper-covered South Wales Hotel.

The hotel opened in July 1858. It was owned by the GWR and the first person to manage it was Thomas Gorley, soon to be succeeded by Edward Williams from Worcester. James Whetton acted as hotel manager from 1871 to 1884, Miss M. Gaskell was manageress in 1891 and Miss Charlotte Wright was in charge from 1895 to 1901. She may still have been the manageress in 1906 when Neyland – and the hotel – suffered the body blow of seeing the Irish ferry service transferred to Fishguard.

Joseph John, who was there from 1914 to 1921, was charged with allowing over 100 Territorial soldiers to be in the premises on a Sunday during the war. The Territorials, who were spilling out into the street, fighting drunk, had descended on the hotel from their camps at Scoveston, Houghton and Pembroke Dock. When asked why he allowed the men into the hotel on a Sunday, Mr. John replied reasonably: 'I was unable to keep them out'. He was fined 40 shillings.

In 1922 the GWR sold the hotel to Milford landowner Sir Hugh Thomas, but following his sudden death a couple of years later it was bought by Sir Frederick Meyrick of Bush, Pembroke. Catherine O'Hara was licensee in 1927 followed by Albert Rabbets who kept the hotel for about five years. Edith Philpin took over and she remained until 1942. The owner and licensee from 1942 until her death in October 1952 was Annie Henderson, although the building's days as an hotel were over by this time.

During the war the premises had been requisitioned and used as a billet for troops, mainly RAF personnel, while in the years immediately after the war they served as temporary council offices. The licence was kept up by Mary Voyle throughout the remainder of the 1950s, but a note in the records for 1954 shows that no licensed trade was being carried on. The hotel was subsequently converted into a hostel for workmen building the Esso oil refinery, but by the late 1960s the building was empty and becoming increasingly derelict, even though the licence was still held 'in suspense'. In 1970 the hotel was pulled down – just seven years after the Beeching axe had fallen on the railway line which had been its *raison d'etre*.

From the South Wales Hotel a track ran westward parallel to the shore, and soon after the arrival of the railway a terrace of substantial properties was built here. This was called Picton Terrace, in what later became known as Picton Road – the name deriving from the estate which owned the land on which the street was built. Three pubs eventually opened along the north side of this terrace, counterbalanced somewhat by the New Milford Temperance Hotel on the opposite side.

The **Mariners'** at 6, Picton Terrace was a pub where the licence seems to have changed hands fairly frequently. John George was in charge in 1861 and from 1867 to 1874 the licensee was Elizabeth Crawford. When she moved along the road to the Picton Castle she was succeeded in rapid succession by James Griffiths and Mrs. Jane Hart. Mary Jane Norton held the licence from 1891 to 1903; her husband was a steward on the Neyland – Waterford steamers. Presumably this was the

An early view of Picton Terrace with the signs for the Mariners' and the Picton Castle plainly visible.

chap who was landlord in 1906 – William Norton. Miss Annie Davies was there in 1910 followed by Mrs. Catherine de Candia, and John Nicholas held the licence in the early 1920s. He was succeeded by Mr. and Mrs. George Keys who held the licence until the pub closed in 1929. The various licensees of the pub had been fined four times for serving after hours and it appears that the magistrates' patience had run out.

The **Picton Castle** two doors further east was a pub-cum-hotel opened in competition to the South Wales Hotel in about 1858 by William John who was still there in 1861. James Miller was mine host in 1863 and William Barnett had charge in 1869 when Miss Fanny Davies from Coedcanlas took over. Elizabeth Crawford was the licensee from 1876 to 1891, followed by Susan Evans from 1899 to 1906 and William James from 1910 to 1933. Margaret James was there from 1935 to 1950 followed by Mrs. Margaret Morgan. The Picton Castle was subsequently converted into the Brunel Quay Hotel which opened in 1985 and thrived for a time under licensees Derek Lee and Dennis Mason but is now firmly closed and boarded up.

The Picton Castle later became the Brunel Quay Hotel, but it is now boarded up.

Despite its name, the **London Coffee House** at 9, Picton Terrace seems always to have been a licensed house; it was certainly selling alcohol in 1870 when it was being run by Mary Vaughan. The pub had been built by stonemason, property developer and occasional innkeeper Jesse Evans, whose name will crop up several times in this chapter. William Hawgood was the licensee from 1875 to 1884 followed by Charles Edwards and Miss Ellen Walsh. A native of Waterford, she had previously run the Coburg and the Pembroke Castle in the town, and she was the licensee of the Coffee House between 1891 and 1914. John Roderick Thomas was in charge from 1923 to 1929 followed by William Boast. From 1932 to 1951 the licensees were Mr. and Mrs. William Thomas, while Dick Jones – a former Rugby League player – was there in the 1950s and James Dorr was in charge during the 1960s. The London Coffee House was converted into a restaurant in the late 1970s but closed altogether a few years later.

The former London Coffee House as it looked in 2006.

A newspaper article in July 1858 announced with some satisfaction that whereas a couple of years previously Neyland had been without a decent inn, it now had three. These were the South Wales Hotel, the Picton Castle and the **Lawrenny Castle** at 17 High Street – named in honour of the other main local landowners, the Lort Phillips family of Lawrenny. Irishman Patrick Connor was the first licensee, although he had great difficulty in obtaining a licence. His was one one of five new licence applications for the Neyland area which came before the local licensing justices in 1857, all of which were opposed by the Rev. Joseph Tombs and all of which were turned down. Connor had better luck the following year and remained in charge until 1862 followed by James Miller – who also had a brief spell at the Picton Castle – and Edmund Stiles. John Davies was there from 1871 to 1880, followed by shipwright Robert Eynon from Lawrenny during the early 1880s.

William Morgan had taken over by the end of the decade, and he continued to run the Lawrenny Castle until his death in 1919; the inn was known as **Morgan's Hotel** for a while during this time. Miss Ethel D. Morgan took over and she was still the landlady in 1923, while George Pocock was licensee in 1927. Claude Hawes was landlord from 1928 until 1941, Edward Frost was there during the 1940s and Kenyon Walters was in charge from the 1950s to 1973. Laurie Burton ran the Lawrenny in 1984, while other licensees included Johnny Rice and Mair and Alan Mason. In recent years the Lawrenny endured an uncertain existence, being closed periodically and even being called the **Blue Marlin** for a time. Its latest closure looks like being the last and the building seems destined to be turned into flats.

Auction signs on the Lawrenny Castle in 2005 spell the end for this once popular pub. Neyland had 13 pubs a century ago; now it has five.

The end of the road for The Warrior.

Almost opposite the Picton Castle was the **Great Eastern** which dated from 1861; it was named after Brunel's great steamship which had spent the winter being repaired on a special grid-iron on Neyland beach. The pub was built and run by Jesse Evans, apparently to capitalise on the vast number of visitors who came to Neyland to view the steamship. When the *Great Eastern* ship left, the Great Eastern pub closed. The premises later became New Milford House – which housed the Institute – later still becoming the Neyland Young Men's and Boys' Club. In the 1970s the building reopened as a pub, the **Viking**, enjoying a brief period of popularity when it housed the Neyland folk club, among other things. The name was later changed to the **Warrior**, again in honour of a ship, but the pub closed in the 1990s and after standing empty for a while the building was turned into residential flats in 2001.

An early 20th-century view of the New Inn, Neyland.
(Picture courtesy of Mr. Simon Hancock)

Nowadays equipped with a new name and a sporting mural, the **New Inn** stands on the corner of St. Clement's Road and High Street. Elizabeth Bendall was licensee in 1866 followed by members of the Hall family and then by former huntsman George Merriman in 1881. Merriman had hunted the Tivyside and Lawrenny packs before retiring to run the pub; he eventually died, aged 90, in 1907, although he had long left the pub trade by this time. Joseph Bendall kept the New Inn from 1884 to 1891 followed by Albert Bendall who handed over to Ellen Walsh in 1898. This lady appears to have been a cousin of the Ellen Walsh who was licensee of the London Coffee Tavern, and she died soon after taking over the New Inn, being succeeded by her sister Miss Mary Walsh. William J. James was the landlord in 1906 and James Downes was behind the bar from 1908 to 1914 followed by Capt. John Setterfield. It was a James Williams house by 1916, when the company advertised: 'New Inn, Neyland to let. First class position and trade. Fully licensed'. There seems to have been a problem finding a steady tenant and Mrs. Elizabeth Brookes, Mr. T.H. Lillis, Mr. W.E. Wignall and Mr. and Mrs. W.J. Jones were all there in the 1920s.

The Joneses stayed until 1935 before moving to keep the Half Moon Hotel in Glannant and Mr. and Mrs. Ivor Lloyd were in charge during the war. The Lloyds were followed by Richard and Florence Mathias who were there from 1948 to 1957. Jimmy Ambrey – son of William Ambrey who kept the Bellevue in Haverfordwest – was mine host from 1958 to November 1962 when he was followed by Andrew Robertson. Florence Sweeney, who was there in the late

1960s and 1970s, once reached the final of a television competition devised to discover 'Britain's perfect landlady'. She didn't win, but returned to Neyland with a consolation prize of a signed picture of the cast of Coronation Street. Recent licensees have included Derick Howells, Dai Vaughan and Melinda Rees. The pub closed in 2005, reopening in 2006 as the Irish themed **Gunning's Bar** complete with a sporting mural on one end.

Top: The New Inn as it looked in 2002
Bottom: A new name for the New Inn – Gunnings Bar.

167

Long-serving landlord of the Coburg, George Rees.

The **Coburg** at 92 High Street was named in honour of Prince Albert, who was the second son of the Duke of Saxe-Coburg-Gotha. Sarah Johns was the licensee in 1867 and John Dalton kept the Coburg from 1878 to 1880. Landlady in 1881 was the Ellen Walsh who later ran the London Coffee House, while Sarah Roderick was there in 1884. A widow named Mary Walsh was there in 1891, helped by her daughter, the other Ellen Walsh (the one who expired at the New Inn). Henry Larkin kept the pub from 1895 until his death in 1910 when his widow took over. At one time the local rugby team used an outbuilding at the Coburg as its changing rooms, the pub having a large tank which contained an ample supply of water for washing off the mud and blood. Thomas Larkin was the licensee from 1920 to 1939 and George Rees, who was there from 1940 to 1962, made and distributed his own brand of potato crisps as a sideline. Dennis and Pat Mason were in charge in the late 1970s before Dennis moved to the Brunel Quay Hotel while Pat continued at the Coburg, eventually clocking up 21 years at the pub. This popular local has changed hands on a number of occasions since she left.

There is a reference in a trade directory to the **Lion** public house, kept in 1875 by Jane Morris. No other reference exists, and it may represent a brief change of name for the Coburg. A short-lived pub was the **Locomotive**, run by Martha Dawkins. It appears to have closed in 1864, in which year auctioneer George Hassell sold off the building and its contents.

Solicitor George Parry owned a considerable amount of land between Honeyborough and Neyland in the 1850s and he was quick to capitalise on the demand for housing created by the arrival of the railway and the need to rehouse the population of old 'Nailand'. He built four terraced streets of 'houses for artisans' and immodestly called his new development 'Parryville'. These streets were originally called South Street, Middle Street, Back Street and Picton Place, later becoming Charles Street, James Street, George Street and Kensington Road. He didn't forget to include a pub or three in his little 'town' and in 1861 the **Milford Arms Tavern** is recorded as being at 'South Street, Parryville, near New Milford'. Oddly, that is the only known reference to a pub of that name.

The Coburg Inn, pictured in 2001.

Like the former Odd Fellows just up the road, the **Forresters** pub in Kensington Road recalls another benefit society with a daft name. The Ancient Order of Foresters established a 'court' in Neyland in 1863 and between 1866 and 1880 George Lewis was landlord of the pub where they met. At that time the Foresters only had one 'r' in the middle; it was described as comprising seven rooms, brewhouse, large tank and garden and was said to be in the best situation in Neyland. Lewis was followed by James Brown between 1876 and 1880, while from 1884 to 1895 John Johns held the licence. Between 1900 and his death in 1929 the licensee was Robert Scurlock, who had actually purchased the pub from George Lewis as far back as 1881; it seems to have been during Scurlock's time that an extra 'r' was added to the pub name. Mrs. Alice Maud Hughes took over and remained the well-respected licensee from 1930 to 1960 after which William Jacob was in charge. More recent publicans have included Dave and Penny Osborne, Colin Baldwin and Arthur Bell, while Hazel Davis is the present licensee.

On the other side of the road, the **Pembroke Castle** was a corner pub on the junction of Kensington Road and Charles Street. Richard Harries was there in 1863, Thomas James was landlord in 1867 and William Smith was in charge in 1871. William Hart kept the pub in 1874 followed by James

The sign on the wall declares that the Forresters has been licensed since 1865.

The Pembroke Castle closed in 1954.

The former Globe – another of Neyland's street corner pubs.

Bowen Llewellyn who was still there in 1879. The ubiquitous Ellen Walsh held the licence in 1884, between stints at the Coburg and the London Coffee House. Charles Evans handed over to Alfred Thomas in 1889 and he was still there in 1895. Mrs. Margaret Thomas was the landlady from 1899 to 1914 and from 1923 to 1929 the landlord was George Davies. When he died the licence passed to his widow Margaret but she died the following year and William Kean was in charge from 1930 to 1954. The licence was not renewed that year.

Back across the road, a block up from the Forresters, was the **Globe** on the next corner. In 1873 this house was owned by Haverfordwest auctioneer Henry Davies, while the licensee was William Smith. Thomas Davies held the licence from 1876 to 1880 while James Bowen Llewellyn was behind the bar in 1884. The Jesse Evans who held the licence from 1891 to 1908 was the son of the pub-building Jesse Evans. In 1908 the licence passed from Evans junior to William Rees, but only after a court order forced Evans to quit the premises, which he was extremely reluctant to do. In 1915 Rees was summoned for serving a few soldiers with a drink shortly after midnight on New Year's Eve. Although the charge was dismissed, the pub was placed out of bounds to the military – a move which cost the landlord an estimated 40 percent of his trade. Rees stayed at the Globe until 1923, but it then changed hands a couple of times before being closed under the redundancy ruling in 1929 when the licensee seems to have been Thomas Arran.

The **Admiral Benbow** at 56, Kensington Road was originally the **Commercial Inn** which was mentioned in 1860 when James Mathias advertised that he had opened new stables at the inn and that horses could be taken at livery. Mathias was still behind the bar in 1866 but the landlady from 1871 to 1875 was his widow Elizabeth Mathias, followed by John Harris and then Richard Eynon. The landlord between 1891 and 1906 was Robert Barter who also hired out carriages and traps and worked part-time as a bill-poster. Mrs. Phoebe Donovan took over in 1909, but the licensee in 1914 was Harry Spicer followed in 1923 by John Spicer who was still there in 1938. Daisy Griffiths was in charge from 1939 to 1945 and Sarah Harkett was licensee from 1945 to 1961. Arthur Lloyd was there in the 1960s followed by John Crumpler in the 1970s and John and Dilas Swales – the ones who changed the name – in the 1980s. The present licensee is Peter Wilson.

The Commercial is now the Admiral Benbow.
Only two surviving Neyland pubs still have their original names.

Somewhere around here was the **Travellers' Rest** which was mentioned in the *Welshman* newspaper in 1856 when Jesse Evans was the landlord. He was still there in 1861 but Mary Rees was the landlady by 1862, Evans having moved to the Great Eastern. Also in the area of Parryville and Honeyborough was the **Salutation**. This was kept by blacksmith William Griffiths in 1861 and by Benjamin Thomas in 1867.

The attractive hamlet of Great Honeyborough is much older than Neyland and grew up around a village green. It seems to have had at least three watering-holes in its time, one of which underwent a name change a couple of years ago. This was originally the **Odd Fellows Arms**, the Independent Order of Odd Fellows being one of the most successful of the 'Friendly Societies' – early fore-runners of today's insurance companies. The Manchester-based Independent Order of Odd Fellows was one of the most popular in Pembrokeshire, and was particularly strong in Neyland where the Odd Fellows built a hall in Charles Street as well as using the pub on Honeyborough Green as a registered office. Elias John was there in 1861 but William Owen was the licensee in 1862, John Evans kept the Odd Fellows from 1867 to 1871 followed by Elizabeth Evans who ran the pub in 1874 and a butcher named John Jabez Davis who was fined ten shillings for serving on Christmas Day 1877. A police officer who visited the pub discovered 'upwards of 20 persons there, singing, whistling and dancing and beer all over the place'. The revellers, he reported sadly, all escaped through the windows when he entered.

The Odd Fellows' Arms in its new guise as the Rose and Willow.

John Howell was landlord from 1891 to 1901 followed by Mrs. Elizabeth Howell between 1906 and 1914. Mrs. Mary Howells was the landlady from 1916 to 1923, Mrs. Eleanor Evans held the licence in 1927 and Mr. W.G. Griffiths was licensee from 1928 to 1930. George Saunders was there from 1931 to 1953 and Annie Saunders was in charge from 1953 to 1961. Bill Wincote was landlord in the 1970s, followed by Dave Osborne and then Diane Ross who handed over to Jimmy Hughes in 1984. Roly Goldthorpe and George Brown were the licensees in the 1990s. The pub closed in 2003 but was reopened by Amanda Jillions and Lea Wilson in autumn 2004 as the **Rose and Willow** – although locals still refer to it as 'The Odds'.

From 1864 to 1891 the landlord of the **Farmers' Arms**, Honeyborough was William Griffiths. The town's first rugby pitch was in a field behind the pub, and the players changed in an outbuilding, much as they did at the Coburg in later years. Mrs. Blanche Davies held the licence from 1895 to 1901 and the landlord thereafter was Thomas James who was succeeded in 1907 by his widow Caroline James. She handed over to Alice Mathias in 1911, Mrs. Emily Ley was in charge after the First World War, while from 1920 to 1929 Mrs. Hannah Lloyd kept the pub. The Farmers' was forced to close that year under the redundancy ruling.

The **Carmarthen Arms** was a Honeyborough beer-shop run by George Thomas in 1863 but nothing else is known about it.

The Farmers' Arms in about 1905, just a few years before it closed.
(Picture courtesy of Mr. Simon Hancock)

Before the building of Scoveston Fort and the construction of a 'military road' from Church Lakes to the fort to facilitate the movement of men and equipment, the main route from Neyland to Milford Haven was along the shore, past Llanstadwell Church and the village of Hazelbeach. There were several pubs and ale-houses along here in the early 19th century, perhaps to cater for workmen who made the daily journey across the Haven to work in the dockyard at Pembroke Dock. The records show that Dan Disney was an ale-house keeper here from 1814 to 1816 while James John ran the **King's Arms** at Hazelbeach in 1819 and William Morgan from Dale ran the **Brig** in 1826. The **Farmers' Arms** was opened by Thomas Rees in 1821, evidently at Hazelbeach, and Richard Rees was the landlord from 1822 to 1828.

In 1861, Jesse Chappell of Hazelbeach was granted a licence to open a new pub. This was probably the **Wellington Tavern** where Joseph Martin held the licence from 1867 to 1874 followed by his widow Elizabeth between 1875 and 1880. She then married David Myers, a navy pensioner, and they ran it as a combined pub and shop. From 1890 to 1901 Elizabeth was running the Wellington on her own, having been widowed for a second time, while the last known landlord was David Lewis who was there in 1906. It is now Valletta Villa.

The Wellington hung up its boots many years ago.

The **Ferry Inn** on the shore at Hazelbeach had been licensed for about 20 years according to a report in the *Pembrokeshire Herald* in 1857, and it seems to have been run for most of that time by George Childs. Although a member of a family of boatmen, Childs was a cabinet-maker by trade and the actual ferryman, James Evans, lived three doors away. (Evans also sold beer and spirits, but he did so without a licence, a fact which landed him with a fine in 1857).

William Evans ran the Ferry Inn from 1861 until 1864 when he handed over to George James. John Davies kept the pub in the early 1870s followed by William Edwards who was the landlord from about 1878 to 1896. George Williams was in charge from 1901 to 1906 and his grand-daughter, Miss

Detail of a painting of the Ferry Inn at Hazelbeach as it used to look.
(Picture courtesy of Mr. Alf Williams)

Appropriately enough the Rosslare ferry is passing the Ferry Inn at Hazelbeach.

Elizabeth Jane 'Lizzie' Edwards was the long-serving landlady from 1910 to 1955 when – at an advanced age – she became Mrs. Lizzie Heatherley. She continued to run the 'Jungle', as the Ferry Inn was known, for a few more years, a feature of the one-room pub at this time being the heavy, steel-clad table under which people would have taken shelter during bombing raids on Pembroke Dockyard. Regulars knew to keep a tight grip on their drinks – the pub counter had a distinct slope and untended glasses had a habit of sliding away.

Former Neyland railwayman David Vaughan took over in the 1960s and completely rebuilt the pub on a much larger scale, taking full advantage of its fine waterside setting. It remains in the same family, being run by his daughter Janet Phillips.

Once a small agricultural village, Waterston was plunged into the petro-chemical age in the 1960s with the building of the Gulf refinery on its doorstep, and it remains very much in the shadow of the energy industry with the recent construction of a terminal to import liquefied natural gas. The village had its share of pubs in the 19th century, although information about them is sketchy. The **Masons' Arms** was opened in 1825 by Charles Esmond – a stonemason, naturally enough. He was still there in 1827 but nothing further is known.

A report in *Potters Electric News* in 1865 referred to landlord John Thomas of the **Weary Traveller**, Little Waterston and he was still listed as a

The Three Crowns in Waterston.

beer-house keeper in 1871. Perhaps the opening of this ale-house was connected with the building of Scoveston Fort during the 1860s, another of the forts built to defend the Royal Dockyard at Pembroke Dock.

Rebecca Morse was in charge of the **Three Crowns** in Waterston from 1851 to 1871, when she was 82, followed by her nephew William Gibby and then by John Comber who was landlord from 1880 to 1884. Isaac Merriman was the landlord of the Three Crowns from 1891 until 1908, followed by his widow Mrs. Rose Merriman who remained in charge until her death in March 1935. William Joseph Merriman took over and was still there in 1945, while Florence Rose Lloyd was there from 1945 to 1955. John Rowe was licensee in 1959 and Charles Lloyd was there from 1962 to 1968 followed by Michael and Pam Murphy. By this time the pub interior had been given a fairly drastic makeover in keeping with the dramatic changes across the road. As one guidebook pointed out: 'The Three Crowns is literally a stone's throw from the great new refinery'.

Brian Smith then ran the pub for a significant period, being in charge throughout Waterston's 'oil age'. However the refinery closed in 1996 and the Three Crowns did not last much longer and had closed by 2000. It is now a private house.

There were two other pubs in the village at different times, about which little is known. One was kept by Letitia Phillips in the 1860s and the other by John Evans in the 1880s.

CHAPTER SIXTEEN

Haverfordwest to Milford Haven
JOHNSTON, TIERS CROSS, STEYNTON, PRIORY & DALE ROAD

Nowadays a large village straddling the main Milford Haven to Haverfordwest road, Johnston was originally a small hamlet of perhaps two dozen cottages scattered around St. Peter's church. Several country lanes joined the turnpike road at this point, so one of the cottages became an alehouse to serve passers-by. This was the **Weary Traveller** which was kept by Anne Jenkins in 1805 and by Nicholas Jenkins between 1806 and 1828. From 1841 to 1875 the landlord was Joseph John, a shipwright by trade, who fell into the hold while on a steamboat passage from Milford Haven to Liverpool in 1868 but lived to tell the tale. The 1881 census shows that the Weary Traveller was being occupied by a farmer of 60 acres named William Harries, with nothing to indicate that it was still being run as a pub.

The arrival of the railway in 1856 had a lasting impact on Johnston. It was the only station on the main line between Neyland and Haverfordwest, and until a branch line reached Hubberston Pill in 1863 it would have been the nearest rail-head to Milford Haven. Despite this ease of access, tourism has never been a feature of the village, and the person who compiled *The Borough Guide to Neyland* in about 1912 struggled to find ways of persuading people to visit Johnston:

> In the village we may lunch and then visit the Fish Manure Works recently established or examine the coal borings now in progress. The Mineral Water Works will be sure to claim notice and repay a visit. ...

One sort of visitor did find Johnston attractive, and that was the Sunday drinker. During the days when pubs were closed on Sundays, it was still permissible to serve drinks on the Sabbath to bona fide travellers – that is, anyone who was obliged to travel more than three miles on business. Naturally this wonderful loophole in the law was exploited to the full by pubs which were just over three miles from centres of population – and Johnston was handily placed halfway between Milford and Haverfordwest. On a Sunday in July 1910, a police officer who kept watch on the **Railway Inn** throughout the day counted no fewer than 114 people entering the premises – all of them supposedly bona fide travellers. As the pastor of nearby Pope Hill Chapel, Mr. E. Lawrence, told the chapel's anniversary service a month later:

> Despite the Sunday Closing Act for Wales, I find that in certain localities there is more drinking taking place on Sunday than on any other day of the week. ...

The Railway Inn had been opened near the station to cater for rail passengers and seems to have replaced the Weary Traveller; quite possibly the licence was transferred. Carpenter Edwin Bowen opened the pub in about 1883 and held the licence until 1901. Mrs. Margaret Bowen was the landlady in 1906 and Thomas Bowen was there from 1910 until his death in 1913 when the licence passed to his brother Martin.

James Williams held the licence of the Railway Inn from 1914 to 1916, in which year, aged 40, he was obliged to attend a tribunal in Haverfordwest to show reason why he should be excused war service. Williams pleaded that he had purchased the Railway at a 'great financial outlay', that his wife was too ill to manage the pub on her own, and that the business would collapse if

A postcard view of the Railway in Johnston when the traffic outside was somewhat less than it is today.
(Picture courtesy of Mr. Peter Flynn)

he were sent to the Front. He was granted an exemption from war service and remained at the pub until 1920. Samuel Ley took over and kept the Railway until 1954, except for two years in the 1940s when for some reason William Preston was in charge. The pub changed hands regularly in the 1950s and 1960s, the better remembered licensees including Fred Setterfield and Jimmy Jenkins, formerly of the ill-fated George and Dragon in Milford Haven. Trevor Morris, Ensor Hadfield and Burt Paterson, now of the Bridge End in Haverfordwest, have been among the licensees of the Railway in recent years, and the present landlord is Peter Flynn. From time to time a shadowy figure wearing a waistcoat appears in the bar; this is the ghost of Sam Ley, still keeping an eye on the pub which he ran for over 30 years.

The Railway in Johnston, pictured in 2005, was once notorious for its Sunday drinking.

To the north of the Railway Inn the main road drops into a valley where there is a modern roadside motel called the **Silverdale Inn**. This was once a marshy area known as Johnston Pond beyond which was the tiny community of Johnston North. This had a roadside cottage inn named the **Vine** where Richard Wilcox was the landlord from 1814 to 1841, followed for at least ten years by his widow Mary. Richard John and his wife Margaret were licensees from 1861 to 1871, after which the pub passed into the Parsell family for a number of years. William Parsell kept the pub in 1875 followed briefly by his widow Marie and then by a relative named John Parsell. His widow Mrs.

A recent view of the Vine Inn.

Alice Parsell was landlady for over 30 years, from 1891 to 1923, and her son Clifford Parsell – a carpenter by trade – held the licence from 1923 to 1946.

John Thomas then had seven years in charge, followed by John Griffiths and the well-remembered Annie Owston who was there from 1954 to 1980. When she retired due to ill health the pub was closed for a few years, before being refurbished and reopened in January 1984. Tommy and Loretta Reynolds were the new licensees, and they were followed in turn by John and Maureen Wright and Fred and Muriel Green. The Vine closed again in 1994 before being rescued a couple of years later by David and Sylvia Lingwood who are still in charge of this popular roadside inn.

Moving towards Haverfordwest, the **Halfway Inn** was near the top of Pope Hill on the left hand side. It was kept in the 1870s by a gardener named John Thomas, but seems to have been quickly superseded by a new inn on the other side of the road, called, unimaginatively, **New Inn**. It was a typical example of a farm cum ale-house where the licensee from 1881 to 1899 was Arthur Williams who also farmed 73 acres.

The former New Inn on Pope Hill, between Johnston and Haverfordwest.

Licensee from 1901 to 1906 was John

Harries, while George Harries was the farmer and innkeeper from 1912 to 1929. Unfortunately for the Harrieses, one of the few neighbouring buildings happened to be Pope Hill Methodist Chapel where the pastor, Mr. E. Lawrence, was a staunch teetotaller. As he once thundered from the pulpit: 'The greatest enemy, the most hideous enemy, that the church has to contend with is strong drink'. The pub seems to have stopped serving after George Harries' day, although the licence was kept up for many years afterwards.

A Green Motors bus outside the Horse and Jockey in Steynton in 1926.
(Picture courtesy of Mr. John Stevenson)

Moving back towards Milford Haven, the familiar crossroads pub near Steynton church, now known as the **Horse and Jockey** but originally the **Horse and Groom**, seems to have been opened in 1810 by William Crispin who remained the landlord until his death in 1831. He was followed by his widow Mrs. Frances Crispin who told a court hearing in 1847: 'I keep a public house in Steynton and have done so these forty years'. The freehold of the pub changed hands in 1851 'together with five other houses together forming a square'. The landlord by this time was farrier and blacksmith Benjamin Howells who shoed horses in the smithy alongside while his wife Margaret served the beer. They were followed in about 1875 by John and Martha Williams, with Martha being in sole charge following her husband's death in 1883. She subsequently married a neighbour, Simon Hire who was the licensee from 1891 until his death in 1905 when his widow resumed command once more. Like Frances Crispin before her, Martha ran the Horse and Jockey for 40 years, finally expiring in 1915.

The Horse and Jockey stands on a busy crossroads.

Joseph Venables took over, followed in turn by Fred James, John Roach, Mrs. Annie Roach and then Julia King. In 1929 she left to run the Bridge End in Hakin and Julia Rhodes took over. Florence Bartlett was there from 1933 to 1951 followed by Wallace George King, Julia Rhodes (again) and William Taylor who took over in 1965. Ron Cox was landlord in 1973, while the pub was much altered during the tenancy of Chris and Sylvie Pettit in the late '70s and early '80s. Since their day the pub has changed hands several times, eventually becoming part of the Punch Taverns chain, and although open for business it was without a full-time tenant at the time of going to press.

The Horse and Jockey is said to be haunted by at least four ghosts, prompting a television company to visit the pub in 2002 with a 'part-time vicar' and a 'white witch' who tried to persuade the rather doleful spirits to quit the premises. They reported 'an overwhelming feeling of sadness and fear' in the pub cellar, but must have failed in their mission because the laments of ghostly children can still be heard from time to time.

This wasn't the only pub in Steynton village, although the waters are muddied by the fact that the new town of Milford Haven, although a couple of miles away, was built within the parish and it can be difficult to distinguish between town pubs and village pubs. However it appears that John Rogers was at the sign of the **Roebuck** (or sometimes **White Hart**) in Steynton village from 1805 to 1816 before moving to Neyland leaving Thomas Rogers to carry on for a couple of years.

It was reported in 1849 that James Davies, innkeeper of 'Stainton Green', had become insolvent with debts of £1,600. His pub is referred to in the 1851 census as 'the **Milford Hotel** in Steynton' but where it stood is a mystery.

A lane from Steynton leads down to Castle Pill, or Prix Pill as it was sometimes called, a sheltered tidal inlet which was used by boatmen long before the town of Milford Haven was thought of. These boatmen would have frequented the ale-house which Elizabeth Sinnett kept at 'Steynton Pill' from 1784 to 1795, the name of which is unrecorded.

Fording Castle Pill at Black Bridge.

At low tide the road to Waterston forded the Pill near an ancient footbridge known as Black Bridge. There were two beer-houses near this crossing place in 1852, one run by John Davies Mathias and the other by Letitia Hughes. Neither pub is named in the records, but the latter was presumably the **Jolly Sailor** at Black Bridge which was being run by Letitia Child in 1861.

On the eastern shore of the Pill stood Castle Hall which was built in the 1770s by John Zephaniah Holwell, survivor and chronicler of the Black Hole of Calcutta. In 1818 the Castle Hall estate was put up for sale following the departure of its then owner, whaling entrepreneur Benjamin Rotch – a leading figure in the early history of Milford Haven. Included in the sale were 'a farmhouse and the **Fox and Hounds** public house, with six cottages contiguous'. David Hughes was the landlord of the Fox between 1811 and 1822 and William Watkins was landlord in 1826.

Benjamin James of the short-lived **Castle Inn**, Steynton, was fined 30 shillings in 1862 for serving out of hours. It appears that by 1871 he had moved and opened another pub nearby, the **New Inn**, a two-room cottage close to Venn Lodge on the side of the road to Waterston from Black Bridge. Blacksmith John Merchant held the licence from 1875 to 1884, Henry

Thomas was there from 1891 to 1895 and Alex Henderson was the landlord from 1900 to 1910 in which year he annoyed the magistrates by altering and extending the premises without their permission. Despite hearing that the pub was 'a useful house of call for wayfarers' the magistrates decided to close it a couple of months later, with £200 compensation being paid to Thomas Palmer of the Sir Charles Whetham, the owner.

The village of Priory grew up around a 12th-century Benedictine priory, built at the head of a tidal inlet which became known as Priory Pill. James Caulfield ran the **Priory Inn** in 1809, presumably in the village. The present **Priory Inn** was opened about 20 years ago in part of the old priory, and for the past 18 years it has been run by Mr. and Mrs, Alf German.

A new pub in an ancient building – the Priory Inn at Priory.

The **Plough** at Priory was being run by 85-year-old Mrs. Ann Harries at the time of her death in 1859. Her son-in-law Benjamin Howell, a weaver from Templeton, seems to have taken over. When the Plough closed in the 1860s it was replaced by the **Masons' Arms**, a well remembered pub at the foot of Priory Hill, opposite the lane which leads over the railway bridge and down to Priory. Thomas Sutton from Little Haven kept the pub and farmed 36 acres in

The Masons' Arms near Priory, now sadly demolished.
(Picture courtesy of Mr. John Stevenson)

1871. Ship's carpenter William Cale from Marloes was the landlord from 1877 to 1901 and the pub was subsequently kept by his daughter Florence and son-in-law John Thomas from Venn, Black Bridge. John Thomas continued to hold the licence until 1939, but since he latterly lived off the premises at Starbuck House it made the Masons' a regular target for night-time break-ins.

William Blockwell took over in 1940, followed by Fred 'Firpo' Hoggins who held the tenancy of this James Williams pub until September 1960 when he left to take over the Sir Charles Whetham in Pill. A former seaman and a local footballer of considerable note, 'Firpo' ran the Masons' with his wife Isabel – always known as Madge – and during their day it was one of the most popular pubs in the area. Eddie Davies took over, followed by Idris Twigg, a much-travelled licensee who later moved to the Welcome Traveller in Tiers Cross before running a couple of Hakin pubs. Several different stories are told about the last days of the Masons', with some people believing that it was closed by the brewery and others that it was the victim of a road widening scheme. Whatever the reason, it had closed by about 1970 and a fire hastened its eventual demolition.

The **Welcome Traveller** still stands in the village of Tiers Cross, which as its name suggests is a village which grew up at a meeting of the ways. Margaret Morgans was the village publican from 1841 to 1861 (when she was 87) and her son David Morgans was there from 1871 to 1895. Henry Davies was licensee

The Welcome Traveller in Tiers Cross as it looked before refurbishment.
(Picture courtesy of Mr. John Stevenson)

from 1900 until his death in 1913, and the licence passed from Jane Davies to Martell Evans in 1916. Frederick Davies was the landlord from 1920 to 1931 and Merchant Phillips – a brother-in-law of William Ambrey of the Bellevue – was there from 1932 to the 1960s. Keen on country pursuits, 'Merch' Phillips was a respected judge of Sealyham terriers and a rider to hounds in his younger days, and the Pembrokeshire Foxhounds would meet regularly at the pub. The much-travelled Idris Twigg was in charge in the 1970s and Keith Wells was the landlord in the 1980s. He made a number of alterations, including the building of a large accommodation block alongside. He was succeeded by Jim Edwards and then by the present licensees, Mr. and Mrs. Jeff Partridge.

A mile or so south-west of the village, the **Three Horseshoes** was at Robeston Cross and – like most pubs with that sign – it was run by a blacksmith. That was William Howells who was there in 1861, although Benjamin Howells was described as a 'public house keeper' in 1864 and Cecilia Howells, probably William's sister, held the licence in 1867. There was a pub at nearby Rickeston Bridge in the 1850s run by William and Esther Evans. The sign isn't known, but the landlord was also a stonemason, so we can perhaps guess what the pub was called. And the records show that **Spread Eagle** was once the name of a property near Lower Hasguard, and this surely indicates that it was a pub at one time.

The Dale Road was the main route into Haverfordwest from the Dale peninsula, and was especially well travelled on market days and fair days. There were a number of roadside pubs along its length to cater for this passing trade, and it seems convenient to group them in this chapter.

A view of the Welcome Traveller in 2005.

The wayside pub known as the **Masons' Arms** at Dreen Hill would have been the first port of call for anyone leaving Haverfordwest. It was mentioned in 1851 when the innkeeper was Sarah Evans, Martha Lewis was there in 1871 and John Evans and his wife Mary-Ann ran this tiny cottage pub in the 1880s. George Beaven was the landlord from 1891 to 1895 and William Stephens was licensee from 1923 to 1950, followed by

A 2004 view of the Masons' Arms, Dreenhill.

his widow Elizabeth Stephens. Their daughter Gwladys took over in about 1955, becoming Gwladys Phillips on her marriage, and she ran the pub until about 1972. The Masons' was notable for not having a bar counter, the beer being tapped into a jug from barrels at the back. Cyril Howe took over and ran the pub for some 15 years, still fetching the beer in a jug when he wasn't tending to his beloved pedigree Weimaraner dogs. Since Cyril and his brother Les departed the Masons' has changed hands four or five times and has changed completely in character, so that nowadays it is as much a steak-house as it is a pub. For a short period in the 1980s there was also a pub-cum-restaurant at nearby **Denant Mill**.

Ratford Bridge is a fair step from the sea, but when William James kept an alehouse here from 1810 to 1828 he called it the **Jolly Sailor**. Half a mile down the road is Solbury Cross where Richard John kept a pub called the **White Hart** in 1841. There was a Walter Jenkins, publican, at 'Solberry' in 1850, while James Pawlett began running the White Hart in the early 1860s. In his day it was a favourite stopping-off point for Dale and Marloes people returning in their farm-carts from Haverfordwest market and the front of the pub would often be so thronged with carts that the roadway would be nearly impassable.

The former White Hart still looks like the country pub it once was.

Sadly, Mr. Pawlett's wife died in the 1870s and he himself went blind in 1878, forcing him to close the pub. He carried on living at the White Hart, eking out a living as a small-scale dairy farmer. In 1892 his daughter moved in with him and they proposed re-opening the pub. However there was considerable opposition to this from the usual temperance quarters, and among the big guns wheeled out to oppose the re-opening was the Fourth Baron Kensington who had once addressed the House of Lords in favour of the Welsh Sunday Closing Act. Telling Roose magistrates that he knew the district well and that he could see no need for a pub at this point, he added: 'If people cannot drive from Haverfordwest to Dale without wanting to go into a public house, it is a very extraordinary thing'. Suitably overawed, the magistrates refused the application and the pub has been closed ever since.

The Flags on the Dale Road near Walwyn's Castle was a pub at one time, and Benjamin Wilcox, mason and publican, was licensee in 1871. It had closed by 1895, because in that year James Jenkins of The Flags was fined for selling beer without a licence.

CHAPTER SEVENTEEN

Milford Haven
HAMILTON TERRACE & VICTORIA ROAD

The town of Milford Haven did not exist until the very end of the 18th century when it was developed virtually from scratch, with three streets running parallel to the Haven on a broad headland between the tidal inlets of Hubberston Pill and Castle Pill. Early settlers included Quaker whalers from Nantucket Island who supplied London with oil for lamplighting and who later came to dominate Milford's brewing industry through the efforts of the Starbuck family. A dockyard was built where ships for the Navy Board were constructed, and various militia regiments were stationed in the town to guard the shipyard. These dockers and militiamen, boatmen and stonemasons provided plenty of trade for the great number of ale-houses which quickly sprang up along the waterfront, and the number of licensed premises in the parish of Steynton – which included Milford Haven – rose from six in 1795 to 24 in 1812.

With a regular boat service to Ireland from nearby Hakin Point, prospects for the new town looked promising, especially when the naval authorities revealed plans to extend the dockyard and turn it into a huge complex of ship-building slips, wharfs, offices, stores and workshops. Unfortunately for Milford this ambitious project was never completed, as the Navy Board failed to agree a purchase price for the land from its owner, Robert Fulke Greville. The dockyard scheme at Milford was abandoned and transferred to land at Paterchurch – now Pembroke Dock – in 1814.

This coincided with the national economic depression which followed the Napoleonic wars and many of the early Milford ale-houses were forced to close, so that in many cases all that is known about them are the sign and the name of the licensee. These early and relatively short-lived Milford Haven pubs included the **King's Arms** (kept by Thomas Lewis from 1805 to 1812); the **Lamb** (William Evans 1812); the **Waterman's Arms** (Anne Reynolds 1810 to 1813); the **Wheatensheaf** (George Lewis 1812); the **White Lion** (Joseph Davies 1808 to 1810, Daniel Evans 1811 to 1812); the **Golden**

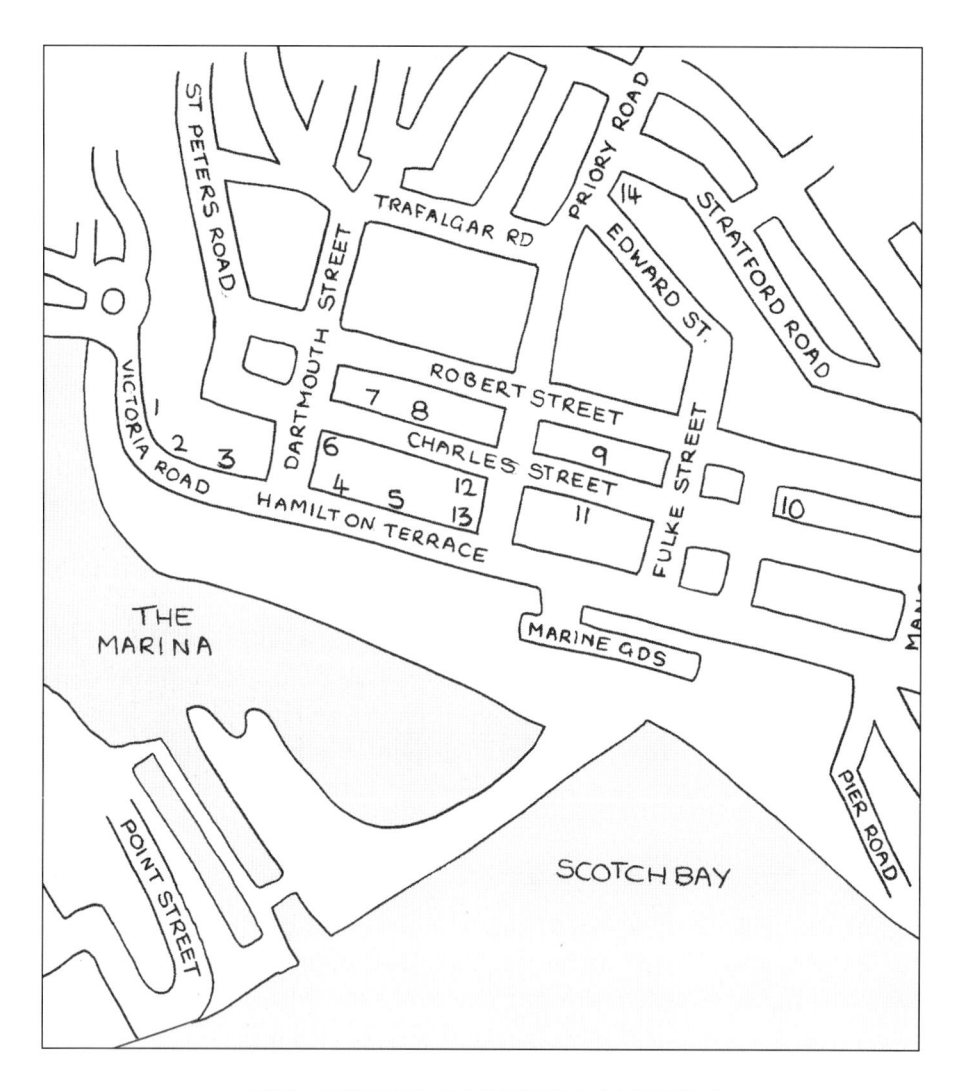

MILFORD HAVEN WEST

(CHAPTERS 17 & 18)

1	Globe	8	Golden Lion
2	Railway	9	Royal
3	Dinas Inn	10	Trafalgar (formerly Spirit Shop)
4	Butchers' Arms	11	George and Dragon
5	Lord Nelson	12	White Lion
6	Commercial	13	Alma
7	Lord Kitchener	14	Victoria

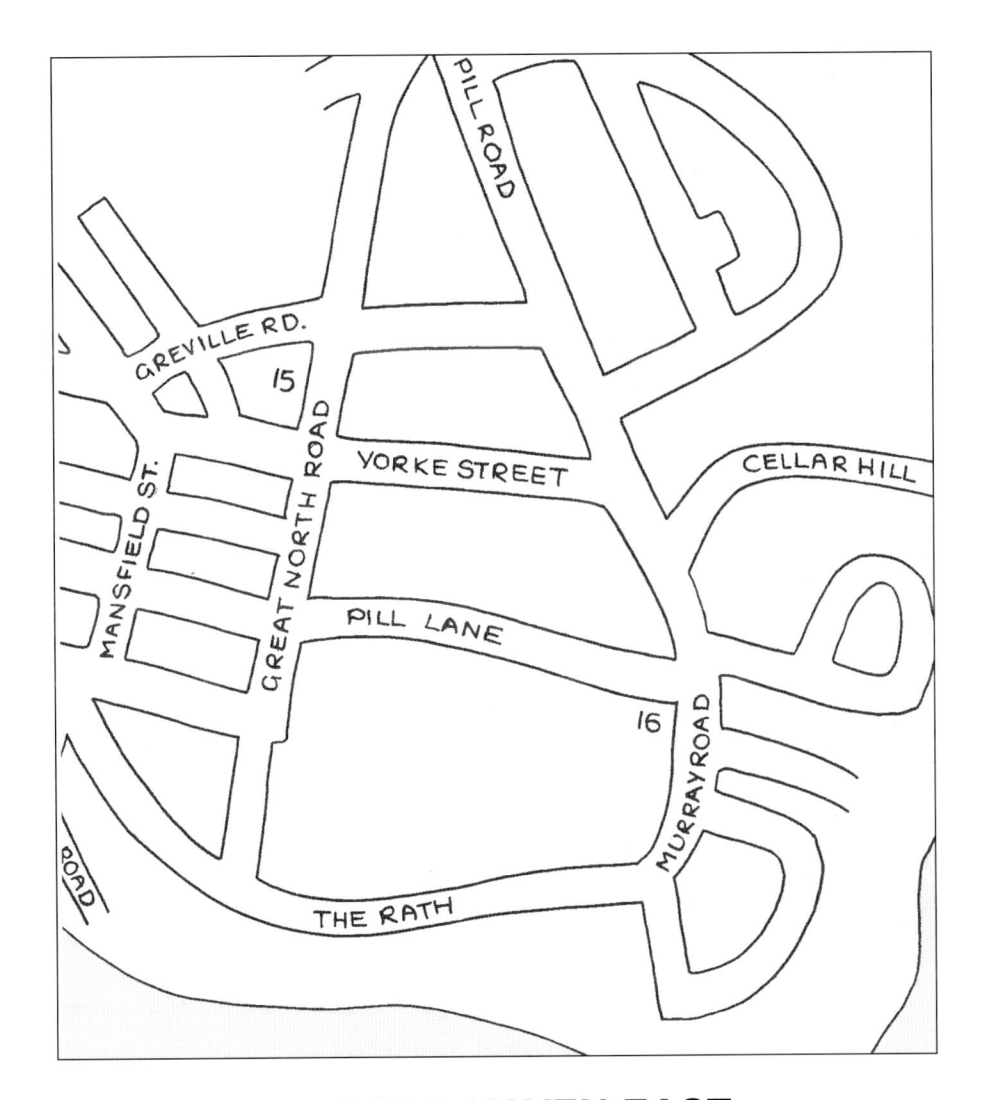

MILFORD HAVEN EAST

(CHAPTERS 17 & 18)

15   Kimberley   16   Sir Charles Whetham

The fishing port in its hey-day.

Anchor (Richard Davies 1814); the **Plaisterers' Arms** (Francis Beazley 1810 to 1812); the **American Arms**, (Joseph Grout 1808 to 1814); the **Britannia** (Thomas Whitfield 1812 to 1813); the **Butchers' Arms** (John Evans 1810 to 1814); the **Recruiting Sergeant** (Samuel Golding Willoughby 1808); the **Coach and Horses** (David Noott 1810 to 1812); the **Waterloo** (John Williams, 1818 to 1820); the **Mariners** (George York Young 1805 to 1809); another **Mariners** (Mary Russell, 1821); the **Jolly Sailor** (James Isaac 1805 to 1811); the **Sloop** (John Davies 1805 to 1806); and the **Anchor** (George Herbert 1810 to 1811).

The next few decades were difficult for the new town, especially as Pembroke Dock also acquired the packet service to Ireland. Plots which had been earmarked for housing were not taken up, trade stagnated, and when Brunel chose Neyland as the terminus of the South Wales railway it seemed like the final kick in the teeth. A local newspaper report in the 1850s summed up Milford Haven as:

> A one-eyed place with its three long, narrow, ill-paved dirty streets and badly managed crossings swept and cleaned only by the wind and rain.

The Milford Improvements Bill of 1857 set out to remedy this state of affairs, introducing gas lighting, paving and mains drainage to the town. Wooden bridges were built across the two Pills and a 750 ft. wooden pier was constructed to allow passengers and cargo to be unloaded from ships without recourse to tenders. At the landward end of this jetty was the Pier Hotel in Marine Gardens, but the pier failed to generate the anticipated passenger trade and the hotel eventually became a private residence.

The belated arrival of the railway in 1863 gave the town new impetus, and a large docks complex was eventually built. Rather by default, this became home to the sixth largest fishing fleet in Britain and the town eventually prospered and grew far beyond its original lay-out. The presence of the docks made Milford and neighbouring Hakin a hard-drinking area, and the temperance lobby was highly active as a consequence. In 1877 the people of Milford and Hakin were canvassed on behalf of an organisation dedicated to stopping the sale of alcohol on a Sunday. Nearly 550 forms were handed out, with 411 of those returned being in favour of Sunday closing and barely a dozen opting to keep the pubs open. However, well over 100 forms were either 'lost or destroyed', probably by people who were too busy drinking to be bothered with filling in forms.

There were 70 convictions for drunkenness in Milford Haven in 1911. At around that time an article appeared in the *Pembroke Dock and Pembroke Gazette* under the heading 'The Drinking Habits of Milford Women'. It painted a bleak picture.

> Years ago it would be considered a disgrace to womanhood to be seen entering a public house – far less to be seen standing at the bar drinking. It is not so today. Women, even young women scarcely out of their teens, enter the public house with no sense of shame or decency. Considerate landlords make special provision for these 'lady' customers by providing 'snugs' into which they may drop without being seen. The sadness of the whole thing is emphasised by the fact that it is amongst the young married women that the drinking habit is most on the increase.

And it wasn't just the pubs which posed a threat to the young married women of Milford while their husbands were away at sea. Each street had its quota of 'old mothers' for whom drink was the automatic remedy for just about any ailment. When acting as midwives they invariably nursed a bottle of whisky under their apron, and they were always ready to prescribe 'a little hot brandy', 'a toothful of whisky' or 'a half pint of best stout' as a sovereign cure for any ailment. Continued the article:

> These old mothers are the curse of the young wifehood of the town. They are often nothing less than a pack of snivelling, evil-smelling dirty boozers who ought to be kicked out of every respectable house on the street. They persuade these young wives to begin the deadly habit of 'nipping' and the young ones spend their husbands' money on these things and the old harpies come in and help them drink it. Many a young, healthy girl has within two years of her marriage become a drunken sot by these means.

An unusual aspect of the pubs of Milford Haven and Hakin is the fact that most came to be owned by Burton on Trent brewers Ind Coope, later part of Allied Breweries. This process began following the death of James Vaughan, a local auctioneer and entrepreneur who had acquired the leases for nine pubs in the town, sub-letting them to tenants. When Vaughan died in 1899, his business was taken over lock, stock and barrel by Ind Coope. The brewery strengthened its stranglehold on the town 20 years later, as explained by Ted Hackett in his *History of the Avondale Hotel*:

> At the end of 1920 when the National Provident Institution started to sell off the Milford Haven estate, most of the estate was sold to Sir Hugh James Protheroe Thomas, but a number of public houses were sold to Ind Coope and Co (1912) Ltd. The Alma, the Avondale, the Commercial, the Dinas Hotel, the George and Dragon, the Globe, the Golden Lion, the King's Arms, the Lord Kitchener, the Quay Stores, the Railway Hotel, the Sir Charles Whetham, the Spirit Shop, the Three Crowns and the White Lion were sold as a job lot for a total sum of £9,400. Because of this purchase Milford Haven and Hakin became 'Ind Coope towns' and later 'Ansells towns'.

The decline of the fishing industry in the 1950s was offset by the growth in the oil industry, with several refineries being built along the Haven. Milford remains a working port, although much of the docks has been redeveloped to include a marina, museum, galleries, shops and restaurants.

Several histories of Milford Haven will tell you that the streets now known as Hamilton Terrace, Charles Street and Robert Street were originally called Front Street, Middle Street and Back Street. Sadly, the truth is not so simple. Front Street or 'First Street' comprised what is now Victoria Road and Hamilton Terrace, while the two streets running parallel to and behind Hamilton Terrace have been described at various times as 'Back of Front Street', 'Second Street', 'Middle Street', 'Third Street' and 'Back Street'. There were various 'Cross Streets' and 'Side Streets' linking the three main parallels, and several decades passed before these were distinguished by individual names. This doesn't make identifying the position of early pubs any easier, but we are on fairly safe ground with grandest of the three streets, Hamilton Terrace, especially as the town's most historic inn still stands proudly at its heart.

In August 1800, Peter Cross announced his intention of opening on September 24 a 'spacious and elegant inn, erected by Sir William Hamilton.' The advertisement added:

> Packets sail daily from Milford and return daily from Waterford. Mail coaches to and from London will be conducted on an improved style.

The building of this 'elegant inn' had been one of the first priorities in the new town of Milford Haven, the establishment of which had been conceived by Sir William Hamilton and brought to reality by his nephew Charles Greville. And in July 1802, Admiral Lord Nelson, the great naval hero, visited Milford Haven with Sir William and Lady Hamilton, attended a dinner at the new inn, and made a speech in praise of the town and harbour. The inn seems to have been known as the **Packet House** or simply **New Inn** in its early days, although it was listed in the licensing records as the **Milford Hotel** when Mr. Cross retired in November 1808. (The sale which followed his retirement included 'a good mahogany-framed billiards table complete; two neat post chaises; four good horses; two colts; two prime milch cows; one fat cow; a number of pigs of the China variety and a large quantity of manure').

Henry Lewis, formerly of the town's Castle Inn, took over the lease of the inn, and in 1810 he changed its name to the **Nelson Hotel** and worked hard to establish the hostelry as one of the more fashionable inns in the county. In November 1811 a ball and supper were held here, given by the officers of HMS *Favourite*. 'Dancing commenced at nine and continued, with little intermission, until one, when an elegant cold collation was served up', reported the *Carmarthen Journal*. And while the younger people then continued dancing through to daybreak, 'others round the social board fought their battles o'er again'.

The Lord Nelson and its gardens dominate this early view of Front Street, now called Hamilton Terrace.

Henry Lewis remained the landlord until about 1821, during which time the trade of the town suffered the severe blow following the removal of the naval dockyard. In a valiant attempt to make the best of a bad job, Lewis launched a one-man campaign to turn Milford into a sea-bathing resort to rival Tenby or Aberystwyth. He created several public walkways overlooking the Haven and even cleared an area of shingle beach where he installed bathing machines. Perhaps not surprisingly, his scheme failed to find much support, and indeed Mr. Lewis seems to have been slightly bonkers in more ways than one. In 1819 he was obliged to pay sixpence in damages to William Green 'for assaulting plaintiff's wife by firing a gun at her'. (At the same Haverfordwest Assizes an unfortunate chap called

William James was sentenced to death for stealing a wether sheep, which all seems a little disproportionate).

Lewis departed to open a pub in Haverfordwest (which he also called the Nelson, although it wasn't a success), and in March 1821 the Nelson Hotel was sold by auction. Included in the sale were chaises, horses and harnesses, the same 'billiards table complete', and 'the coppers and utensils belonging to the large brewery carried on there'.

Edward Pritchard was the landlord from 1821 until his death in 1845. A noted breeder of enormous pigs, he slaughtered a hog in 1843 which weighed 32 score and 14lb – a record for Pembrokeshire. He was a popular and respected licensee and had previously run the **Milford and Waterford Coffee House** in the town; he also had charge of the Green Dragon in Pembroke for a spell. The Nelson was the meeting place of the Milford Haven freemasons from 1821 onwards, partly because 'Brother Pritchard's zeal in the cause of masonry is not to be surpassed', as a newspaper of the time noted. In 1822 Mr. Pritchard married his bar-maid, Charlotte Morgan, and they ran the inn together until his death in 1845.

On the day of his funeral, a large crowd gathered outside the Nelson, partly to pay their last respects, and partly because it had been rumoured that the coffin would have to be lowered from one of the upper windows of the hotel. To the disappointment of the Milford ghouls, it was discovered that the coffin had been taken downstairs the previous evening. When the funeral did get underway it was one of the biggest ever seen in the town, with twenty carriages following the hearse. Pritchard's widow Charlotte took over as landlady and also held the office of local postmistress, since the mail coach stopped at the inn. In 1848 the coach house at the Nelson played host to an unusual guest – an elephant belonging to Hylton's Menagerie which was touring the country. During his stay the elephant managed to escape from the coach house and rumbled up and down Hamilton Terrace for a while before being recaptured by keepers wielding pitchforks and hot-irons.

Following Charlotte Pritchard's retirement in 1855 the inn underwent a thorough overhaul. According to the *Milford Haven and Haverfordwest Telegraph* in 1856:

> The ball-rooms, with the new saloons in course of erection, are hastening towards completion. No expense has been spared in fitting it up as a first class hotel.

With the new look came another new name – the **Lord Nelson Hotel** – and the person who oversaw the refurbishment was new proprietor, Miss Louisa Davies. William Ryder Durant from Taunton was landlord from 1861 until his death, aged 51, in 1870. Joseph Ball, James Whetton and Henry

A solitary horseman passes the Lord Nelson.
(Picture courtesy of Mr. Roger Davies)

Rance all had short spells in charge, before the energetic Thomas Palmer became proprietor in 1878. The Nelson was described in the 1880s as a 'family and commercial hotel overlooking the Haven and New docks; omnibus meets all trains'. Palmer left in 1895 to run the Sir Charles Whetham in Pill – which he built – and Alfred Keeping was the hotel manager between 1900 and 1906 for brewers Truman, Hanbury, Buxton and Co. who were by then the owners.

Charles Crosbie was in charge from 1919 to 1921 by which time – it being the hey-day of the fishing industry – the Lord Nelson, was busy every night of the week. The long-serving manager of the hotel from 1921 to 1953, Bill Hyde from Reading, is remembered as running a tight ship. Trawler skippers and owners would be permitted to drink in the hotel's upmarket Blue Room, while deckhands, dockers and other riff-raff were directed into the public bar. It was said of him: 'He frowned deeply at female customers and discouraged them'.

Bill Hyde was followed in fairly quick succession by John Hyde, James Hall and Vernon Paice. With the coming of the oil industry, a further public bar was created from the former post office alongside, specifically to cater for the hard-drinking construction workers; it earned the dubious nickname 'the Bucket of Blood'.

In the 1960s and '70s the Nelson was run by Mr. and Mrs. Robbie White who saw to it that Nelson maintained its dual role as a first rate hotel and as a

Trawlermen stop for a chat outside the Lord Nelson.
(Picture courtesy of Mr. Roger Davies)

place where local people could drop in for a drink and a meal. Among the notable people who chose to stay here at this time were Lord Snowdon, the artist Graham Sutherland, Tory leader Ted Heath, and most of the cast of the television series *The Onedin Line* which was filmed locally. In June 2000 the hotel was purchased by Principality Developments Ltd, headed by Nick Laing, becoming part of the Innkeeper Wales chain. In February 2005 it changed hands again, being purchased by S.A. Brain, the Cardiff brewers.

Although the most prestigious, the Nelson wasn't the only inn on the front, and the **George**, which was run by James Evans from 1810 to 1817, was a house of some note. In May 1818, the *Carmarthen Journal* reported that 'Burton Jun.', the young English juggler, conjuror, bird trainer and ventriloquist, would be giving a performance 'in the large room' at the George.

Grace Hyman took over the running of the inn later that year, and shortly afterwards changed its name to the **Commercial Hotel and Packet House**. It was a substantial property, possessing a brewhouse, coach houses and stables, thirteen bedrooms, three parlours, a bar and a billiards room. In the early 1820s there was a regular coach service connecting the inn with London, the route being via Brecon, Worcester and Oxford. Grace Hyman remained the landlady until her retirement in 1828, when an advert described the inn as being 'opposite the Slip'.

James Murphy seems to have taken over the business, but without success, as in 1832 'the property formerly known as the Commercial Inn, Front Street, Milford' was offered for sale as a private dwelling. It seems to have remained unoccupied for a few years before being purchased and reopened by John and Margaret Wade who were there during the 1840s. Their nephew John Brown took over as licensee of the Commercial in the 1850s and was responsible for extending the premises in 1855 as the town began to perk up as a result of the Improvements Act. However the pub must have closed soon afterwards and by 1861 Brown was working as a 'timekeeper at the Battery'. It later became a lodging house and may have stood on the corner where Barclays Bank now stands.

Two doors along from the Commercial was the **Railway Tavern** which opened in about 1850. It was run by John Scale and was short-lived because Scale was declared insolvent in 1852. Meanwhile Holden's *Annual Directory* for 1811 refers to the **Milford Hotel and Packet House** run by William John, He had been the licensee from 1805, but the licensing records show that the business had closed even before Holden's *Directory* made it into print. The inn is thought to have been in Front Street.

In September 1810, the *Carmarthen Journal* carried an advertisement which ran:

> **Union Hotel**, Milford Haven. John Barber returns his sincere Thanks to the Nobility, Gentry, gentlemen Travellers and Others for the liberal encouragement he has met with since he opened the above Inn, and begs to inform them he has made considerable improvements for their accommodation.

These improvements included laying in a stock of choice wines and spirits. Barber had opened the Union Hotel in 1809 and he ran it until 1817 when it appears to have closed; again this inn is thought to have overlooked the Haven. Meanwhile a trade directory for 1830 mentions the **Union Packet** run by Ann Rees, but this was probably a different place.

Near the corner of Hamilton Terrace and Dartmouth Street stood the **Spirit Vaults** where Simeon Johns was wine and spirits merchant from 1861 to 1871. Daniel Lloyd Davies carried on the business during the 1880s, but it seems to have developed into a pub by the time John Williams was there from 1895 to 1899. He handed over to his son James, while from 1914 to 1923 Alfred Bowen held the licence of this W.H.

Tom Smedley with two of his grandchildren outside the Spirit Vaults.
(Picture courtesy of Mr. John Smedley)

George toehold in Milford. George Pocock was there in the late '20s and William Horan kept the Spirit Vaults for most of the 1930s. Retired trawler skipper Thomas Smedley took over in 1938 and remained the publican for well over 20 years; his son Albert and daughter Vera Jacks also became a well-known licensees in the town. In the early 1970s the pub was incorporated into the neighbouring Haven Hotel, becoming the hotel's back bar.

A general view of Victoria Road and Hamilton Terrace, with the fishing port buzzing with activity. Many of the pubs in town were supplied with beer and spirits from the Quay Stores on the left.

Victoria Road is the continuation of Hamilton Terrace down the hill towards Hakin, the station and the dock gates, and with so much passing trade it was prime territory for the opening of a string of pubs including – confusingly enough – the Dinas Inn and the Dinas Arms. Publican and sawyer Thomas Morris was the landlord of the **Dinas Inn** during the early 1850s followed by his widow Martha Morris from 1858 to 1861. Daniel Jeffs was there between 1864 and 1867, at which time the pub was noted for its skittle alley and for the fact that it was the meeting place of the local Order of Foresters. The local Starbucks Brewery evidently owned the pub at this time and announced that the lease was up for grabs in 1869; John Doherty took it on, with Mary Doherty being licensee in 1871. John Paulett was running the place by 1874 followed by carter and carrier Richard Venables in 1880 and Joseph Angrove in 1884.

The Dinas was then closed for a number of years before being reopened by Alfred Bowen in about 1899. Robert E. White – a son of Henry White who formerly ran the Pembroke Dock Brewery – was in possession from about

The Dinas Inn can be seen in the centre of this early view of Victoria Road, just beyond the shipbuilding slip.

1904 to 1909 followed by Joseph J. Evans between 1910 and 1923. Elizabeth Evans was there in the late '20s and George McKay ran the pub from 1930 to 1956. Being nearly opposite the dock gates, the pub was popular with trawler crews, and it is said that disputes between crewmen would often be settled with a fist-fight in the yard behind the Dinas. John Freatby took over as licensee in the late 1950s, being followed in 1965 by Hilda Freatby. The Dinas – pronounced locally 'Die-nass' – closed in the early 1970s, apparently because the licensee was less than enamoured at the change in clientele which had seen the trawlermen superseded by the roughnecks and roustabouts who had arrived with the oil industry.

References to the **Dinas Arms** further down Victoria Road are confusing and contradictory. Maria Harries appears as landlady in

No longer a pub, the Dinas is still an attractive building.

various trade directories from the 1850s to 1867, although the 1861 census clearly shows William and Maria Lewis running the inn. And it gets more confusing: *Potter's Electric News* reported in 1868 that Mrs. Mary Rees, Dinas Arms, Milford Haven, had been granted the transfer of her licence since the house she occupied was on land required for the mineral railway which was being built to connect the town station with Newton Noyes pier. Evidently the pub did move, because in a trade directory for 1870 the Dinas Arms is recorded in Stephen Street (*sic*) with David Jenkins in charge, and in the 1871 census the Dinas Arms appears in Dartmouth Street with Catherine Jenkins in charge – after which, mercifully, there are no further references.

Before the railway finally reached Milford Haven in 1863 it was the practice of local inns to send coaches to meet trains at Johnston station in order to pick up passengers, and competition for trade could sometimes be intense. On one occasion in 1862 the rivalry boiled over into a punch-up between the coachman from the Lord Nelson and his opposite number from the **Rose and Crown**, a chap called G. Raymond who was fined ten shillings for assault.

Thomas Morris (son of the Thomas Morris from the Dinas Inn) had been granted a licence for the Rose and Crown in Victoria Road in 1861 and he was still the landlord in 1867 when the pub was closed and later pulled down to make way for the new mineral line mentioned above. The licence was transferred to a new house to be called the **White Lion** in Priory Street. The Rose and Crown may have stood opposite the Dinas Arms.

The younger Thomas Morris was obviously determined to run a pub near the station, because he was in charge of the **Railway** in Victoria Road from 1871 to 1880.

The Railway as it looked in 2002.

204

In 1875 a soldier named George Pardie was charged with stealing a concertina from the pub. The only remarkable thing about the case was the soldier's single previous conviction 'for knocking down a man on Milford bridge and stealing a conger eel from him' – evidently a slippery customer.

Subsequent licensees of the Railway included Joseph Carter in 1881, Jules Morel in 1891 and Charles Hundredmark from 1892 to 1914. Mr. Hundredmark was German by birth but was a naturalised British citizen; he had arrived in Milford Haven in the 1880s to act as butler and waiter at the Lord Nelson Hotel. A prominent freemason, he was the oldest licensee in the town when he died in 1914. By 1923 the landlord was John Warlow and George Westenborg was there from 1928 until the last war. A descendant of 'Tom the Dutchman' Westenborg who came to Milford to work as a rigger on the *Great Eastern*, he was succeeded by Marian Westenborg.

Gwyn Harries, formerly of the Wexford and Waterford Packet in Hakin, took over in 1951 and ran the Railway for many years. The pub closed recently and was in the process of being converted into 'luxury apartments' as this book went to print.

A couple of doors down, near the bottom of the hill stands the **Globe**. This was part of the Quay Stores, the owner of which, James Johns, acted as general merchant and occasional innkeeper between 1861 and about 1878, at times installing managers to run the pub, including Julia Soady and William Phelps.

An early picture of the Globe with the Quay Stores on the left.
(Picture courtesy of Mr. John Stevenson}

The Globe had undergone a couple of name changes by the time this photo was taken in 2005.

The business was then taken over by local entrepreneur James Vaughan who built up a busy trade in coal and potatoes as well as running a wine, spirit and ale store, acting as auctioneer and dealing in second-hand furniture. In 1886 he rebuilt the Quay Stores on a much bigger scale and also refurbished the adjoining inn which became the Globe Hotel. Over the course of the next decade James Vaughan acquired the leases of nine licensed houses in Milford and Hakin, sub-letting them and supplying them from the Quay Stores where he was the local agent for Ind Coope's Pale Ale, Burton Ales and Irish Stout.

Vaughan recruited various tenants to run the Globe, including Edward Evans, Frederick Handcock and William Tonner who was there from 1886 to 1895. When Vaughan died in 1899, his flourishing little empire was bought by Ind Coope. George Phelps Eynon had just taken over as licensee at the Globe and he remained in charge until 1940, by which time he was the oldest publican in the town. A native of the horse-racing village of Lawrenny, he was a fine horseman and always had a couple of hunters in his stables. He rarely ventured out without his usual garb of breeches, leggings, hacking jacket and bowler hat.

Miss Lily Williams took over and conducted the business with the help of a sister for a dozen years, while Albert Smedley, formerly of the White Lion, was licensee from 1952 to 1971. The Globe remains open, even though it has suffered something of an identity crisis in recent years, becoming in turn the **Galleon**, the **Buccaneer** and now the **Llan-y-mor**.

CHAPTER EIGHTEEN

Milford Haven

PILL, CHARLES STREET, ROBERT STREET & PRIORY STREET

Long before the town of Milford Haven was built, the village of Pill stood overlooking the Haven and the inlet of Castle Pill. The Royalists built a fort here in 1643, but it fell to a besieging Parliamentarian force the following year, after which the village lapsed back into obscurity for 150 years. When Milford Haven was built, Pill gradually became a suburb of the new town, albeit one with a fiercely independent identity which it retains to this day.

Martha Powell of Pill dispensed good ale in the village between 1805 and 1818, but the sign of her inn has not come down to us. However we do know that the **Lugger**, which stood on Pill Green, was run by David Jones in 1805 and by Sarah Jones in 1811. Meanwhile Henry Davies of Cellar Hill, Pill, was a publican in 1841.

The **Swan** was run by Thomas Thompson from 1795 to 1811 and then by John Roberts for a couple of years. Henry Harding was the landlord from 1814 to 1827, and since he was also a butcher in Pill the pub is included here. James Sexton kept the Swan between 1830 and 1835 followed by Hannah Symmons but there is no sign of the pub after 1840.

In 1870, three years after the death of Col. Robert Greville, the Milford Haven estate passed out of the hands of the Greville dynasty and into the hands of the National Provident Union, to which the estate had become heavily in debt. And in January 1881 the trustees of the National Provident Union granted a lease to Thomas Palmer, licensee of the Lord Nelson Inn, for a cottage, two gardens and seven fields in Pill. With the docks starting to take shape at last and other projects promising to turn Milford into a boom town, Palmer obviously intended to develop this land. He even had dreams of opening a new pub here, but he was initially thwarted by a clause in the lease which stated:

> That any building for the time being erected thereon would not be used as an inn, public house or beer house or for the sale of intoxicating liquors unless the same be in connection with the business of the Lord Nelson Hotel.

How Palmer got around that restriction isn't known, but it may be no coincidence that the purpose-built pub he erected later that year on his land in Pill was called **Sir Charles Whetham** – which just happened to be the name of the chairman of the National Provident Union! Sir Charles, who was Lord Mayor of London in 1879, was also for a brief period in the early 1880s chairman of the Milford Haven Railway and Estate Company.

Overturning the clause in the lease was just one of Palmer's problems – he also had to persuade the magistrates to grant him a licence. Opposing his application was an uncomfortable alliance of temperance agitators and local publicans worried about increased competition, and Palmer's first application for a licence was turned down. The following year, 1882, he tried again, and with the magistrates mindful of major developments, which included a new iron and steelworks employing 200 men at Castle Pill, they decided there was a case for a new pub in Pill and approved the application. John Rees was the first landlord at the Whetham and he remained there until Palmer himself took over in about 1897. As well as being a property developer, Palmer seems to have been something of an entrepreneur, because his advert in a trade directory for 1901 stated:

> Wine, sprit, ale and beer merchant and bottler; agent for Alsopp's and Bass' celebrated ales and stouts in cask or bottle; livery stables; carriages of every description; carting agent to the Great Western Railway Co; letters and telegrams promptly attended to.

This picture of the Sir Charles Whetham may date from the 1950s.
(Picture courtesy of Mr. John Stevenson)

Robert Snewin, formerly of the ill-fated St Dogmell's Arms in Hakin, was landlord in 1909 and Mrs. Martha Snewin was licensee from 1910 to 1914. The Whetham was well known at this time for its 'snug' – a tiny bar where the local womenfolk could go unobserved to sip gin or buy a jugful of ale to carry home. It was also the headquarters of the town's association football team which played on the Pill Field behind the pub. Matt Kingston kept the Whetham from 1923 to 1931 while Henry Clarke was licensee from 1932 to 1944. He was succeeded by Alexander McKay, while Edward Peter McKay was there during the 1950s. Fred 'Firpo' Hoggins and Charlie Myhill both had significant spells in charge, after which the Whetham changed hands fairly frequently and was even closed for a time before being refurbished and reopened in 2005.

The Whetham as it looked in 2001.

The **New Inn** in Pill was kept by Thomas Cole from 1810 to 1813 and by John Adams in 1815. It closed the following year. However by the 1860s there was a new **New Inn** on the fringe of the Pill area, in the developing Great North Road, where the first licensees were Thomas Thomas and his wife Jane. From 1880 to 1884 Charles Richards was landlord and Mrs. Lucy Lloyd was there during the 1890s. John White took over in 1898, having moved from running the brewery in Cosheston when his first wife, Jessie, died. He immediately refurbished and extended what had previously been a relatively small pub, and as the Boer War was making headlines at that time he changed the name to the **Kimberley** to celebrate the lifting of the long-running siege of the town in February 1900. John White had numerous sons and daughters, so he invited his late wife's sister Annie Marie to move to the Kimberley to help look after them. She became John White's second wife, and the son she bore him, christened Octavius, was to become well known throughout Pembrokeshire as Ocky White, the Haverfordwest department store owner. John White subsequently moved to Cheltenham and the pub was taken over by his son Richard E. White who was described in 1918 as 'cinema proprietor, farmer and licensed victualler'.

The interior of the Kimberley with a poster advertising 'The Bad Girl of the Family'.
(Picture courtesy of Mr. John Stevenson)

Richard was succeeded at the Kimberley by his sister Frances, a remarkable lady who was widowed four times – the first time when she was running the Golden Lion in Charles Street. Her second husband, William Williams, died in 1926 after which she married George Picton who only survived for eleven months before dying at the age of 66. Undaunted, Frances married for a fourth time, becoming Mrs. Frances Armstrong in 1932. This time her husband, John Armstrong, was a hale and hearty 50-year-old and he survived until 1953, the redoubtable Fanny passing away one year later.

It is said that the pub was sold to wine merchants James Williams of Narberth at this time on condition that the tenancy would be held for life by Fanny's daughter by her second marriage, Miss Mary Williams. Always known as 'Miss Mary', she duly ran the pub in a no-nonsense fashion until her death in 1979, refusing to allow women in the public bar and having an aversion to serving the crewmen of oil tankers who would invariably be sent on their way. 'Miss Mary's brass piano' became a feature of the pub, this being the nickname for the splendid brass till which adorned the bar counter. Another unusual feature was the copper 'rum warmer' where Miss Mary would heat up tots of rum for her favoured regulars, many of whom worked all hours on the docks, unloading catches from the trawlers' icy holds, sorting the fish and packing them into crates.

The Kimberley was previously the New Inn.

Some present-day regulars are convinced that Miss Mary is still a ghostly presence in the pub, in which case she will have seen quite a few changes since her demise. Dai and Vicky Evans took over in 1980, and during their time the interior was modernised and given the usual James Williams open plan make-over. John Adams was licensee for much of the 1990s and Eric Thomson, the present landlord, has been in charge of this popular local since 1999.

Charles Street has been much altered since this photo was taken in about 1910.

It seems fairly certain that the early names 'Back of Front Street', 'Second Street' and 'Middle Street' all refer to the thoroughfare now known throughout its length as Charles Street. While the eastern end of this terrace housed the families of shipwrights and mariners, the western end was always much more commercial and this was where the market and most of the pubs were to be found. Charles Street was much altered during the oil boom of the 1960s and early 1970s with unlovely blocks of shops replacing a number of the older buildings, including at least one pub.

Most of the pubs in the street – indeed, the vast majority of the original houses – were on the north side, facing the Haven. Starting at the Dartmouth Street corner, the first pub along on the left was the short-lived **Nelson Tap**, which appears to have had no connection with the Lord Nelson Hotel. Innkeeper and post-horse proprietor Daniel Mayo ran the Nelson Tap in 1871. The pub passed to Thomas Bowen in 1872 but seems to have closed within a short time.

William Mumford opened an ale-house in Middle Street in 1806 and since he was a cooper by trade it was natural that he should name it the **Coopers' Arms.** His widow Frances Mumford was the licensee from 1822 until her death in 1846. On June 4, 1829 about 200 members of the Society of Ancient Britons assembled at their club room at the Coopers' Arms and – preceded by the Hakin Amateur Band with colours flying – marched to Steynton Church for a service. On their return to the Coopers' they were served dinner by landlady Mrs. Mumford. This was apparently accompanied by 'strong cwrw da' and as a consequence 'the afternoon was spent with the greatest hilarity'. Elizabeth Mumford was landlady from 1850 to 1852, but there is no mention of the inn by 1858. It seems to have stood in this part of the street.

In the days when Milford pubs brewed their own beer, a local Police Sergeant made a practice of regularly appearing at the door of certain houses with a two-gallon jar. It was part of his job, he said in his best official voice, to test the quality of the brew ... One of his ports of call would have been the **Lion** which was five or six houses along from the corner. Morris Johns (formerly of the Golden Lion) held the licence from 1850 to 1858 and Jane Johns ran the Lion in 1861. Benjamin Owen was licensee from 1867 to 1871, followed by Elizabeth Vaughan who was still the landlady in 1876. Thomas Hughes was there from 1877 to 1880 followed by Mrs. Jane Morris between 1884 and 1894.

William Davies had not long taken over the licence when for some reason the pub closed in about 1896. It reopened a couple of years afterwards as the **Lord Kitchener**, the new name honouring the field marshal who had just gained a peerage after his triumph at the decisive battle of Omdurman in the Sudan. William

An early 20th century view of the Lord Kitchener in Charles Street.
(Picture courtesy of Mr. John Stevenson)

The interior of the Lord Kitchener.
(Picture courtesy of Mr. John Stevenson)

Macfarlane became landlord in 1899 and Mrs. Ellen Macfarlane was the landlady from 1906 to 1909. In that year she became Mrs. Ellen Harries and she continued to hold the licence until 1927. Ernest Youe was there for about four years and Benjamin Joyce held the licence from 1932 to 1940. Jack and Lily Hudson took over and they were still there in 1957, Mrs. Hudson – 'Diamond Lil' – being remembered as 'a big woman, very strict'. Derek Picton took over and ran the pub for a lengthy spell, while present licensee Alan 'Moochie' Power has been at the 'Kitch' for about 15 years.

Landlord of the **Golden Lion** from 1837 to 1844 was a butcher called Morris Johns who seems to have moved to open the Lion just down the road. His sisters Charlotte and Martha Johns then kept the Golden Lion from 1850 to 1861, with Charlotte being in sole charge between 1867 and 1892. James Williams held the licence from 1895 to 1901 while former Milford Haven AFC player William Davies had not long taken over as landlord when he died at an early age in 1906 – the first of the four husbands his wife Frances outlived. Her second husband was William Williams, and they ran the Golden Lion until 1924 when they moved to the Kimberley. From 1924 to 1936 the landlord of the Golden Lion was Alfred Rust, followed by Daniel Whisby. Fred Thomas was the licensee during the 1940s, and there was another

An early 21st-century view of the Lord Kitchener.

The Golden Lion as it looked in about 1910.

William Davies in charge in the early 1950s. Subsequent licensees have included Ken Warrington – a former RAF officer with a wooden leg and a handlebar moustache who ran a very strict pub – Thomas Brewerton and Cecil Jacks. The pub suffered two name changes in recent years, becoming

The Golden Lion had become the Orange Tree by 2005.

Champers and then the **Orange Tree**, and was closed at the time of going to press.

A butcher called William Barrell (Barzell in some accounts) held the licence of the **Dolphin** in Charles Street from 1818 to 1830. In the 1830s the Dolphin was the regular setting for inquests into unfortunate sailors who had fallen into the docks – sometimes as a consequence of spending too long in the Dolphin. In 1826 the St. George's benefit society held a dinner here 'with plenty of cwrw da' followed by a dance at the Commercial Inn in Hamiton Terrace. The society had been formed in 1821 and was still going strong in 1844, with 200 members signed up. The local Odd Fellows also met here in 1845, and one of the 'brethren' – another butcher by the name of John Greenish – held the licence between 1835 and 1851. The place must have been awash with friendly societies, because during his time the Milford Royal Victoria Female Society, 200-strong, used to meet in their club-room at the Dolphin. They were apparently a group of 'very respectable and extremely well-dressed females'. The pub, which seems to have been a couple of doors along from the Golden Lion, closed in the 1850s.

The **Cardigan Arms** was opened in 1827 by Thomas Morris who was still the landlord in 1830; this name may have changed, because between

1840 and 1844 Thomas Morris was landlord of the **Cross** on the junction of Charles Street and Priory Street. He later moved to open the Dinas in Victoria Road. Thomas Watts ran the **Fishguard Arms** beer-house from 1870 to 1875 and this also seems to have been on one corner of this busy junction.

Also in Charles Street, between the junctions with Priory Street and Fulke Street, was the **Royal** which was kept by a widow named Mrs. Elizabeth John from 1899 to 1903. The landlord in 1906 was Charles Morris followed by Richard E. White between 1909 and 1913 and Albert Thomas who was there from 1914 to 1916 when the licence passed to E.F. Thomas. Arthur Fisher was there in the 1920s and early '30s; following his death in 1934 his widow Alice Fisher took over the licence. Probably the best-remembered licensee was ex-boxer Frank Moody who took over in October 1936 and remained licensee until 1959. The Moody family was from the Valleys but Frank and

The Royal Hotel in Charles Street.
(Picture courtesy of Mr. John Stevenson)

his brothers travelled around south Wales with the fairground boxing booths, eventually settling in Pembrokeshire where they ran successful pubs in Fishguard, Haverfordwest and Milford Haven. Fred and Maureen Dytor took over the Royal in 1959 – 'It was a hard act to follow', Mrs. Dytor recalled – and they ran the pub for six years before moving to Hubberston. Milford was still a busy fishing port at the time, and as Mrs. Dytor remembered:

> The trawlermen were lovely fellows. We used to open up at 7.30 every morning, which was strictly illegal but we had back steps which the men could use. On winter mornings they would troop in and have a couple of glasses of something to warm them up before going to sea, and sometimes a bottle to take with them. "I'll pay you later," they would say – and they always did.

The Royal changed hands a few times after the Dytors left and eventually closed. For the past 25 years it has been a card shop.

Charles Price was the landlord of the **New Inn,** Middle Street, between 1805 and his death, aged 55, in 1818. Hannah Price was the landlady from 1819 to 1827 and Susannah Symmons was licensee between 1828 and 1841. In 1815 the New Inn was burgled by a chap called David Thomas who stole a silver spoon, a silver watch and about £6 in cash. At the following Haverfordwest Assizes Thomas was sentenced to death for the crime. The New Inn was also the scene of a burglary in 1832 when thirty shillings in silver were stolen. 'Mr. Venables, the constable from Haverfordwest, has been employed to trace the robbery, but nothing has yet transpired to lead to the detection of the delinquent,' reported the *Welshman* newspaper. This much-burgled inn seems to have stood in this part of the street.

A new role for the Royal.

There were at least three licensed premises named after Queen Victoria in the town at various times and William Smith was running the **Victoria** in

Middle Street between 1839 and 1844. Again this pub seems to have been between Priory Street and Fulke Street, although it is difficult to be certain.

Cabinet-maker Thomas Symonds was granted a new licence by Roose magistrates in 1861 for a house at 41 Charles Street. This became known as the **Spirit Shop** and David Davies was there from 1870 to 1891. James Hart, later to open the Victoria Hotel, was the licensee from 1895 to 1897, Herbert Smith held the licence from 1909 to 1920 and Mark Robson ran the Spirit Shop from 1927 to 1940. Herbert Nicholls, who was the popular licensee from 1941 to 1956, is remembered for always sounding a ship's bell instead of crying 'Time'. By this time the pub was known to its regulars as the 'Devon', this being the name of a local trawler, the crew of which frequented the pub. Popular with visiting servicemen during the war, the 'Devon' was famed for its collection of naval cap-bands. Mr. Nicholls was followed by Gordon Jones and James Horan who took over in 1965. Dickie Marchant and Eddie Thomas both had spells in charge, but the pub was closed for a few years before David John arrived from the Victoria in 1992. He refurbished the pub and reopened it under a new name, the **Trafalgar**, in honour of the town's Nelson connections. The licensee for the past seven years has been Monica Vink.

The Trafalgar still carries the sign of its former name, the Spirit Shop.

There were very few pubs on the south side of the street, but these seem to have included the **Eagle Spirit Vaults** where William Stephens was in charge from 1851 to 1873. The **Whale** may also have stood in Charles Street, this being an apt name for a pub in what was once a whaling port. Stephen Martel was the landlord from 1806 to 1827 and was still in business as a grocer and draper in 1835, but trade directories are silent as to whether the pub was still going as well. And on his death, aged 64, in 1837, Mr. Martel was described merely as 'shopkeeper'.

The **New Quay Arms** also seems to have stood on the Haven side of Charles Street. This beer-house was the scene of a massive punch-up in June 1867 between a gang of railway navvies and local police officers called to eject them from the pub. Two policemen were badly beaten-up and six of the navvies later appeared in court on assault charges. David Davies was the landlord at the time, presumably the chap who later ran the Spirit Shop.

On the Market Square stood the **Commercial** which was accessible both from the Square and from steps leading up from Dartmouth Street. Mrs. Jane Prior seems to have been the first licensee; she was landlady from 1881 to 1899. William Hart had charge for a few years, and Tom Lewis was the landlord from 1906 until his death in 1919 when his daughter Gertrude took over. James Bussby ran the Commercial from 1923 to 1930 and Thomas Lloyd was there from 1931 until after the Second World War. Cecil Jacks and his wife Vera were licensees in the 1950s and '60s before moving to the Golden Lion. The pub closed in the late 1960s and is now a tattoo parlour with flats behind.

There were two entrances to the Commercial. This shows the Market Square frontage.

Dartmouth Street was the most westerly of the town's 'cross streets'. The **Sloop and Railway** in upper Dartmouth Street was a somewhat seedy beer-shop cum boarding house where David Mathias was the landlord in 1858. It was kept in 1861 by Mary Wagner and her three dressmaker daughters followed by Hannah Rees in 1867. By 1868 the pub was being run by a widow by the name of Elizabeth Antwis and regularly regularly figured in court cases. In 1869, John Child of the Sloop and Railway was charged with punching his wife Elizabeth. When he pointed out that his wife and daughter had been hitting him with iron bars at the time the case was dismissed.

The second of the 'cross streets', and the most important as far as boozing was concerned, was the central Priory Street and there was a little cluster of pubs on the right hand side going down Charles Street towards Hamilton Terrace.

Oldest of these was the **Bristol Trader** where John Hughes was the landlord from 1812 to 1840 and Elizabeth Hughes was licensee until her death, aged 75, in 1843. Thomas Hughes was there from 1844 until 1847 when he was jailed as an insolvent debtor. Nathaniel Hall was the licensee from 1850 to 1852 and John Roberts was there in 1858. In 1861 the licence passed from

This picture shows the regulars at the White Lion in Priory Street, drinking a toast to Albert and Evie Smedley on their last day at the pub in June 1952. The Smedleys, who later ran the Globe in Victoria Road, are standing in the doorway between the two men in caps. Several well-known Milford characters appear in the photograph, including Billy John, Joe Utting, Howard Phillips, Dick Reid, Hughie 'Bull' Best, Jack 'Jumbo' James, Billy Picton, Billy Davies the barber, Dick Albrow, and 'Johnny the Indian'.
(Picture courtesy of Mr. John Smedley, who is the young lad in the cap)

John Denton to a widow named Eliza Johns, and later that year two of the lodgers at the inn were described as 'firemen aboard the *Great Eastern*'. The pub seems to have closed a couple of years later.

When the Rose and Crown in Victoria Road was pulled down in 1867 to make way for a railway line, the licence was transferred to a new house called the **White Lion** in Priory Street. This was located more or less on the site of the old Bristol Trader. One of the first licensees was Charlie Lister who had come to Pembrokeshire with the *Great Eastern* and decided to stay; in later years he ran the Criterion pub in Pembroke Dock. The White Lion's longest-serving landlord was Theophilus Evans who kept the pub from 1875 until his death in 1906. He was succeeded by Thomas and Gertrude Marchant who were still there in 1912, while Gilbert Hart was licensee in 1914. Benjamin Robert Joyce was the landlord in the 1920s and Albert Smedley was there in the late 1930s and '40s before moving to take over the Globe in Victoria Road – although his wife Evie's name appeared over the door during the war years. The Smedleys left in 1952, and soon afterwards brewers Ind Coope closed the pub. It is now The Windjammer Café.

The Windjammer Café now occupies the premises which once housed the White Lion.

Next door down was the **Coburg** where Martha Saies was landlady from 1840 to 1844. She seems to have given up the licensed trade soon afterwards to run a bakery at the premises, which she did for many years afterwards.

Mary Ann Davies kept the **Alma** in Priory Street from 1858 – just four years after the battle in the Crimea after which it is named – until 1861. The Alma was one of the places where an early dentist in the town by the name of Dick Byers practised his trade. Rather than wait for patients to come to him, Dr. Byers apparently sought them out in the town's ale-houses. Finding a suitable pain-racked victim he would operate on the spot, yanking out the offending molar with a pair of pliers while the other drinkers in the pub looked on, clapping and cheering. He charged threepence a time for this service, but sportingly refused to accept any money if he removed the wrong tooth by mistake.

The Alma is still going strong after 150 years.

The Alma changed hands fairly frequently in its early days, and licensees included David Jenkins, Joseph Green, Mary Edwards, Thomas Hales and Fred White. The pub was greatly improved and enlarged in the late 1880s by local wine merchant James Vaughan who had built up a small portfolio of pubs in Milford and Hakin, and a plaque on the wall dated 1890 seems to be a legacy of this refurbishment. From 1891 to 1895 the licensee was Mrs. Elizabeth Smith and from 1898 until his death in 1915 it was William Davies. His widow Mrs. Lil Davies carried on running the pub until 1937 and Thomas Parsell Roberts was there during the war. Harry Roberts – like Thomas Roberts, a former licensee of the Wexford and Waterford Packet – was in charge during the 1950s, with Alfred John taking over in 1962. Leslie Roberts was there in the 1970s and another well-remembered licensee was Gwyn Bevan.

Like several Milford pubs the Alma closed for a time in the 1990s, perhaps a legacy of the downturn in the local oil industry and the closure of the Mine Depot at Newton Noyes. It was rescued by David John, who had previously revitalised the 'Devon'. He bought the Alma from Ansells, refurbished it, and got the business up and running again before moving on. The pub is now back in brewery hands, being owned by S.A. Brain of Cardiff, and the licensee for the past few years has been Phil Dow.

In 1911, dispensing chemist John Davies Harries applied for permission to sell spirits off the premises from his chemist's shop on the corner of Hamilton Terrace and Priory Street. The Rev. D. Garro-Jones and the Milford Total Abstinence Society were quick to object; as they told the local magistrates:

> If your lordships grant this licence there will be a great deal of surreptitious drinking amongst women. There is too much at present. There is many a woman who would not dream of going to a public house who would go to such premises as these, connected with a chemist's shop, because her neighbours might think she went in for syrup this or elixir that or some medicine or other. It is well known that such a licence as this is the curse of the country generally.

Evidently impressed, the magistrates refused the application; the building is still a chemist's shop.

A few years ago, workmen carrying out alterations to the **George and Dragon** – a pub on the corner of Charles Street and Barlow Street – discovered human bones hidden in a bricked up alcove. Legend has it that they were the remains of two crewmen from a ship which had called at Milford in the early 1800s. The men had died of fever and their bodies had been hastily concealed to trick the authorities who would otherwise have placed the ship in quarantine and prevented it leaving. William Wade kept the pub from 1835 until his death in 1842 at the age of 32. During this time the Odd Fellows of the Loyal Mariners' Lodge established their lodge room at the inn and it was sometimes referred to as 'the Mariners' hotel'.

The George and Dragon in the 1950s, as seen from Charles Street.
(Picture courtesy of Mr. John Stevenson)

Ann Wade was landlady from 1844 to 1858, Elizabeth Hall was there in 1861 and Benjamin Davies from Whitland held the licence from 1867 to 1871. Landlord William Llewellyn died in 1873 and Catherine Llewellyn was the landlady in 1875. John Vaughan was there in 1881 and James Prior

The hill outside the George and Dragon is still known to locals as 'Dragon Hill' although the pub is long gone.
(Picture courtesy of Mr. John Stevenson)

was landlord between 1891 and 1914. Former docks engineer Albert Thomas then took over, but died in 1918. Mrs. Mabel F. Jenkins ran the pub in 1923, after which it was run for a few years by Herman Westenborg and then by William Westenborg.

Edward Edwards was there from the late '30s to the mid-'50s, followed by James Jones and Jimmy Jenkins who took over in 1963 but left to run the Railway in Johnston when it became apparent that the George and Dragon was to be demolished as part of a major redevelopment scheme for Charles Street.

Running parallel to Charles Street, residential Robert Street has always been served rather badly for pubs, and the few that did exist were located to the west of the Priory Street junction. Stonemason John Jones ran the **Masons' Arms** in Robert Street from 1840 to 1852, while Martha Whittow ran the **Victoria** in Robert Street between 1851 and 1871 when she was 84. The landlady in 1875 was her daughter Hannah Phelps but the pub had closed by 1881.

The **Farmers' Arms** in Robert Street was kept by David Johns between 1844 and his death in 1860. Milford Haven was still a relatively rural settlement in those days and the pub doubled as a farmhouse with sixty acres of farmland. When William Johns succeeded his father he seems to have dispensed with the pub trade.

Priory Road is the northerly extension of Priory Street and became an important artery as Milford grew with the opening of the docks; over 400

The Victoria in Priory Road, photographed in 2002.

houses were built in the 1890s. To cater for this growing population James Hart built the **Victoria Hotel** in Priory Road in 1897 – Victoria's jubilee year – and ran it until his death in May 1911. A Devonshire man, he had come to Milford in about 1885 to work on the building of the docks and by 1891 he was licensee of the King's Arms in Hakin. He later ran the Spirit Shop before building the Victoria, the third pub of that name in the town. It was a substantial corner house and in 1906 he advertised that he was hiring out horses and traps, coaches and carriages (suitable for weddings and funerals), brakes, wagonnettes and governess carts. The traps, it was proudly announced, were fitted with 'India Rubber Tyred Wheels'. His widow Emma succeeded him, while from 1923 to the last war Gilbert Hart kept the pub. He was followed by William Thompson and the long-serving William Berryman.

At some stage the interior of the Vic was given the open-plan treatment by the owners, Felinfoel Brewery, and David John was there from 1988 to 1992 when he moved to the 'Devon'. Licensees then came and went in regular succession and the pub suffered as a result. Present licensee Helen Crumpler has worked hard in the past six years to re-establish the Vic as a locals pub, serving the neighbouring community, and she was rewarded when the readers of a local newspaper voted it 'Pub of the Year' in 2005. Throughout all the changes there has been one regular at the Vic – Percy the pub ghost, thought to be the restless spirit of a guest who died in the hotel many years ago.

Inevitably there are a few Milford pubs which have defied all efforts to trace them, not to mention any number of beer-shops about which all that is known is the name of the householder. There were two inns called the **Castle**. Henry Lewis ran one in 1808, but he left soon afterwards to take over the town's flagship inn which eventually became the Lord Nelson. Thereafter the Castle was run for a couple of years by George Lewis, presumably a relation of Henry. Jane Hallett opened another **Castle** in 1827, but closed it again soon afterwards. Whether either of these pubs was the same as the **Ship and Castle** where James Saies was the landlord in 1822-24 is impossible to tell. And no trace has emerged of two pubs recorded in 1835, the **Royal William** where the landlady was Ann Hall and the **Three Crowns** run by grocer William Hogan. Similarly impossible to pin down is the **New British Spirit Shop** where Eliza Bennett was dispensing the gin in 1852.

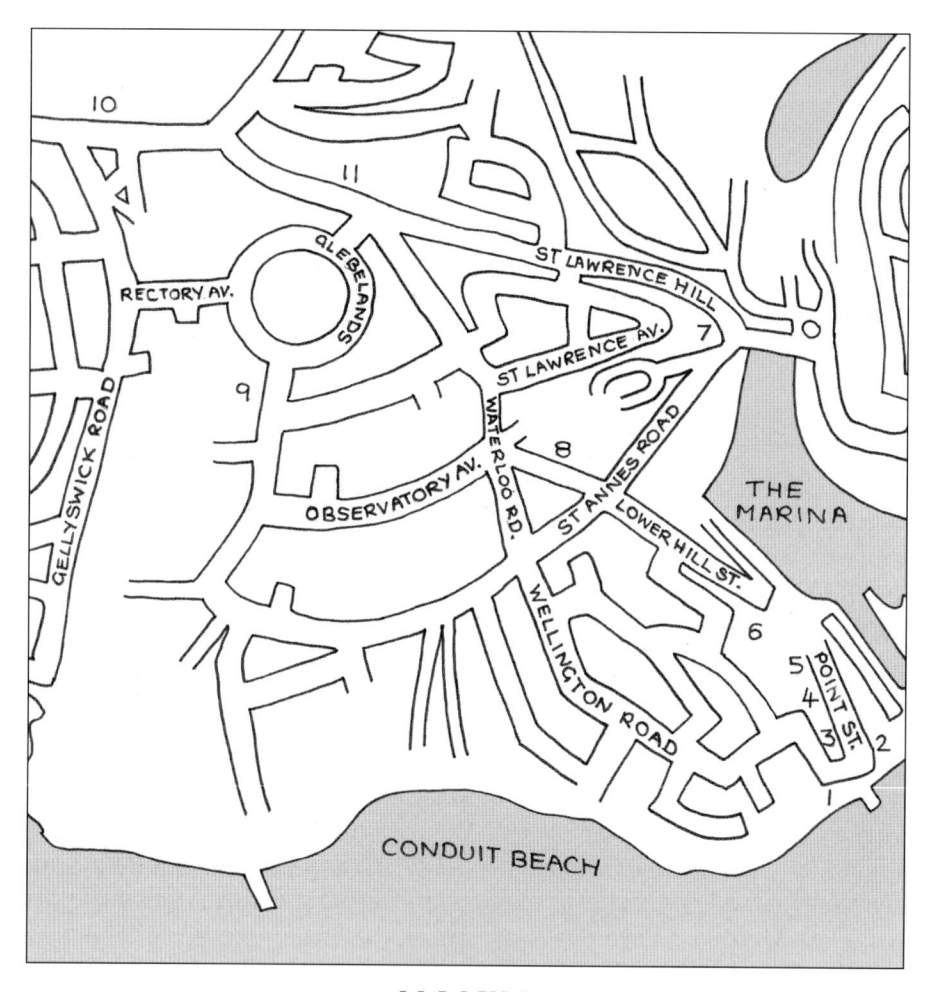

HAKIN

(CHAPTER 19)

1	King's Arms	7	Bridge End
2	Sloop	8	Avondale
3	St Dogmell's Arms	9	Observatory
4	Great Eastern	10	Three Crowns
5	Wexford and Waterford Packet	11	Masons' Arms
6	Heart of Oak		

CHAPTER NINETEEN

Hakin & Hubberston

Hubberston and Hakin face the town of Milford Haven across what was once the tidal Hubberston Pill, now an area of docks and modern infill. Hubberston grew up slightly inland, centred on the medieval parish church, while neighbouring Hakin had its own quay and brewery by the mid-18th century. A lease dated 1746 refers to:

> An old quay and ground at Hakin and the brewhouse built thereon and springs of water at the same place and commonly called Ship Style Slade.

Hakin began to expand rapidly in the late 18th century along the shore of Hubberston Pill, and particularly around Hakin Point. This had become one of the chief landing places in the Haven and in 1771 an Act of Parliament authorised the repair of the turnpike road from Tavernspite through Haverfordwest and Tiers Cross to Hakin Point. Ships from Bristol and Liverpool increasingly landed goods and passengers here – usually via rowing boat tenders – and a packet service was set up to carry the mail to and from Waterford in Ireland. It is recorded that a coach carrying the Irish mail left Hubberston every morning, arriving in London 48 hours later.

Previously there had only been a few fishermen's cottages in the Hakin area, but these were soon converted into ale-houses to provide refreshment for travellers and new buildings rapidly followed. One passenger who arrived at Hakin Point from Liverpool in 1772 recorded:

> At seven we landed in the village, which is very small and irregularly built (the houses being all constructed of a rough stone) and consists only of a few little public houses.

It has been claimed that every other house in Hakin was licensed at one time – and that all the other houses were selling beer without a licence. Certainly, in 1779 a number of people in Hubberston parish were convicted of selling ale and strong beer without being authorised to do so. (Hakin remained a hot-bed of illicit drinking well into the 20th century; in 1918 two women were fined for running shebeens in Lower Drang).

By 1784 there were ten licensed ale-houses in the parish, most of them straggling along the track which led along the shore of the Pill from the Point, while by 1795 the first of the Nantucket whalers had arrived to colonise the area and plans for the smart new town of Milford Haven were well advanced. This was to be built across the Pill from Hakin, superseding the old fishing village and initiating a rivalry between the two communities which still exists to this day. The number of hostelries on the Hakin side had risen to 13 by this time, including a rudimentary inn. When the compilers of the *Cambrian Guide* landed at Hakin Point in 1800 after a boat journey from Pembroke they were not impressed by this establishment. 'Hubberston did not induce us to stay longer than was sufficient to recruit ourselves', they wrote. 'We found the dirty inn pre-occupied by unfortunate Irish refugees'. Sadly, if prudently, they did not name the inn.

By 1812, with Hubberston Pill buzzing with shipbuilding and whaling activities, there were no fewer than 21 fairly rough and ready ale-houses on the Hakin side of the inlet. However Hakin, perhaps even more so than Milford Haven, was hit hard by the decision of the Navy Board to transfer its dockyard from Hubberston Pill to Paterchurch in 1814. Many ale-houses closed for want of trade, with several licensees moving upriver to open new pubs in upstart Pembroke Dock.

As was the case in Milford Haven, all we are left with in many instances are the names of these early and often short-lived Hakin ale-houses and their licensees, with only a rough idea of where they were in business. The following were all known to be operating in the early 19th century: The **Arloch Castle** kept by William Evans from 1806 to 1812; the **Britannia** (Thomas Davies 1812 – 1815, Martha Adams 1816); the **Lord Nelson** (Benjamin Giles 1805 – 1809, Hannah Giles 1810); the **Flying Dragon** (Elizabeth Anderson 1809 – 1813); the **Harp and Crown** (Michael Lee 1805 – 1818); the **Jolly Sailor** (Philip Stephens 1810 – 1813); the **Blue Boar** (John Rees 1812); the **Pembroke Arms** (William Husband 1805 – 1816, Ann Husband 1817 – 1818); the **Sailmakers' Arms** (William Brown 1807 – 1809); the **Mermaid** (William Owens 1810 – 1812); the **King's Head** (Andrew Wing 1805 – 1809); the **Coach and Horses** (Elizabeth Morgan 1806 – 1814); the **Rope Walk Castle** (John Morgans 1805 – 1808); the **Old Packet House** (Martha and Hannah Beynon 1813 – 1816); the **New Inn** (John Davies 1814 – 1817) and the **Waterman's Arms** (John Williams 1808 – 1821).

A further blow followed in the 1830s when the Irish packet service was transferred up the river to the new Hobbs Point pier at Pembroke Dock. This again would have accounted for a number of Hakin hostelries, and there seems to be no trace of the following pubs after about 1835: The **Butchers'**

Arms (John Davies); the **Brother Sailor** (Elizabeth Hughes); the **Navy Tavern** (William Phillips); the **Champion** (Anne Richards and John Richards); the **Lion** (Peter Jenkins, William Phillips, Thomas Philpin) and the **Brig** (Mary Godman).

Despite these setbacks, shipbuilding and ship repair continued on the shores of the Pill while the docks developed in fits and starts, eventually becoming home to a large fishing fleet. The economy of the area recovered and thirsty wharf-rats, deckhands and fish-packers provided more than enough custom for the multitude of Hakin pot-houses. Naturally the area became a target for the temperance movement – 'Hakin is Hell on Earth', a local chapel minister once declared – and the first pub in Pembrokeshire to lose its licence under the redundancy ruling was the St. Dogmell's in Point Street.

The Rev. John Evans, who arrived in Hakin from north Wales in 1913, soon found himself suffering from culture shock. 'I have seen more drunkenness in Hakin during the few months I have been there than in the same number of years in Pwllheli!' he spluttered. This outburst prompted a spirited retort from a loyal Hakin resident in the *Milford Haven and Neyland Gazette* the following week:

> Hakin is not Pwllheli, thank goodness, and if we prefer a little beer to ginger pop and a good beef steak to a Bath bun we are surely nothing the worse for that. It requires stamina, endurance and physical courage of no ordinary type to pile up the credit of a community, the deeds of daring which have given Hakin a place in the making of history. Hakin is a name to conjure with, and only a fool would dare question its supremacy in the world of intellect and daring.

The **King's Arms** still stands at the foot of Chapel Street, virtually on Hakin Point, and until fairly recently was the headquarters of the local yacht club as well as being a focal point of the Lifeboat Regatta. Henry Merritt was licensed to keep an alehouse in Hubberston in 1795 and this was probably the King's Arms since someone of that name is known to have been the landlord there from 1805 to 1825. Elizabeth Griffiths was licensee between 1828 and

An early view of Hakin showing the long straggle of Point Street with its pubs and shipyards.

The King's Arms on Hakin Point.

1835, while coastguard pensioner William James was there in the 1840s and early '50s. He didn't always run the pub, however, delegating that job to his niece Sarah Davies. William Leonard, waterman and licensed victualler, was the landlord between 1858 – when the pub is thought to have been substantially rebuilt – and 1875 and Charlie Codd was there in 1880.

The premises were further improved and enlarged in the 1880s by local wine merchant James Vaughan of the Quay Stores. James Hart from Appledore was licensee in 1891 before going on to build the Victoria Hotel in Milford town. Jesse Warren held the licence from 1895 to 1898, fish merchant Dan

Lester was licensee in 1901 and Causey Whittow was there from 1906 to 1909. Jeremiah Coughlin kept the pub from 1909 to 1923 having previously run the Heart of Oak, and Holman Jenkins was licensee from 1927 to 1939. Alexander McKay was landlord during the war, after which William Kenrick was in charge for nearly 20 years. Fred Dow and William Jewels were licensees in the 1960s, by which time the Kings' Arms had become a 'singalong' pub with a brand new Hammond organ. Like most of the pubs around Milford, the King's Arms was an Ansells house at this time and subsequent tenants included Teddy Powers and Idris Twigg. Current licensees are Harry and Bernadette Hutchings who purchased the pub from the brewery nearly 20 years ago.

The **Globe** was in the area where Point Street and Chapel Street meet near the Point. Martha Beynon opened the Globe in 1818, having previously run the Old Packet House, and continued to run it until 1840, while Hannah Thomas – possibly a sister – was landlady from 1841 to 1852. It was still open in 1859, because in that year a well-known local drunkard named George Howells was making such a nuisance of himself in the pub that he was hit over the head with a poker by a woman named Mrs. John. Although Howells died shortly afterwards, Mrs. John escaped any blame, the jury at the inquest deciding that Howells had died of 'erysipelas caused by intemperate habits'. This incident seems to have rung down the curtain on the Globe.

The **Pilot Boat** was launched in 1827 by James Johns. In 1830 the Hakin Benefit Society met 'at the sign of the Pilot' and marched to Hubberston church led by the Hakin Amateur Band. On their return, the society members enjoyed what the *Carmarthen Journal's* correspondent pompously described as 'a quantum sufficit of the good old beverage, cwrw da'. James Johns was still the landlord at the time, but the pub had closed by 1835. Its exact location cannot now be determined, but it seems to have been in the area of Chapel Street and the Point. Also in this vicinity, alongside a small shipyard, was the **Shamrock** where the landlady from 1867 to 1875 was Elizabeth Hogan, a member of a prominent local family of shipbuilders. The pub doubled as a grocery shop.

From Hakin Point a narrow lane of houses and cottages once followed the shore of Hubberston Pill. Originally called Hakin Street, this later became Point Street, a dockside thoroughfare inhabited by seamen and sail-makers, ships' carpenters and riggers, lodging house keepers and ships' chandlers; it was also home to a vast number of inns and pot-houses.

A plaque on the wall of the Heart of Oak pub laments the fate of Point Street.

It was the hub of Hakin past
With buildings and people of renown!
Sadly the era was not to last –
First cut off, then needlessly knocked down.

Looking south along Point Street with the Docks Company fence on the left.
(Picture courtesy of Mr. John Stevenson)

The 'cutting off' occurred in the 1870s when Milford Docks were built. Most of the properties on the shore side of Point Street were demolished and a solid fence was built in their place, grimly separating the remaining houses from the new Hakin wharf and dry dock. Further demolition followed during the 20th century, usually prompted by Docks Company expansion schemes. Some of these schemes never came to fruition and parts of the old street, where buildings were 'needlessly knocked down', remain as waste ground to this day.

In 1825 the *Carmarthen Journal* reported that a public house called the **Sloop** in 'Hakin Street' had been damaged in a gale. A gig-boat had been caught up by the wind and blown through the bay window of the pub which stood at the Haven end of the street, about 40 yards from the King's Arms. Thomas Phillips was landlord from 1805 to 1830 while from 1835 to 1858 the landlady was Mary Phillips. She was assisted in running the Sloop by her daughter Elizabeth Alpass, whose husband – a master mariner – was at sea for long periods. Emma Rickaby or Kirkby was licensee in 1861 and William Lewis was there from 1867 to 1870. Between 1871 and 1881 the pub was run by Corbetta Brown while her husband – whose name appears to have been Charles – was on the high seas. When the Sloop closed isn't known, but it was reported in 1905 that the licence had lapsed.

Houses in Point Street peer over the Docks Company fence.

The **Ross and Wexford Arms** was next door to the Sloop and John Beynon was landlord in the 1820s. The pub was run by the Johns family between 1827 – when Thomas Johns took over – and the 1870s, but with the menfolk evidently at sea for long periods the pub was sometimes in the charge of a chap called James Edwards. Elizabeth Johns was the licensee between 1867 and 1875 followed by John Peterson. In 1877, with the building threatened with demolition by a new docks development, Peterson attempted to transfer the licence to the nearby Fishguard Arms – where the licence had lapsed – but without success.

There were three pubs more or less in a row at this point, and next door to the Ross and Wexford Tavern was the **Three Tuns** which was run by Thomas Rees in 1808 and by Mary Richards from 1810 to 1813. Thomas Rees was back in charge from 1815 until his death in 1826 when Elizabeth Rees took over and she was still there in 1835. It was run by pilot James Hancock and his wife Margaret between 1840 and 1861 but seems to have closed in the 1860s.

It's difficult to determine the exact location of the many pubs of Point Street, but the **Hibernia** seems to have been the next ale-house along the way. Ann Scott was the landlady in 1823, followed in 1825 by Lavinia Scott who was still there in 1830. Butcher William Phillips, formerly of the Lion, was in charge from 1835 to 1851 helped by his daughter Ann Phillips who later became the licensee in her own right. By 1861 the pub was being run by 65-year-old John Mathias, a former master mariner who had 'swallowed the anchor' and he was still there in 1875.

Next door to the Hibernia was the **Carpenters' Arms** which was opened by Thomas Roberts in 1811. It had become the **Shipwrights' Arms** by 1819 and Roberts remained the landlord until 1824. He was followed by baker and innkeeper Ann Roberts between 1825 and 1851. Landlord and grocer between 1858 and 1875 was Robert Payne, followed in fairly quick succession by George Scotton, Thomas Morgan and shoemaker Thomas Evans who seems to have been in charge when the pub closed in the 1890s.

Close by was a short-lived pub called the **Prince of Wales**, the only reference to which appears on the 1861 census when it was run as a sideline by tailor William Lewis. He was still on the premises 20 years later, but by then he was being described solely as 'tailor'. Meanwhile Hakin grocer George Phillips launched the **New Sloop** two doors along in about 1844, only for it to founder the following year when Phillips died.

A couple of doors further along was the **St. Dogmell's Arms** which was kept by a mariner from St. Dogmael's named William Griffiths and his wife Mary between 1841 and 1871. Their daughter Miss Ann Griffiths kept the St. Dogmell's from 1875 to 1890 and William Jones was there from 1895 to 1901. In 1905 this was one of numerous buildings acquired under an Act of Parliament by the Milford Docks Company with a view to demolition, perhaps in connection with the building of a new mackerel market. Attempts were made to transfer the licence of the St. Dogmell's to the Sloop, recorded above, where the licence had been allowed to lapse. However, this plan met fierce opposition from various local temperance groups as well as from the Royal Mission to Deep Sea Fishermen, which wanted the licence expunged altogether. It was the very first case to be considered by the newly-constituted Redundancy and Compensation Committee, and the licensee, Robert Boyd Snewin, fought long and hard against the loss of his livelihood, producing a petition signed by 300 people in favour of keeping the licence alive. However it was to no avail. Hakin at that time had a licensed house for every 254 residents – too many, according to the authorities (who conveniently failed to include the visiting trawler crews in their figures) – and the St. Dogmell's was the pub to be sacrificed. The committee set the amount of compensation to be paid at £457; the owners demanded £2,000 and an appeal court later judged that the sum should be £1,295.

The **Blue Anchor** – sometimes referred to simply as 'Anchor' was opened by Isaac Mathias in 1809 and he was still licensee in 1835. At the time of the 1841 census he was living in the vicinity of the St. Dogmell's and was described as a 'waterman', aged 60, having apparently given up the licensed trade.

Ship's carpenter William Huzzey, a member of a family of shipwrights and publicans from Burton Ferry, ran the **Spirit Shop** in this part of Point Street in the early 1860s, but it was apparently a short-lived enterprise.

The next pub along the way seems to have been the **Sailor's Return**. Details about this pub are sketchy, but it was probably opened in the 1840s by a widow named Sarah Kearnes, later being run by her daughter Anna Maria and her Nova Scotia-born husband Alexander McKay during the 1850s.

A carter and labourer called James Grunnah opened the **Wexford Tavern** in about 1855 and was still in charge in 1870. His widow Jane held the licence in 1871, followed by the couple's widowed son-in-law John Peterson in 1875. He subsequently moved to the Ross and Wexford Arms and by 1881 the Wexford Tavern stood empty, awaiting demolition.

Close by was the **Newport Castle** where Griffith Howell was the first known landlord in 1835. John Mathias was the landlord from 1844 to 1852 followed by Joseph Williams in 1861 and Sarah Thomas who was behind the bar in 1867. By 1870 she had given up selling beer, being described as a 'shopkeeper' in a trade directory of that year.

The nearby **Great Eastern** was named in honour of Brunel's mighty steamship which visited Neyland in 1861. Landlord of the Great Eastern in 1870 was John Thomas, and by coincidence the *Great Eastern* steamship actually entered the newly-built Milford Docks in 1874 and spent several years moored just a stone's throw from Point Street. The licensee of the Great Eastern in 1875 was E.R. Hutchinson, also described as 'brewer and maltster, Milford Brewery'. He had left by 1884 to be replaced by William Thomas. Fisherman James Gray and his wife Jane kept the pub from 1898 to 1905, in which year – like the St. Dogmell's – it was acquired under the Act of Parliament by the Milford Docks Company with a view to demolition. A proposal to transfer the licence of the Great Eastern to new premises to be built nearby was rejected by Roose magistrates who felt there were more than enough beer-shops around the docks. They agreed with a local chapel minister who declared of Milford trawlermen: 'Sober, they are as fine a body of men as one could wish to find. Drunk, they are unmanageable!'

In 1820, the freehold of a dwelling in Hakin called the Caernarvon Castle was up for sale, the tenant being Archibald Hall. There is no indication that this was a public house, nor whether it had any connection with the Point Street pub called **Caernarvon Castle** where Joseph Anderson was the landlord from 1844 to 1852 and Mary Anderson was in charge from 1858 to 1861. In 1871 the local magistrates heard that the house had been 'badly conducted for some time' and suspended the licence which was held at the time by Ann Griffiths. However, they relented two weeks later and allowed the landlady's widowed sister, Mary Allen, to run the pub. Between 1873 and 1875 the landlord was John Thomas and he was followed by the widowed Elizabeth Thomas and then William Owen Thomas. The pub closed in 1886.

William Brown, a pilot, was the landlord of the **Yarmouth Arms** hereabouts from 1841 until his death 'at an advanced age' in 1849, after which it was run for a few years by his widow Eleanor. (From 1810 until 1835 William Brown had run a pub in Hakin called the **Ship and Brig**, but whether that was a different place or the original name of the Yarmouth Arms is impossible to determine).

At 56 Point Street was the **Sailors' Home** run in 1851 by Margaret Saunders and between 1857 and 1867 by seaman and innkeeper Francis Squire. And three doors along was the **Carpenters' Arms**, evidently not the earlier Hakin pub of the same name. Charles Smith was landlord in 1835 followed by John and Mary Rees (or Reece) who were there from 1841 to 1861.

The **Fishguard Arms** seems to have occupied 65 Point Street. Elizabeth Morgans, who opened the pub in 1817 and ran it until 1852, regularly catered for meetings and dinners of the Hakin Friendly Society. Landlady in 1862 was Martha Harries, William Rosen ran the pub in 1867 and William Dimmock was the landlord from 1870 to 1875. The licence appears to have lapsed shortly afterwards, and a determined attempt by John Peterson to revive the pub came to nothing; it was standing empty in 1881.

The **Rose and Shamrock** is a difficult pub to pin down. Mary Davies was the landlady from 1840 to 1844 but no-one of that name appears as a publican in the 1841 census. However the census does list a Mary Davies, shopkeeper, in Point Street, sharing the address with a Margaret Owen, publican. On this evidence the Rose and Shamrock is included at this point.

The northern end of Point Street with the Wexford and Waterford Packet in the centre of the picture.
(Picture courtesy of Mr. John Stevenson)

The **Freemasons' Tavern** at 73 Point Street was the scene of an inquest in November 1855. Landlord between then and 1861 was Henry Merritt, auctioneer and baker and presumably a relative of the Henry Merritt who once ran the King's Arms. The pub seems to have closed in the 1860s.

Two doors along, at 75, Point Street, was one of Hakin's earliest alehouses. This was the **Waterford Pacquet** which was run by the Owens family for several years – presumably Robert and Catherine Owens who are known to have kept an inn in Hubberston Parish between 1784 and 1795. It seems to have been closed for a few years before being reopened in 1813 by John Morris. Martha Morris was the landlady from 1821 to 1841, while Mary Ann Morris, who was in charge from 1844 to 1864, refurbished and enlarged the premises at some stage, changing the name to the **Wexford and Waterford Packet**.

Mary Morris handed over to Elizabeth Vaughan who was still there in 1867 and the landlord from 1871 to 1898 was James Vaughan, a wine merchant and entrepreneur who subsequently ran the Quay Stores and acquired a small portfolio of local pubs. So busy was he with these other affairs, in fact, that the running of the Wexford and Waterford Packet was usually left to his wife Margaret. Frank and Martha Carpenter saw in the new century at the pub and Thomas Jenkins was landlord from 1906

One of Hakin's earliest hostelries, the Wexford and Waterford Packet shortly before demolition. The more recent Heart of Oak in the background is still going strong.
(Picture courtesy of Mr. John Stevenson)

241

to 1911, James Barker was there briefly in 1911 and Matt Kingston held the licence from 1912 to 1914.

A strapping young chap named Walter Charles Harries tried to take over the licence during the war years but the local magistrates were having none of it. 'No man should apply for a public house licence who is of military age' they admonished him. William Greenish took over instead, while in the 1920s Thomas Lloyd kept the pub. Thomas Parsell Roberts was the landlord between 1931 and 1938, followed in a steady succession by Lilian Hudson, Harry Roberts, Joe Roberts and Gwyn Harries. The Wexford and Waterford Packet became the last of the Point Street pubs to close when the licence was not renewed in 1952. Shortly afterwards this sturdy old Georgian pub was demolished along with the remaining properties in Point Street, apparently as part of a Docks Company scheme to build dry docks capable of taking oil tankers.

Point Street ended near where the **Heart of Oak** still stands at the foot of Lower Hill Street. A fine, traditional Hakin pub, with a lively dockside flavour, the Heart of Oak was run by Mary le Hunte from 1840 to 1845 when it was a meeting place of the 'Good Samaritans' benefit society. James Davies was landlord in 1850 followed by Ann Phipps, a relative of the le Hunte family, who was in charge from 1856 to 1871. Ship's carpenter Charles Davies was the landlord between 1875 and 1891; when he left, James Vaughan of the Quay stores advertised for new tenants. 'A splendid opportunity for a persevering couple' declared the advert. William Bough was landlord in 1895 and Thomas Hitchings held the licence in 1901.

From 1904 to 1906 Richard E. White – son of John White of the Kimberley – was the licensee and Jasper Wootton held the licence from 1909 to 1914. In that year the pub survived a determined attempt by the local temperance brigade to have it closed, chiefly on the grounds that there were five pubs within 400 yards. The solicitor for the owners – brewers Ind Coope – pointed out that that the house 'was a good and commodious one and did a considerable trade' and the magistrates voted to keep it open. In 1923 the landlord was H. Jenkins and Thomas Childs was there from 1927 to 1938. Billy Briggs took over in 1939 and kept the pub for 20-odd years, and Irishman Jimmy Murphy was in charge by 1961. He ran the pub for several years with his wife June, a daughter of Towyn Francis of the Three Crowns in Hubberston. Then, as now, the Heart of Oak was popular with the crews of ships docked in the harbour, and Mrs. Murphy can remember ships' cooks serving the crewmen their meals in the pub, having tired of waiting for them to return to their vessels at mealtimes.

Mr. and Mrs. Murphy eventually moved to Pembroke Dock where they took over the Railway Inn in London Road (and immediately changed its

The Heart of Oak is a popular dockside pub.

name to Kerry Arms). They were succeeded by Pat Carrington, while other recent licensees have included John Horton, Bobby Morgans and Mike Jackson. For the past 14 years the Heart of Oak has been run by Tim Caddey and the pub is well worth visiting for its unusual collection of fishing and shipbuilding artefacts, most of them suspended from the ceiling.

Bridge Street was a continuation of the old 'Hakin Street', running from the junction with Lower Hill Street towards the bridge over Hubberston Pill. Originally a ferry crossed the Pill at high tide, with just a rather slippery footbridge over the stream at low water. A high-level wooden toll bridge was constructed in the 1850s, making communications considerably easier, and the present bridge is the fourth in line. Like Point Street, much of Bridge Street became a victim of the docks expansion and also like Point Street it had its share of pubs. These included the **Commercial**, where a widow named Anne Allen was licensee in 1861. It must have closed a couple of years afterwards, because *Potter's Electric News* in 1868 refers to 'a house in Hakin formerly known as the Commercial Inn'.

The Commercial was at number 15, while two doors along was the **Shipwrights' Arms** where James Davies was landlord in 1844 and Charlotte Davies was in charge between 1858 and 1880. William Evans was landlord in 1884. Next door was the short-lived **Plough** which was kept by Isaac Williams in 1861.

The **Bridge End** inn was built to greet people as they crossed into Hakin. James Havard, publican and iron moulder, seems to have been the chap who opened it in the late 1850s, shortly after the completion of the wooden bridge. When John Bowen applied for the renewal of the licence in 1867, it was refused on the grounds 'that the house is very badly conducted, rows very frequently occur there and it is the resort of women of evil repute'. Joseph Green attempted to reopen the pub the following year, but again the magistrates stood firm, this time pointing to the fact that there were 'about 16 licensed houses in the neighbourhood'. However Green persisted and by 1870 the pub was open once more. Bridge toll collector John Doherty was the

The Bridge in Hakin as it looked in 2001. It was rebuilt in the 1930s.

landlord in 1875 and from 1881 to 1901 it was John Thomas, a haulier from Little Haven, the pub being known as the **Bridge Hotel** by this time. Thomas G. Hebblethwaite ran the Bridge in 1906 in which year the licence passed to William Roch of St. Ishmaels. The landlord from 1909 to 1923 was Thomas Roch and John King kept the Bridge from 1926 until his death in 1930.

Julia King then moved from the Horse and Jockey in Steynton to take up the tenancy, but shortly after her arrival the original pub had to be demolished since it stood in the way of the approach road to the new bridge over the Pill. The present Bridge Inn was built nearby by local builders Phelps and Owens, and Julia King carried on as licensee until after the Second World War.

William Rackley was there during the 1950s while recent licensees have included Malcolm Hawkins and Tony and Eileen Hunt who were there from the late 1980s to 2004.

While most Hakin pubs were either on the Point or along the shore, there were a few others a little further inland including the **St. David's Arms** which was in Hakin Back. Jane Griffiths was there in 1814, followed by John Morris, William Garnett and Martha Garnett who was in charge from 1824 to 1826. Martha Watkins held the licence from 1827 to 1830 followed by John Thomas who was there from 1835 to 1844. The **Ship at Launch** was also at Hakin Back; Thomas Roberts ran it from 1805 to 1809. before moving to open the Carpenters' Arms.

Avondale House in Upper Hill Street was once an upmarket private residence, complete with stables, coach-house and servants quarters. The last family to live there were the Kelways, but in 1907 Mr. George Kelway was approached by James Gray, landlord of the doomed Great Eastern pub in Point Street. As noted earlier, the Great Eastern was due to be demolished and Mr. Gray had failed to obtain permission to build a new pub to replace it. Consequently he suggested converting the Avondale into a pub.

The Avondale was previously a private house with its own grounds.

Mr. Kelway agreed, and an application was made to transfer the licence of the Great Eastern to the Avondale. As ever, the usual suspects came out in force to oppose the transfer, especially as the old National School stood next door, and the magistrates turned down the application. However an appeal, which was heard in Haverfordwest a couple of months later, overturned the magistrates' decision and the new pub opened in about 1908.

Initially it seems to have been called the Great Eastern, but local people still called it the **Avondale**, so that is what it became. James Gray was fined ten shillings under the wartime 'no treating' legislation but remained landlord until about 1924. It was very much a fishermen's pub at the time; women were not encouraged and were restricted to the 'snug' which had a separate entrance. Henry Clarke was landlord in the late '20s, followed by William Davies who handed on to Alexander McKay, a former bookmaker, in 1936. When he moved to the King's Arms in 1940 the new licensee was Billy Cridland, during whose time the ghost of a woman began to make occasional appearances in the pub.

Former Brentford and Swansea Town footballer Billy Sneddon took over in the late 1940s, being followed by James and Barbara Evans. Barbara Evans was in sole charge by 1963, becoming Barbara Davies on her marriage to Gordon Davies. Saturday night was live music night in the 1960s, the resident house band being 'Michael John and the Avondale Neversweats' with support from 'The Two Wallies'. Keen pool player Idris Twigg was landlord in the 1970s – the local pool league still contests the Idris Twigg Trophy – and John and Maureen Nicholas were there in the 1980s during which time major internal reconstruction work was carried out, changing the layout of the pub and making the former entrance to the 'snug' the new front door. Since 1992 the licensees have been Susan and Edgy Cooper.

Other Hakin pubs are impossible to locate. John Morgan was the landlord of the **Cardigan Castle** in 1844 and a chap of that name was still running a beer-shop in Hakin in 1852, although its whereabouts are unknown. The *Carmarthen Journal* for 1831 recorded the death of George Davies of the **Three Compasses**, Hakin, presumably an ale-house, while a single reference also exists to the **Alma** in Hakin where John Troy was apparently the landlord in 1864.

Between Hakin and Gellyswick is Conduit Beach. There used to be a small but distinct community behind the beach, known as Conduit, with its own farm and its own pub – the **Three Mariners**. Mary Morris was landlady from 1821 to 1825 followed by Eliza Hughes. Further information is hard to find, but the pub seems to have survived until the 1850s when it was run as a beer-shop by rope-maker William Evans.

A new licence was granted at Roose Licensing sessions in 1861 for a pub at Half Ploughlands, Gellyswick – close to where building work was under

The long-serving Thomas Rees outside the Masons' Arms in Hubberston which he ran for over half a century.
(Picture courtesy of Mr. John Stevenson)

way on the barracks and gun battery of Fort Hubberston. No doubt the pub – the **Navy Inn** – where James Thomas from Mathry was landlord from 1861 to 1871, profited from the presence of a well-paid workforce on the doorstep, especially as the fort was not completed until 1865. The Navy Inn seems to have closed in the 1870s and the local yacht club now stands on the site of the small row of cottages known as Half Ploughlands.

Stonemason William Warlow ran a pub in 'Ubberstone' in 1840. This was the **Masons' Arms** – a small cottage pub on the right-hand side of the road from Hakin Bridge to Hubberston village, at the top of Hubberston Hill. Thomas Rees from St. Ishmael's became landlord in 1852 and ran the pub for a remarkable 58 years, also farming 30 acres. During this time he only chalked up one conviction – for serving after hours in the 1870s. Landlord Rees kept up his ties with his home area and the Masons' was a regular port of call for people from the Dale Peninsula who would stop off to exchange news and drink beer out of the blue and white mugs which were a feature of the pub. In later years Dale and St. Ishmael's men, who worked on the Milford trawlers, would leave their pushbikes at the Masons' before going to sea. At the end of the trip they would collect their bikes and pay Mr. Rees sixpence for storage.

The owner of the Masons' Arms was A.V.W. Stokes of St. Botolphs, and he received £670 compensation when the pub's licence was withdrawn in

*The Three Crowns in Hubberston is on the left
of this photograph from the early 1900s.*
(Picture courtesy of Mr. John Stevenson)

*The Three Crowns at Hubberston had been modernized and extended when
this photograph was taken 2002.*

1910 under the redundancy ruling. Thomas Rees, who was 90 by this time and the oldest tenant on the St. Botolphs estate, received just £80 to compensate him for the loss of his only means of livelihood.

Master mariner Thomas James ran the **Farmers' Arms** at 1, Hubberston Terrace in 1861, but in 1865 the pub was advertised as being to let in *Potters Electric News* and seems to have closed at this time.

The **Weary Traveller** was kept by William Morgan from 1851 to 1861 but was taken over by Thomas Childs in 1868. He changed the name to **Three Crowns** and it remained the Childs family pub for many years. Thomas' widow Margaret Childs held the licence from 1881 to 1891 and her son, John Childs was the landlord from 1901 to 1923. Mrs. Ann Childs was landlady from 1923 to 1927, followed for eight years by Miriam Childs. Her brother John Childs took over the licence in 1935 and was still there in 1943. Towyn Francis succeeded him, and his name was still over the door in 1962. The oil industry was just starting and, as one of the nearest pubs to the Esso Refinery, the Three Crowns enjoyed a busy time being popular with site workers who used it to socialise and to hold strike meetings. Mr. Francis left to run Y Polyn, a country pub near Nantgaredig, since when the Three Crowns has changed hands several times with George Rider and Stanley Boyes being among the licensees.

Charles Greville, Milford's founder, was an amateur scientist and astrologer and a fellow of the Royal Society. He decided to endow his new town with a college specialising in mathematics and the sciences, the centrepiece of which would be a well-equipped observatory. The college was built

Observatory Hall has been a pub since the 1960s.

on a site overlooking Gelliswick Bay and consisted of a central observatory with a number of small buildings leading off it, plus a large house for the college superintendent. Before the college was officially opened, however, Charles Greville died and the costly project was later abandoned, with the observatory becoming a ruin.

The large house alongside was turned into a farmhouse, but with the building of a sprawling council housing estate after the last war the farm lost its land and became a private house. By the mid 1960s it was standing empty, its potential as a pub being spotted by Fred and Maureen Dytor of the Royal in Charles Street. They went from door to door with a petition enlisting support for the proposal, which was readily forthcoming, and the **Observatory Hall** opened as a pub in 1965.

The new pub quickly benefited from its position near the Esso refinery site, and Mrs. Dytor can remember lining up pint after pint of Guinness on the counter to greet the Irish site-workers when they finished their shift. The Dytors remained at the 'Obs' for eight years before selling the pub to the Courage Brewery and moving to the Bush at Robeston Wathen. It then changed hands several times before current licensee Bruce Paton took over and established the 'Obs' as the popular local which it is today.

CHAPTER TWENTY

West of Milford Haven
HERBRANDSTON, ST. ISHMAEL'S, DALE & MARLOES

Now obliterated by oil refinery installations, Little Wick was both a bay and a tiny community on the road between Gellyswick Bay and South Hook Point. John Withers from Berkshire ran the **Half Way Inn** at Little Wick in the early 1860s, and no doubt this ale-house was opened to cater for the workmen building the fortifications at South Hook Point and on Stack Rock island – gun batteries designed to protect the Royal Naval Dockyard at Pembroke Dock from seaborne attack.

Herbrandston itself is an attractive village, especially the older part around St. Mary's Church and the village green. Primarily a farming community, it also had links with the sea by means of the tidal Sandy Haven Pill. It is also a rare example of a 'Thankful Village' – one where all the village sons returned home alive from the two great wars. There have been several licensed houses in the village over the years, but information about the earlier ones has proved difficult to find.

From 1810 to 1827 the landlord of the village's **New Inn** was George Wort, but in 1828 he left to run the Barley Sheaf in Pembroke Dock and the pub was taken over by Rees Jones. The **New Inn** where William Lloyd was landlord from 1861 to 1881 seems to have been a different place. By 1891 it was being run by Mrs. Emily Kearney but it had closed by the turn of the century.

Elizabeth Williams and her daughter Martha Williams were innkeepers in the village between at least 1841 and 1851. There is a newspaper reference in 1854 to the **Horse and Jockey** in Herbrandston, which could have been their inn. Grace John was listed as publican on the 1841 census, but there is no clue as to the sign of her pub, while the only reference to the **Cross Inn** seems to occur in a conveyance dated 1876.

Journeyman stonemason John Sutton was living in West Row, Herbrandston in 1851, and at some stage he decided to open the **Masons' Arms.** He was the landlord of this cottage ale-house from 1871 to 1880 and

Building work under way on the Foxhounds on Herbrandston Green.
(Picture courtesy of Rowena John)

his widow Mrs. Elizabeth Sutton ran the pub from 1881 to 1891. Like the New Inn it had closed by 1901, which is probably one reason why plans for a brand new pub on Herbrandston Green were submitted for approval in September of that year. The **Foxhounds** was duly built and opened by Jack James in 1903. He was fined £1 in May 1905 for permitting drunkenness on his premises, but he and his wife Sarah remained the licensees until the pub closed in May 1933. The Foxhounds was a magnet for troops who were stationed at South Hook during the First World War and they could occasionally cause problems. As one local resident recalled:

> Sometimes when the militia men got nasty Mrs. James would put them in their place. She was only a small woman but she was not afraid of them.

The licence was kept up for a few years after the pub's closure, but in 1940 it was not renewed.

It is rare in Pembrokeshire to find a purpose-built 20th century pub; most are conversions of existing buildings. Herbrandston, however, boasted two such pubs – the Foxhounds mentioned above and the more recent **Taberna**. This modern inn was designed and built by local carpenter and builder Reg Mathias in 1963 – just as the oil industry was taking off in the area.

*The motoring age comes to Herbrandston.
The Foxhounds is on the right.*
(Picture courtesy of Josie Owens)

*The Foxhounds has been a private house
for 70 years.*

A Pembrokeshire pub with a Latin name - the Taberna.

Mr. Mathias apparently arrived at the unusual pub name one night while helping his young nephew Robert with his Latin homework, discovering as he did so that the ancient Romans called an inn a 'taberna'.

Mr. Mathias and his brother Billy subsequently ran the Taberna for nearly 15 years, since when it has changed hands a few times while also acquiring a restaurant and a reputation for good food, notably when Ann Cooper was licensee in the mid 1990s.

In the 1970s, Fred and Maureen Dytor of the Observatory Hall in

Hubberston bought an old farmhouse in Herbrandston and applied for permission to turn it into a small hotel, pub and restaurant. The planning process was so protracted that the Dytors – having sold the 'Obs' – were obliged to spend three years running the Bush at Robeston Wathen while the bureaucrats chewed over the plans. Eventually permission was granted and the **Sir Benfro** became a reality, although sadly Fred died just as the building work was being completed. Maureen took charge of the business and remained the popular licensee of the Sir Benfro for nearly 30 years until her well-earned retirement a couple of years ago. The attractive hotel and its outbuildings were soon demolished by the new owners who had other plans for the site.

Sandy Haven Pill at low tide.

In 1813 William Garnett opened the **New Tavern** on the western shore of Sandy Haven inlet, at one end of a rowing-boat ferry which operated at high tide only. Garnett left a couple of years later to run a pub in Hakin, but Sandy Haven soon acquired another pub, because by 1826 the **Sloop** was being run by a widow named Mary Griffiths and she was still there in 1828. 66-year-old Mary Davies was innkeeper in 1851 and her son Benjamin was the licensee from 1861 to 1881.

In the autumn of 1894, the Sloop was visited by George Mason, who later wrote of his visit in his book *Historical Sketches of Pembroke Dock*.

> On landing from our yacht in the upper part of Sandy Haven, we proceeded along the shore until we reached a small cottage called the Sloop Inn. On entering the Inn for refreshments, we were somewhat astonished on reading a bill for sale of the Inn, to find what an extraordinary long lease it had. The

landlord of the Inn explained it as follows: 'You see, gentlemen, when the lease was made many years ago, scholarship did not count for much in these parts. The man who drew out the lease used figures and not letters to express the years. It was intended to be for nine hundred and ninety-nine years, but he put down 900, then 90, then 9, which read 900,909 years'.

The landlord also told Mason:

> I've just returned from Carmarthen Asylum to which I was sent after the wreck of the Loch Shiel, through the blessed cases of whisky coming in on the shore, which I and others drank like drinking water.

(The *Loch Shiel* was the Australia-bound merchant vessel which ran aground on Thorn Island on January 30, 1894, shedding its cargo of Scotch whisky – much of which was later washed up around the entrance to the Haven. One young beachcomber drank himself to death).

The repentant whisky drinker must have been George Morgans who was landlord from 1891 to 1898. He was followed by Howard Powell between 1901 and 1906 and Charles Mathias who was there in 1910. James Spicer was behind the bar in 1914 and John Gullam or Gwilliam kept the pub from 1916 to 1921 when Edward Stradling took over. In March 1924 George and Annie Hooper

Regulars in The Sloop in 1940. Back row: Bob John, George Hooper (landlord), Mrs. Hooper, Iris Hooper (daughter), Ernie John and his father Davy John, and Billy Mathias whose brother Reg built the Taberna. Front row: Trevor Jones, Sidney Roach and Albert Edwards.
(Picture courtesy of Mrs. Ruth John)

The building in the middle of the row was once the Sloop Inn

were granted a licence for the Sloop; he was the last to run a ferry across the creek, charging threepence a time. He would also collect thirsty customers from the Herbrandston shore for free and row them back across as necessary, depending on the state of the tide. (One regular from the village would announce to his family each evening that he was 'going cockling down Sandy Haven'. It was a fairly transparent excuse for visiting the pub – but he usually managed to return with a handful of cockles tied up in a damp handkerchief to back up his story!).

George Hooper remained the licensee until the mid-1950s when the property and the licence passed to next door neighbour Mrs. Lilian Beer, a member of a family of shipowners which for many years operated a small fleet of coastal traders from Sandy Haven Quay. It is said that she disapproved of the pub and only acquired it in order to close it down; certainly it was reported in 1962 that the Sloop was closed, although the licence was still being kept up.

Further west, St. Ishmael's is a largely agricultural village at the head of a valley leading down to the small beach of Monk Haven on the north shore of Milford Haven. The village had one ale-house in the 1780s, kept by Thomas Lewis and later by Jane Lewis, while John Elliot held an ale-house licence between 1795 and 1809; unfortunately no pub name has come down to us.

However we do know that the **Mariners** in St. Ishmael's was kept by Anne Morgans from 1812 to 1816 followed by William Laugharne in 1817. There is no record of a pub in the village in 1818, but by 1820 William Laugharne was in charge of the **New Inn**, presumably the pub which Elizabeth Laugharne is recorded as running between 1822 and 1824. In 1825 a stonemason named William Roch was running the only pub in the village;

The two trees in the centre of this old postcard view of St. Ishmael's may provide a clue as to why an early village pub was called The Elms.

naturally he called it the **Masons' Arms**, which may well have been a re-naming of the former New Inn.

William Roch was still a publican in 1861, but by now his pub was called **The Elms**. Presumably this was the house opposite the village post office which is still called The Elms. There is also a reference in a trade directory to a short-lived pub in the village called the **Castle** which was kept by John Roach in 1867.

The Elms is now a private house.

Whitewashed from doorstep to chimney-pot – the Brook in St. Ishmael's as it looked a century ago.

Brook House was the home of John Lewis in 1861, but by 1867 he had converted it into the **Brook** inn – perhaps because The Elms had closed. The landlord from 1871 to 1895 was master mason Lewis Rees who was fined 10s. in 1893 for selling watered-down whisky. Thomas Roch kept the pub from 1901 to 1906 and from 1910 until his death in April 1948, aged 69, the licensee was Thomas Hughes. His daughter Gladys Hughes took over, becoming Mrs. Gladys Dillon in 1952, and she still held the tenancy of this James Williams house in 1967.

A feature of the pub at this time was the pig-sty in the garden where pigs were fattened to be slaughtered and salted down each autumn. These pigs were invariably fed on slops of beer and as a result they lived their brief lives

The Brook in 2006.

in a permanent state of mild inebriation. For some curious reason each successive pig was named Dennis, so that 'give it to Dennis' became a catch-phrase in the pub for unwanted beer.

Morris Allen, Malcolm Rowlands and George Jackson were among the tenants of James Williams who succeeded Mrs. Dillon, while the longest-serving licensee in recent years was Joan Morgan-Salmon who ran the Brook on her own following the death of her husband Hugh. During her time at the pub it was much altered internally, being given the regulation James Williams 1980s' make-over.

Dale village is attractively situated facing up the estuary, with a sand and shingle beach and some fine houses along the old quay wall – at least two of them former inns. In centuries past it was a busy sea-trading and fishing village, with a sideline in smuggling and spiriting away cargoes from wrecked ships, but nowadays it relies mainly on the tamer trade of tourism.

In the past the area had a reputation for producing booze of various kinds, and there is a reference to a brewhouse in the village in 1705. According to *The History of Haverfordwest and Some Pembrokeshire Parishes*:

> One family of the name of Runwa, now died out, are said to have done quite a flourishing trade as brewers, sending a considerable quantity of ale to Liverpool.

There is also a tradition that a man named Evan Williams, a member of a Dale family well known for its skill in making whisky, emigrated to America in the 1700s and founded a distillery in Kentucky which is still flourishing. Certainly Dale had more than its fair share of ale-houses in the early 19th century. Dale Roads, like Angle Bay across the Haven, was often full of sailing schooners and ketches anchored and waiting for the right weather to put to sea, and the crews would sometimes row ashore for a couple of beers and a plate of bread and cheese, providing useful trade for these cottage pubs. During and after World War Two, there were Royal Naval air bases at Dale Aerodrome and HMS Harrier (Kete) which provided plenty of custom for the Griffin – the sole survivor of the many village pubs.

The earliest of these was kept by Lewis Sandivan or Saundison between 1784 and 1806, although the name on the sign isn't recorded. By 1795 there were three ale-houses in the parish, Sandivan being joined by William Harries and Thomas Symmons, while by the early 1800s there were half a dozen ale-houses. One of these was the **New Inn** which was run by Richard Mathias between 1806 and about 1814. Confusingly there was a second ale-house in the parish called the **New Inn** at about this time, run by Anne Symmons; the location of these ale-houses isn't known.

The sea front at Dale with the Brig on the left and the Griffin on the right.

Jeremiah Hays was the landlord of the **White Hart** in Dale from 1806 to 1813. He was also a registered fisherman, living in South Street. The **Sloop** in Dale was kept by John Morgans from 1808 and 1810, while Anne Morgans ran the **Jolly Sailor** in the village in 1811 before moving to open the Mariners in St. Ishmael's. William Morris, another registered fisherman, opened an ale-house called the **Prince William** in Dale in 1808 but it only survived for a couple of years, and another short-lived village pub was the **George** where James Harries was landlord in 1815-16. William Morgan ran the **Swan** in 1813 and the **Three Mariners** in 1815 – possibly the same place under a different name. William Hall kept the Three Mariners in 1820 followed by Mary Hall in 1821.

An elderly lady called Dinah Geary kept an ale-house at Dale Cliff in 1841. According to the excellent history of the village produced by Dale W.I., this pub may have been called the **Drum and Monkey**. And the presence of the local place name **Blue Anchor** indicates that there was a pub of that name hereabouts in the distant past.

Mariner and fisherman Thomas Hall ran the **Black Lion** from 1806 to 1815, followed by Margaret Hall in 1816 and Elizabeth Hall in 1818 and 1819. She is then recorded as being licensee of the **Brig** in 1820 and of the **Ship** from 1822 to 1828 – probably all of them being the same place.

By 1841 the Brig on Brig Quay was the home of Charles George and his wife Mary, she acting as innkeeper. Their daughter Eliza married a tailor called George Roach and he subsequently held the licence from 1861 to 1874. From 1881 to 1887 the licensee was a Chelsea Pensioner by the name of John Joseph Kent. Kent had spent nearly 30 years in the Royal Artillery, having been discharged with the rank of Master Gunner, and had apparently

The Griffin shelters behind the sea wall.

served in the Crimea. His wife (or widow) Mary was licensee in 1895 but by 1901 Tommy Jacks from Llangwm was in charge.

By 1906 George Davies was running the Brig as a tenant of Narberth wine merchants James Williams, the pub being owned by Col. Lloyd-Philipps of Dale Castle. In 1910 the licensee retired and due to a misunderstanding the licence was allowed to lapse. James Williams applied to have the licence reinstated the following year but the magistrates were having none of it and the Brig has remained closed to this day.

Thomas Morgans was the landlord of the **Three Horseshoes** from 1821 to 1823 and, as the name implies, this was once the home of a blacksmith complete with smithy alongside. However, when a fisherman called William Thomas took over the pub in 1824 he changed the name to the **Griffin** for reasons which are not now apparent. He was in charge until 1841 and ship's carpenter John Jones was the landlord from 1851 to 1895, supplementing his income by helping to build ships on the seafront and running a fishing vessel. Arthur Bowen was the landlord in 1906 and George White was there from 1910 to 1915; when he died the licence passed to his widow Mrs. M.E. White.

In 1923 the landlady was Mrs. Sarah Jane Saunderson, Alice Snelling was there in 1927, by which time it too was a James Williams house, and Lewis Lewis was landlord from 1930 to 1950. During the war the Misses Lewis who were behind the bar scrupulously rationed the beer, which was in short supply, the ration being two pints per person a night; Mary Lewis ran the pub herself for half a dozen years in the 1950s. Charles English was in charge of the Griffin from 1957 to 1963 and during his time the pub was extensively refurbished – partly at the insistence of the magistrates who were concerned at the near absence of toilet facilities. John Peebles, formerly of the Belle Vue in Haverfordwest, took over in 1964 and he was succeeded in turn by Mr. and Mrs. George Horwood and Mr. and Mrs. W. Tamsett. Dennis Blackman arrived from the Lobster Pot in Marloes in 1975 and ran the pub for ten years, followed in turn by Mr. and Mrs. P. Backhouse, Mr. and Mrs. Alan Cosnett and the present licensees, Mr. and Mrs. Rob Mathias. (Mr. Mathias has already featured in this chapter; it was his Latin homework which gave rise to the name of the Taberna in Herbrandston).

Once a village of crab and lobster fishermen, Marloes still has close links with the sea and with the Pembrokeshire islands; boats for Skomer leave from nearby Martin's Haven. More unusually, the area was once famed for the leeches which were gathered in Marloes Mere and sold to medical practitioners. The attractive clock tower in the village was built in 1904 in memory of the fourth Baron Kensington of nearby St. Bride's Castle, the local squire and a prominent temperance campaigner. It was in

1889 that his wife, Lady Kensington, opened the new Temperance Hall in Haverfordwest, close to the Kensington town house in Tower Hill, and it is probably no coincidence that Marloes was without a pub for many years.

This wasn't always the case and Francis John ran an ale-house in the village in 1808-09. Elizabeth Laugharne also ran an ale-house in the parish at around that time, but no names have survived of these early hostelries (although it would be nice to think that one was called 'The Leech-gatherers' Arms').

The first genuine Marloes pub name that appears in the records was the **King's Arms** where John Beynon held a licence from 1811 to 1813. The **Fishermen's Arms** was opened by John Roberts in 1813 and he remained in charge until 1828 when he was succeeded by Mary Roberts. References also exist to the **Masons' Arms** which was opened by John Edwards in 1828 and to the **Royal William** where a meeting of farmers and tradesmen took place in 1850 to discuss the merits of Protectionism as opposed to Free Trade. The **Farmers' Arms** was an ale-house on the north side of the village run by Thomas Phillips in 1861.

Smithy Cottage is thought to have been the Blacksmiths' Arms in the 1860s.

The **Blacksmiths' Arms** in Marloes was a two-room ale-house at the far end of the village with just a parlour and kitchen. William Jenkins, a blacksmith by trade and a man of 'portly dimensions', was the landlord from the 1850s to 1875. On one occasion two police constables entered the pub after hours to find the landlord still serving. Part of his defence was that he was still operating on 'local time' and did not realise that licensing hours had to be enforced according to the new-fangled 'railway time'.

On another occasion three gunners with the Antrim Artillery Militia, stationed at Dale Point, called at the pub. As the ale and porter flowed they began dancing Irish jigs to tunes played on a whistle. The diversion this caused allowed one of the artillerymen to sneak into the kitchen of the pub, break open a drawer and steal silver coins and gold rings. A police officer was soon on the trail of the culprit, finding him hiding up to his neck in a duck-pond near Hasguard, and he was sentenced to three months' hard labour. According to local tradition the Blacksmiths' Arms is now Smithy Cottage.

In 1870 William Davies Vittle obtained a licence for a pub in Marloes which seems to have been called the **Sailors' Home,** although it was known locally as the 'Raggy Down'. It was a fairly unruly place, being the haunt of poachers who roamed the St. Brides estate in search of rabbits and other game, and its far from spotless reputation may have prompted the local squire to take action. According to a letter from Mr. T. Martin which appeared in the *West Wales Guardian* in 1987:

> There were two pubs [in Marloes], the Blacksmiths' Arms and the Raggy Down, and Lord Kensington closed them both together after finding the village men roaring drunk in the village one night!

The opening of the Lobster Pot meant that Marloes was no longer 'dry' after nearly a century.

Marloes was without a pub for many years until the aptly-named **Lobster Pot** opened in November 1962. There had been objections to this purpose-built pub from Mr. Charles English, licensee of the Griffin in Dale, who claimed it would be 'disastrous to his trade'. However the licensing authorities were unmoved and gave the go-ahead to William Rees of Glebe Lane, Marloes, to open the pub. He ran it for a number of years while Mr. Dennis Blackman was there in the early 1970s. Ironically, perhaps, he left to run the Griffin, showing that Mr. English's fears were unfounded. Since then the Lobster Pot has changed hands on several occasions while remaining popular with villagers and holidaymakers alike.

CHAPTER TWENTY-ONE

West of Haverfordwest
THE HAVENS

The picturesque village of Little Haven is squeezed into the valley at the head of a sandy inlet. These days it is very much a holiday centre, with a far larger population in the summer than in the winter, and the inlet is busy in season with small pleasure craft and a few lobster boats.

Unlikely as it now seems, this was once the heart of a mining area, with anthracite from the workings at Strawberry Hill and elsewhere being exported on coasting vessels which were beached in the sheltered bay. However as early as 1814 the beach was being described as 'a celebrated bathing place', popular with the local gentry who built seaside homes here. Agriculture also played a part, and the village had its own hiring fair. This was held on 1 November and was known as the 'Runaway Fair' since most of the men seeking work had previously been hired at Portfield Fair in October, only to have fallen out with their new employers within a couple of weeks. The village even had its own police station with a single cell; it is said that the constable's wife would periodically lock her husband in this cell when he rolled home drunk from one of the village pubs.

In the days when Sunday drinking was forbidden, the pubs in the Havens acquired a reputation for bending the law. On one August Sunday in 1924 the licensees of three of the four pubs in the two villages were caught serving beer by Detective Constable Thomas and all three were later fined. The war years brought mixed blessings to Little Haven's three hostelries. On the one hand the RAF and Czech airmen who were stationed at Talbenny were good customers, but on the other hand beer was in short supply during the war and the airmen often drank the village dry, leaving nothing for the thirsty locals.

Publican and baker John Prosser ran the **New Inn**, Little Haven, from 1851 until his death in 1855. He was followed by his son, James Prosser, who was there until at least 1867. When he died his widow Ann Prosser took over the running of the pub, subsequently marrying William Phillips of Pembroke who was described as a 'farmer of 82 acres and innkeeper and grocer' in 1881.

A general view of Little Haven at the beginning of the 1900s, with the Swan on the left and the Castle on the right.
(Picture courtesy of Mr. Roger Davies)

The New Inn had become a Sunday drinking den by the 1890s, being well placed to take advantage of the 'bona fide traveller' loop-hole. The increase in the tourist trade (or possibly this Sunday drinking) led to the New Inn adding a six-stall stable block on the opposite side of the road in 1891. Landlord at this time was William Rees from St. Ishmael's. Carpenter John Russan was there in 1895 and in 1901 the licensee was a collier named William Thomas.

Noted for the ancient well in its beer-cellar, the New Inn became the rather grandly named **St. Bride's Hotel** in about 1904, and Thomas (or William) Stanford was the licensee in 1906. James and Jane Truscott held the licence between 1910 and 1923 followed by Mary Truscott while William Edgar Evans – always known as 'Sam' – and his wife Ada were there from 1928 to 1940. A member of a long-established Little Haven family, Mr. Evans always made a big event out of the the annual pig-killing day at the pub, dressing up in a black suit and top hat for the solemn 'Funeral of the Pig'. At the end of the day Mrs. Evans would cook faggots for the whole village to enjoy.

On one Sunday the St. Bride's was the subject of a raid conducted by police officers from Haverfordwest. Fortunately Sam and Ada had been tipped off about the impending visit (by the village constable!) so the pub was empty of customers when the raid took place. Ada served the town policemen with a consolation meal of ham and eggs, which they ate in the front part of

The St. Bride's, Little Haven, as it looked in the 1950s.
(Picture courtesy of Mrs. Barbara Chester)

the house – unaware that Sam was busily serving his regular customers from the back yard, sending up bottles of beer in a basket to the cliff-top garden behind the inn.

When Sam and Ada retired in 1940 the pub was taken over by their daughter and son-in-law Alec and Florrie Norman who were there throughout the war. Elizabeth Headley and James Griffiths then had stints in charge, while George and Barbara Chester were licensees from February 1952 until 1956, Mrs. Chester having been born in the nearby Swan Inn when it was kept by her parents, William and Katie Evans. When the Chesters left, the pub changed hands every couple of years with the licensees including George Gray and Francis Sell. In 1963 Eric Bradley moved from the Swan in Haverfordwest to take over the St. Bride's and he ran it throughout the 1970s, followed by his daughter Joan and son-in-law Phil Giles (now licensees of the Royal Oak in Pembroke) who were there for nine years. George Moody, formerly of the Royal in Broad Haven and the son of George Moody of the White Lion in Haverfordwest, subsequently kept the pub for a dozen years until his recent retirement.

The name of the **Swan** in Little Haven seems to come from Alexander Swann who ran a pub in Little Haven from 1795 to 1817; certainly Mary

The Swan Inn, Little Haven in the 1950s.
(Picture courtesy of Mrs. Barbara Chester)

Swann was landlady of the Swan from 1826 to 1828. By 1841 the licensees were a miller named George Max and his wife Mary, and Mary was still running the pub in 1851. Their daughter Letitia Max was the landlady from 1861 to 1895 helped by her sister Susan Max and Susan had taken over by 1901, running the pub with the help of her widowed sister Esther Owens. John and Mary Mills were licensees from 1910 to 1927 followed by Archie Phillips and then by William George Evans.

When Mr. Evans took up a post at Talbenny Airfield in 1939 he was obliged to give up the licence of the Swan, so it was his wife Katie ('Molly') Evans whose name was over the door until 1959. Among the regular visitors to the Swan at this time was royal photographer Norman Parkinson who delighted in photographing the village characters in the pub. Stan Lewis then held the tenancy of this James Williams house until 1965 followed by Cliff Wilkinson who was still there in 1973. Wing Commander George Nelson-Edwards, previously of the Trewern Arms in Nevern, took over the tenancy in May 1974. A former fighter pilot and a cordon bleu chef he built up the pub's reputation for good food during his ten years in charge. Beryl and Glyn Davies arrived from the Ship in Solva in 1987, and when they retired in early December 2004 the closure of this attractive and popular pub was announced shortly afterwards, provoking a great deal of dismay – and opposition – in the local community and further afield. The future of the Swan was still in the balance as this book was being prepared for publication.

Swan song ... The Swan closed a couple of years after this photograph was taken in 2002.

Just a stone's throw from the Swan, but in a different parish, is the **Castle** Inn, so named for no obvious reason. It seems to have begun life as the **British Hotel**, under which name it was run by John Owens in the early part of the 19th century. William Crunn kept the inn from 1823 to 1841, latterly assisted by Jane Banner, and Crunn seems to have been the one who renamed it Castle Inn. By 1851 Jane Banner was the licensee in her own right and she too changed the pub sign, because the 1861 census names her as licensee of the **Griffin**, Little Haven. The new name can't have stuck, however, because the inn appears as 'Castle' in a trade directory of 1867, with Jane Banner still holding the licence

William Phelps, a Dorset man, took over in January 1871 and held a house-warming dinner to mark the event. Dinner was advertised as being on the table at 3 o'clock and tickets were three shillings each. Phelps ran the pub from 1874 until his death in 1898 and his widow Mrs. Sarah Phelps continued to run it until 1906, after which Alan Medlicott was in charge. William John Horam was in charge during the First World War and licensees in the 1920s included Erskine Paul, Reginald Russell and William Philpin, while Mr. and Mrs. John Max Owen – 'Jack Max' – were the licensees from 1931 to 1939. Ethel McClaren held the tenancy of this James Williams house from 1940 to 1964 when local builder Roger Gibson and his wife Gladys took over. The Gibsons were still there in 1979.

*One of the most haunted pubs in Britain, the Castle Hotel,
as it looked before recent alterations.*

John Nelson-Edwards (son of George) and his wife Sue were in charge in the early 1980s when the Castle was described as one of the most haunted pubs in Britain. Doors would open and close, ghostly footsteps would be heard and the figure of a First World War soldier would materialise from time to time. It was suggested that in years gone by the bodies of drowned sailors who had been washed ashore on the beach would be laid out in the Castle Inn to await burial, resulting in a glut of restless spirits wandering about the place.

During Mike Harries' time as landlord the regulars were more interested in horses than spirits, a consortium of locals having shares in a thoroughbred called Stack Rock which won several races on the Flat. However the ghosts

The Castle in Little Haven photographed in 2002.

hadn't gone away for good, and Jim Stark, who was licensee in 1997, reported hearing 'strange noises which chilled the blood' and that objects kept being moved mysteriously around. The Castle was extensively refurbished in 2001, since when it has been run by Malcolm and Mary Whitewright – Mary being another daughter of Eric Bradley of the St. Bride's – and the ghosts still enjoy alarming the waitresses from time to time.

The **Waterloo** was a cottage ale-house in the alleyway behind the Castle Inn. John Owens was licensee in the 1820s, presumably after leaving the British Hotel. Much altered, the building survives as Waterloo Cottage. The **Lion**, also on the Walton West side of the village, is a puzzling place. John Williams held a licence for this pub in 1817-18 and again in 1823-24, but there is no mention in the licensing records of either pub or landlord between these dates – or afterwards.

There was also an ale-house in the village kept by William Allen between about 1806 and 1828, although the name is not recorded. The Pevsner guide to the buildings of Pembrokeshire states that the Manor House just off Grove Place was previously an inn before being rebuilt in the early 19th century, so presumably this was where William Allen was the innkeeper.

Also a coal-mining village at one time, neighbouring Broad Haven began to emerge as a seaside resort (complete with bathing machines) in Victorian times, as visitors discovered the wide sandy beach. Finding accommodation was a problem, however, and it was stated in 1851:

Broad Haven has changed beyond all recognition since this picture was taken in the 1950s.

The want of a suitable inn or hotel has been a great drawback in constituting Broad Haven a renowned bathing station.

There had been a pub in the village in the 1820s, serving the colliers. That was the **Three Cups** where Henry Cole was the landlord from 1808 to 1822 and Damaris Cole was in charge from 1823 to 1828. And while Little Haven developed as a resort during the 19th century, Broad Haven continued to depend more on the coal industry, so it was mainly for the coal workers that mineral agent William Powell ran the **Three Mariners** from about 1850 to 1874. The pub stood in the vicinity of Sandyke Road and the Slash Pond, and *The Welshman* newspaper reported in 1889 that it had been 'destroyed' in the late 1870s and not replaced.

Thereafter the village was without a pub for at least 15 years, with attempts to remedy the situation being regularly defeated in the courts. On one side were a group of people, mainly Haverfordwest businessmen, who thought that an inn would encourage tourists to visit the village and boost the economy; in the other camp were a group of local landowners who tended to treat the beach as their personal playground and had no wish to share it with the riff-raff.

Haverfordwest wine and spirit merchant and local historian John Brown built himself a grand house in Broad Haven in the 1880s called Sedgmere

The Royal was formerly a private house known as Sedgmere Villa.

Villa. He later decided to convert it into a small hotel, and in August 1889 the local magistrates granted him a licence for the 'Western Hotel'. However this decision was overturned by the county licensing committee under pressure from the landowning faction.

John Brown died the following year and Sedgmere Villa was purchased for £550 by another familiar figure – W.D. Phillips, the Haverfordwest licensee and journalist. He changed the name to the **Royal** and opened the hotel on 26 May 1892, promising 'well-aired beds'. He still couldn't promise beer, though, and there was a prolonged fight over the licence – a battle Royal, so to speak. Twice the local magistrates granted him a licence; twice the big-wigs on the county licensing committee overturned this decision.

'My chief opponent is, I know, rich and powerful, but I believe ultimately that right will triumph over might', thundered Phillips in the local press. And so it proved, because by 1898 the Royal was licensed and in the hands of Haverfordwest wine merchants W.H. George who installed tenants to run the business.

Mrs. Mary Ann Davies, formerly of the Stag in Haverfordwest, held the licence from 1898 to 1901. Landlord in 1906 was William Edwards, by 1910 William Jones was in charge, and in 1916 the inn was run by Mrs Annie Oliver with the help of her husband Harold. W.G. Evans was there in 1924 and Louis Nortier was licensee from 1927 to 1935. In that year Roose magistrates dealt with an application to transfer the licence from Mr. Nortier to a widow from Milford Haven named Ivy Foster. They approved the transfer despite the remarks of Police Supt. C.B. James who wondered rather sniffily if it was 'suitable to trust the licence of such an important house as the Royal, Broad Haven, to a widow'. Mrs. Foster was still in charge in 1939 but George Hunt had taken over by the 1940s. Harriet Hunt succeeded him, becoming Harriet Farmer in 1948.

Daniel Smith was in charge by 1950, but Catherine Smith held the licence from 1953 onwards. The wonderfully-named Jack Whip was there in the 1960s and George and Brenda Williams were running the pub as tenants of James Williams in the early 1980s. They left to run the Pump on the Green in Spittal, since when the Royal has changed hands several times and has been greatly refurbished; licensees have included Sheila McConnell and George Moody.

The **Broad Haven Hotel** was a landmark on the seafront for many years before being demolished to make way for apartment buildings as part of the recent sweeping changes which have transformed the village. The

The sands of time were running out for the Broad Haven Hotel when this picture was taken in about 1995.

The Galleon was converted into a pub from a seafront café.

hotel only acquired a full justices' licence in December 1961, when Richard Richards managed to convince the magistrates that it would boost the tourist trade. He was granted the licence on condition that he gave up running the Cabin Club, a members' only bar close to the hotel. Eifion Morgan ran the hotel in the 1970s and he was followed by Anthony Sage who was the popular licensee for nearly 20 years. He sold the 34-bedroom hotel in 1987 'for a sum believed to be in excess of £350,000' to a London-based property developer, after which its fortunes declined. Chris and Kathy Ross bought the business in 1994 and worked hard to restore it to its former status, but the building eventually fell victim to the large scale redevelopment of the area.

In the mid-1980s, James Campbell and Robert Curtis converted a seafront tea-room into a pub called the **Galleon**. Former merchant navy captain Geoff White and his wife Heather took over in about 1990 and built up the restaurant side of the business so that today the Galleon is well known both as a restaurant and a pub.

Broadway, where the road from Haverfordwest splits to serve the two Havens, was a rather bigger village at one time than it is now; the 1861 census shows some 20 properties, including two beer-houses. William James ran the **Bush Inn**, Broadway, in the 1850s, also farming 50 acres, but when he died in 1863, aged 67, the farmhouse pub seems to have died with him. It may have been at the present Elderbush Farm. At the other end of the village was the **Rising Sun** where James Thomas was the landlord in 1861 and also kept a small shop. Charles Davies and his wife Mary were there in 1871 but the pub seems to have closed when he died some time in the 1870s and by 1881 it was listed as a 12-acre smallholding.

Bibliography

Much of the information in this book has been gleaned from old newspapers, notably the *Welshman*, the *Carmarthen Journal*, *Potter's Electric News*, the *West Wales Guardian*, the *Pembrokeshire Herald*, the *Pembroke and Pembroke Dock Gazette* and the *Haverfordwest and Milford Haven Telegraph*.

The various trade directories have also proved very useful, particularly those published at various times between 1811 and 1925 by Slater, Kelly, Pigot, Holden and Hunt.

General
Ale and Hearty, Alan Wykes, 1979.
Drink and the Victorians, Brian Harrison, 1971.
Farmhouse Brewing, Elfyn Scourfield, 1974.
The English Pub, Peter Haydon, 1994.
The English Pub, Michael Jackson, 1976.
The Old Inns of England, A.E. Richardson, 1934.
Prince of Ales - The History of Brewing in Wales, Brian Glover, 1993.
The Pubs of Leominster, Kington and North-west Herefordshire, Ron Shoesmith and Roger Barrett, 2000.
Victuallers' Licences, Jeremy Gibson and Judith Hunter, 1997.
Welsh Pub Names, Myrddin ap Dafydd, 1991.
The Wordsworth Dictionary of Pub Names, Leslie Dunkling and Gordon Wright, 1994.

Pembrokeshire
A Vision of Greatness, Ken McKay, 1989.
The Builders of Milford, Flora Thomas.
The Borough Guide to Neyland, E.J. Walker, 1912.
The Changing face of Haverfordwest, Bill Richards, 1992.
Dale....an Illustrated History, compiled by Dale Women's Institute, 2000.
Descriptive Excursions Through South Wales and Monmouthshire, E. Donovan, 1804.
Discovering Pembrokeshire Country Pubs, Richard Jago and Nigel John, 1981.
The End of the Line, Desmond N. Davies, 1997.
Freystrop and Folk, compiled by Beryl Davies, 2004.
A Guide to Pembrokeshire Inns and Pubs, Michael Fitzgerald.
Haverfordwest Charities, with Numerous Interesting Local and Historical Notes and Useful Information.

Haverfordwest in Old Picture Postcards, Sybil Edwards, 1997.
Haverfordwest, compiled by Haverfordwest Civic Society, 1997.
Historical Sketches of Pembroke Dock, George Mason.
History of the Avondale Hotel, Hakin, Ted Hackett.
A History of Haverfordwest, edited by Dillwyn Miles, 1999.
The History of Haverfordwest and Some Pembrokeshire Parishes by John Brown, revised and extended by J.W. Phillips and F, Warren, 1914.
The Inn Crowd, C.I. Thomas (publ.).
Little Haven Conservation Statement published by the Pembrokeshire Coast National Park, 2001.
Llangwm Essays and Sketches, A. Dudley Edwards, 1974.
Marloes – A Miscellany of its History, W. Grenville Thomas, 1992.
Memories of Haverfordwest, John Mathias, 1945.
Milford Haven in Old Picture Postcards, Jack Warburton.
Neyland and Llanstadwell in Old Postcards, Simon Hancock.
Nicholson's Cambrian Travellers' Guide, 1840.
Old Haverfordwest by W.D. Phillips, 1925.
The Pembrokeshire Election of 1831 article by David Williams in *The Welsh History Review*, Vol. 1, 1960.
Pembrokeshire, the Forgotten Coalfield by M.R. Connop-Price, 2004.
The Pevsner Guide to the Buildings of Pembrokeshire, Thomas Lloyd, Robert Scourfield and Julian Orbach, 2004.
Photographic Memories of Neyland and Llanstadwell, Simon Hancock, 2005.
The Place-names of Pembrokeshire, B.G. Charles, 1992.
Portfield Fair, Charles E. Sinnett.
A Proud Centenary – Neyland in 1900, Simon Hancock, 2000.
The Railways of Pembrokeshire, John Morris, 1981.
Rings and Rosettes, Derek Rees, 1977.
Rosemarket, Geoffrey Nicolle, 1982.
Shipbuilder and Publican - article by Terry Belt about the Deans of Burton Ferry.
A Short History of the Vine Inn, Johnston, E.A. Hackett, 2001 (unpublished).
A Short History of Llangwm, Miss E Morgan (unpublished).
The Story of Milford, J.F. Rees, 1954.
The Story of the Milford Haven Waterway, Sybil Edwards, 2001.
The Town and County of Haverfordwest and its Story, G. Douglas James, 1958.
William Roblin – A Pembrokeshire Murderer, article by Andrew J. Roberts in Vol. 7 of the *Journal of the Pembrokeshire Historical Society.*
Wales' Maritime Trade in Wine During the Later Middle Ages (Maritime Wales, 1992), K Lloyd Gruffydd.
The Welsh Sunday Closing Act 1881 (Article in The Welsh History Review, December 1972), W.R. Lambert.
The Western Telegraph 'Then and Now' Series
The Journal of the Pembrokeshire Historical Society, numbers 10 and 11.
West Wales Historical Records, Vol. VIII.

Index

In the following index all pub names, old and new, are indexed – where there has been name changes they are cross-referenced and shown in brackets. 'Inn' is not normally used in the title (apart from 'New Inn'). To avoid confusion the parish or village is shown for country inns; in Haverfordwest and Milford Haven the street name is included. Page numbers in bold type indicate the main entry for that inn.

Admiral Benbow (Commercial), Neyland	**172**
Agricultural Arms (Greyhound and Agricultural), Albert Street, Haverfordwest	**125**
Albion, Dew Street, Haverfordwest	**90**
Albion, North Street, Haverfordwest	**57**
Alma, Hakin	**246**
Alma, Dew Street, Haverfordwest	**81**
Alma, Priory Street, Milford Haven	196, **223**
American Arms, Milford Haven	**194**
Anchor (Blue Anchor), Hakin	**238**
Anchor, Hook	**144**
Anchor, Little Milford	**141**
Anchor, Merlin's Bridge	**140**
Anchor, Milford Haven	**194**
Angel, Bridge St./High St./Castle Square, Haverfordwest	**70**
Angel, Church Street, Haverfordwest	**59**
Angel, Neyland	**159**
Apollo, Haverfordwest	**20**
Arloch Castle, Hakin	**232**
Avondale, Hakin	15, 196, 245, **246**
Bar Charlie, Dark Street, Haverfordwest	**101**
Barking Shark, Quay Street, Haverfordwest	**74**
Barley Mow, Grove Row, St. Thomas' Green, Haverfordwest	**120**
Barley Mow, Prendergast East, Haverfordwest	**38**
Barley Mow, Rosemarket	**151**
Barley Sheaf, Rosemarket	**151**
Bear (Plough, Champion), Market Street, Haverfordwest	70, **105**
Bell, Upper Market Street, Haverfordwest	**108**
Bellevue (Horse and Jockey), Dale Rd./Haven Rd., Haverfordwest	82, **128**, 132, 166, 188, 262
Black Bear, Tower Hill, Haverfordwest	**104**

Black Horse, Bridge Street, Haverfordwest	56, **63**
Black Horse, Llangwm	**148**
Black Lion (Brig, Ship), Dale	**260**
Black Lion, Dew Street, Haverfordwest	**85**
Blacksmiths' Arms, Marloes	**263**
Blayney's Irish Bar, Quay Street, Haverfordwest	**74**
Blue Anchor, Dale	**260**
Blue Anchor (Anchor), Hakin	**238**
Blue Boar, Dew Street, Haverfordwest	**80**
Blue Boar, Hakin	**232**
Blue Marlin (Morgan's Hotel, Lawrenny Castle), Neyland	**164**
Boars Head, Dew Street, Haverfordwest	**86**
Boot and Shoe, Bridge Street, Haverfordwest	**61**
Bridge End (Bridge Hotel), Hakin	**244**
Bridge End, Bridge End Square, Haverfordwest	**43**, 90, 92, 181
Bridge End, Merlin's Bridge	**140**
Bridge Hotel (Bridge End), Hakin	**244**
Brig (Black Lion, Ship), Dale	**260**
Brig, Hakin	**233**
Brig, Hazelbeach	**175**
Bristol Trader, Quay Street, Haverfordwest	**72**, 97
Bristol Trader, Priory Street, Milford Haven	**222**
Britannia Arms, Dew Street, Haverfordwest	**90**
Britannia, Hakin	**232**
Britannia, Milford Haven	**194**
British Hotel (Castle, Griffin), Little Haven	**269**
Broad Haven Hotel, Broad Haven	69, **274**
Brook Inn, St. Ishmael's	**258**
Brother Sailor, Hakin	**233**
Brunel Quay Hotel (Picton Castle), Neyland	**163**
Buccaneer (Globe, Galleon, Llan-y-mor), Victoria Road, Milford Haven	196, 205, **206**
Bull, Prendergast, Haverfordwest	**39**, 87
Bumbies and Flies (Crown), Old Bridge, Haverfordwest	**45**
Bumble Bee, Little Milford	**141**
Bunch of Grapes, Dew Street, Haverfordwest	**90**
Bush, Broadway	**275**
Bush, King St. (Hill St.), Haverfordwest	**116**
Bush, Upper Market Street, Haverfordwest	**110**
Butchers' Arms, Burton	**154**
Butchers' Arms, Hakin	**232**
Butchers' Arms (Jolly Sailor), Dew Street, Haverfordwest	**89**
Butchers' Arms, Prendergast, Haverfordwest	**36**
Butchers' Arms, St. Mary's St./Dark St., Haverfordwest	**99**
Butchers' Arms, Hamilton Terrace, Milford Haven	**194**
Caernarvon Castle, Hakin	**239**
Cambrian, Cambrian Place, Haverfordwest	**28**
Cambrian, Old Bridge, Haverfordwest	**46**
Cardigan Arms, Charles Street, Milford Haven	**217**
Cardigan Castle, Hakin	**246**

Carmarthen Arms, Cartlett, Haverfordwest	17, **25**
Carmarthen Arms, Honeyborough	**174**
Carpenters' Arms (1) (Shipwrights' Arms (1)), Hakin	**237**, 245
Carpenters' Arms (2), Hakin	**240**
Carpenters' Arms (Square and Compass), Cartlett, Haverfordwest	**22**
Carpenters' Arms, Dew Street, Haverfordwest	**85**
Carpenters' Arms, Uzmaston	**135**
Castle, Castle Square, Haverfordwest	6, 20, 21, **66**, 94, 95, 97, 125, **128**
Castle (British Hotel, Griffin), Little Haven	**269**
Castle (1), Milford Haven	197, **228**
Castle (2), Milford Haven	**229**
Castle, St. Ishmael's	**257**
Castle, Steynton	**185**
Cat and Bagpipes, Dew Street, Haverfordwest	**81**
Champers (Golden Lion, Orange Tree), Charles Street, Milford Haven	**217**
Champion, Hakin	**233**
Champion (Bear, Plough), Market Street, Haverfordwest	**105**
Church, Llangwm	**148**
Coach and Horses, Hakin	**232**
Coach and Horses, St. Martin's Place, Haverfordwest	**93**
Coach and Horses, St. Mary's Street, Haverfordwest	101, **103**
Coach and Horses, Milford Haven	**194**
Coachmakers' Arms (Mail Coach), Cartlett, Haverfordwest	**28**
Coburg, Shut Street, Haverfordwest	**87**
Coburg, Priory Street, Milford Haven	**223**
Coburg, Neyland	163, **168**, 171, 174
Colliers' Arms (Cross), Freystrop	**143**
Colliers' Arms, Hook	**146**
Commercial, Hakin	**243**
Commercial, Old Bridge, Haverfordwest	**46**
Commercial, Merlin's Bridge	**139**
Commercial, Market Square, Milford Haven	**221**
Commercial (Admiral Benbow), Neyland	**172**
Commercial Hotel and Packet House (George), Front Street, Milford Haven	88, 196, **200**, 217
Coopers' Arms, Charles Street, Milford Haven	**212**
Cottage, Llangwm	**149**
County Hotel (Salutation Hotel), Picton Place, Haverfordwest	**30**
Court House, Shipman's Lane, Haverfordwest	**120**
Cromwell Arms (Railway), Barn Street, Haverfordwest	**126**
Cross (Colliers' Arms), Freystrop	**143**
Cross, Herbrandston	**251**
Cross, Charles St./Priory St., Milford Haven	**218**
Crown, Kensington Gardens, Haverfordwest	**126**
Crown (Bumbies and Flies), Old Bridge, Haverfordwest	**45**
Crown, Quay Street, Haverfordwest	**73**
Denant Mill, Dreenhill	**190**
Dinas Arms, Victoria Road & Stephen St./Dartmouth St., Milford Haven	202, **203**
Dinas Inn/Hotel, Victoria Road, Milford Haven	196, **202**, 204, 218
Dolphin, St. Mary's Street, Haverfordwest	101, **103**

Dolphin, Charles Street, Milford Haven	**217**
Dragon, Hill Street, Haverfordwest	**115**, 148
Drovers' Arms, Prendergast, Haverfordwest	**36**
Drum and Monkey, Dale	**260**
Duke of York, Bridge End Square, Haverfordwest	**45**
Dungleddy, Old Bridge, Haverfordwest	**49**
Eagle Spirit Vaults, Charles Street, Milford Haven	**221**
Elms (Masons' Arms, ?New Inn), St. Ishmael's	**257**, 258
Falcon (? Wheatsheaf, St. Martin's, Jolly Seaman, Wheatensheaf), North Street, Haverfordwest	**58**, 59, 127
Farmers' Arms, Prendergast, Haverfordwest	**41**
Farmers' Arms, Hazelbeach,	**175**
Farmers' Arms, Holloway, Haverfordwest	**55**
Farmers' Arms, Honeyborough	**174**
Farmers' Arms, Hubberstone	**249**
Farmers' Arms, Marloes	**263**
Farmers' Arms, Robert Street, Milford Haven	**227**
Farmers' Arms, Uzmaston	**135**
Feathers, Market Street, Haverfordwest	**105**
Ferry (Jungle), Hazelbeach,	**175**
Ferry House, Neyland	**159**
Fiddlers'/Peddlars' Arms, City Road, Haverfordwest	**128**
Fisherman's Arms, Llangwm	**147**
Fishermen's Arms, Marloes	**263**
Fishguard Arms, Hakin	237, **240**
Fishguard Arms, Old Bridge, Haverfordwest	20, **49**
Fishguard Arms, Charles St./Priory St., Milford Haven	**218**
Fishguard and Cardigan Arms, Bridge Street, Haverfordwest	**62**
Flags, Nr. Walwyn Castle	**190**
Fleece, High Street, Haverfordwest	**79**, 88, 101
Flying Dragon, Hakin	**232**
For(r)esters, Neyland	**170**
Foresters' Arms, Bethany (Foresters) Row, Haverfordwest	**22**
Fountain, Holloway, Haverfordwest	**57**
Fountain, Prendergast, Haverfordwest	**37**
Four-in-Hand, Barn Street, Haverfordwest	**125**
Fox and Hounds, Hill Street, Haverfordwest	88, **111**, 113
Fox and Hounds, Steynton	**185**
Foxhounds, Herbrandston	13, **252**
Freemasons' Tavern, Hakin	**241**
Friars' Vaults, Castle Square, Haverfordwest	**65**, 108
Galleon, Broad Haven	16, **275**
Galleon (Globe, Buccaneer, Llan-y-mor), Victoria Road, Milford Haven	196, 205, **206**
Gamekeeper's Arms, Merlin's Hill, Haverfordwest	**120**
George, Dale	**260**
George, Prendergast, Haverfordwest	**36**
George (Commercial Hotel and Packet House), Front Street, Milford Haven	**200**
George and Dragon, Upper Market Street, Haverfordwest	**109**

George and Dragon, Charles St./Barlow St., Milford Haven	181, 196, **225**
George's (Three Horseshoes), Market Street, Haverfordwest	**106**
Gibbs' Gin Shop (Spirit Vaults), High Street, Haverfordwest	**77**
Glaziers' Arms, Bridge Street, Haverfordwest	**61**
Glen, Merlin's Bridge	114, **138**
Globe, Hakin	**235**
Globe, Upper Market Street, Haverfordwest	**110**, 118
Globe (Galleon, Buccaneer, Llan-y-mor), Victoria Road, Milford Haven 196, **205**, 206, 222, 223	
Globe, Neyland	**171**
Gloster Arms, Mariners' Square, Haverfordwest	**100**, 101
Golden Anchor, Milford Haven	**191/194**
Golden Ball, City Road, Haverfordwest	**128**
Golden Lion (Champers, Orange Tree), Charles Street, Milford Haven	196, 210, 213, **214**, 217, 221
Golden Slipper (?Sailors' Arms), Quay Street, Haverfordwest	**74**
Great Eastern, Hakin	**239**, 245
Great Eastern (Viking, Warrior), Neyland	**165**, 173
Green Dragon, Cartlett, Haverfordwest	**34**
Green Dragon, Slebech	**133**
Greyhound, Mariners' Square, Haverfordwest	**91**, 113
Greyhound and Agricultural (Agricultural Arms), Albert Street, Haverfordwest	**125**
Griffin (Three Horseshoes), Dale	259, **262**
Griffin (Castle, British Hotel), Little Haven	**269**
Grove, Hill Street, Haverfordwest	113, **115**
Gunning's Bar (New Inn), Neyland	**166**, 168
Half Way Inn, Little Wick	**251**
Halfway, Johnston	**182**
Hammer and Gavel, Old Bridge, Haverfordwest	**52**
Harp and Crown, Hakin	**232**
Haven Hotel, Milford Haven	**202**
Haverfordwest Arms, High Street, Haverfordwest	**79**
Haverfordwest Tavern (Plasterers' Arms), Dew Street, Haverfordwest	**89**, 110, 120, 128
Heart of Oak, Hakin	**235**, 242
Hermit, Uzmaston	**135**
Hibernia, Hakin	**237**
Hibernia, Shut Street, Haverfordwest	**87**
Hideaway Bar (Tudor Cellar Bar), Hill Street, Haverfordwest	**116**
Homeward Bound, Uzmaston	**133**
Hope and Anchor, Quay Street, Haverfordwest	**73**
Horse and Groom (Horse and Jockey), Prendergast, Haverfordwest	**38**
Horse and Groom (Horse and Jockey), Steynton	**183**
Horse and Jockey (Bellevue), Dale Rd./Haven Rd., Haverfordwest	71, **128**
Horse and Jockey (Horse and Groom), Prendergast, Haverfordwest	**38**
Horse and Jockey, Herbrandston	**251**
Horse and Jockey (Horse and Groom), Steynton	**183**, 244
Hotel Mariners (Mariners', Three Mariners'), Mariners' Square, Haverfordwest	20, 68, 88, **93**, 110
Huntsman, Rosemarket	**154**
Ivorites' Arms, Old Bridge, Haverfordwest	**48**
Ivorites' Arms, Prospect Place, Haverfordwest	**33**, 49,

Ivy Bush, Market St./Hill St., Haverfordwest,	**108**
Ivy Cottage, Merlin's Hill, Haverfordwest	77, **121**
Jolly Sailor, Burton Ferry	**156**
Jolly Sailor, Dale	**260**
Jolly Sailor, Hakin	**232**
Jolly Sailor (Butchers' Arms), Dew Street, Haverfordwest	**89**
Jolly Sailor, Llangwm	**148**
Jolly Sailor, Merlin's Bridge	**140**
Jolly Sailor, Milford Haven	**194**
Jolly Sailor, Ratford Bridge	**190**
Jolly Sailor, Steynton	**185**
Jolly Seaman (? Wheatsheaf, St. Martin's, Wheatensheaf, Falcon), North Street, Haverfordwest	**58**
Jungle (Ferry), Hazelbeach	**175**
Kensington Arms, Dew Street, Haverfordwest	**90**
Kimberley (New Inn), Great North Road, Milford Haven	**209**, 214
King's Arms, Hakin	228, **233**, 236, 241
King's Arms, Dew Street, Haverfordwest	79, **87**, 89, 95, 96, 111
King's Arms, Hazelbeach	**174**
King's Arms, Marloes	**263**
King's Arms, Milford Haven	**191**, 196
King's Head, Hakin	**232**
King's Head, Dew Street, Haverfordwest	**85**
Lamb, Dew Street, Haverfordwest	82, **86**
Lamb, Milford Haven	**191**
Lamb and Flag, Freystrop	**142**, 143
Lamb and Flag, Cartlett, Haverfordwest	**28**
Lamb and Flag, Dew Street, Haverfordwest	**86**
Lawrenny Castle (Morgan's Hotel, Blue Marlin), Neyland	**164**
Limeburners' Arms (Weary Traveller), Jubilee Row, Haverfordwest	**34**
Lion, Hakin	**233**, 237
Lion, Little Haven	**271**
Lion, Merlin's Bridge	**140**
Lion (Lord Kitchener), Charles Street, Milford Haven	**213**
Lion, Neyland	**168**
Lion Spirit House/Lion Vaults (White Lion (2), Ra Café Bar, The Bar), Dew Street, Haverfordwest	**82**
Liverpool Arms, Dark Street, Haverfordwest	**101**
Llan-y-mor (Globe, Buccaneer, Galleon), Victoria Road, Milford Haven	196, 205, **206**
Lobster Pot, Marloes	16, 262, **264**
Locomotive, Neyland	**168**
London Coffee House, Neyland	**163**, 166, 168, 171
Lord Kitchener (Lion), Charles Street, Milford Haven	196, **213**
Lord Nelson, Hakin	**232**
Lord Nelson Hotel (New Inn, Milford Hotel, Packet House, Nelson Hotel), Hamilton Terrace, Milford Haven	197, **198**, 204, 205, 207, 212, 229
Lugger, Pill Green, Milford Haven	**207**

Mail Coach (Coachmakers' Arms), Cartlett, Haverfordwest	28
Mariners' (Hotel Mariners, Three Mariners'), Mariners' Square, Haverfordwest	20, 68, 88, **93**, 110
Mariners (1), Milford Haven	**194**
Mariners (2), Milford Haven	**194**
Mariners', Neyland	**162**
Mariners, St. Ishmael's	**256**
Market Cellars, Market Street, Haverfordwest	**105**
Masons' Arms, Dreenhill	**189**
Masons' Arms, Cartlett, Haverfordwest	**22**
Masons' Arms, Dew Street, Haverfordwest	**90**
Masons' Arms, Herbrandston	**251**
Masons' Arms, Hubberstone	**247**
Masons' Arms, Marloes	**263**
Masons' Arms, Robert Street, Milford Haven	**227**
Masons' Arms, Priory	11, **186**
Masons' Arms (The Elms, ?New Inn), St. Ishmael's	**257**
Masons' Arms, Waterston	**177**
Mermaid, Hakin	**232**
Milford Arms (Mill-Ford Arms), Cartlett, Haverfordwest	**26**
Milford Arms Tavern, Neyland	**168**
Milford Hotel (New Inn, Packet House, Nelson Hotel, Lord Nelson Hotel), Hamilton Terrace, Milford Haven	**197**
Milford Hotel, Steynton	**184**
Milford Hotel and Packet House, Front Street, Milford Haven	**201**
Milford and Waterford Coffee House, Milford Haven	**198**
Mill, Cartlett, Haverfordwest	28, 36, 76
Mill-Ford Arms (Milford Arms), Cartlett, Haverfordwest	**26**
Miracle,	16
Morgan's Hotel (Lawrenny Castle, Blue Marlin), Neyland	**164**
Nag's Head, St. Martin's Place, Haverfordwest	**91**
Narberth Arms, Cartlett, Haverfordwest	**23**
Navy Inn, Hubberstone	**247**
Navy Tavern, Hakin	**233**
Nelson, Cartlett, Haverfordwest	**32**, 198
Nelson Hotel (New Inn, Milford Hotel, Packet House, Lord Nelson Hotel), Hamilton Terrace, Milford Haven	67, **197**, 198, 204, 205, 207, 212, 229
Nelson Tap, Charles Street, Milford Haven	**212**
New Anchor, Hook	17, 143, **145**
New Black Horse, Holloway, Haverfordwest	**57**, 63
New British Spirit Shop, Milford Haven	**229**
New Inn (1), Dale	**259**
New Inn (2), Dale	**259**
New Inn, Hakin	**232**
New Inn, Old Bridge, Haverfordwest	**51**, 116
New Inn, Portfield, Haverfordwest	**130**
New Inn (Whale), Portfield Gate, Haverfordwest	**130**
New Inn, Prendergast, Haverfordwest	**36**
New Inn, Upper Market Street, Haverfordwest	96, **109**

New Inn (1), Herbrandston	**251**
New Inn (2), Herbrandston	**251**
New Inn, Johnston	**182**
New Inn (St. Bride's Hotel), Little Haven	**265**
New Inn, Llangwm	**148**
New Inn, Lower Freystrop	**142**
New Inn (1), Merlin's Bridge	**140**
New Inn (2) (?Commercial), Merlin's Bridge	**140**
New Inn (Kimberley), Great North Road, Milford Haven	**209**, 214
New Inn (Packet House, Milford Hotel, Nelson Hotel, Lord Nelson Hotel), Hamilton Terrace, Milford Haven	**197**
New Inn, Middle Street, Milford Haven	**219**
New Inn, Pill, Milford Haven	**209**
New Inn, Nash Mountain	**149**
New Inn (Gunning's Bar), Neyland	**166**, 168
New Inn, Rosemarket	**151**
New Inn (?Mason's Arms), St. Ishmael's	**256**
New Inn, Steynton	**185**
New Inn, Uzmaston	**135**
New King's Arms, Prendergast, Haverfordwest	**36**
New Market, High Street, Haverfordwest	**80**
New Put Up, Barn Street, Haverfordwest	**126**
New Quay Arms, Charles Street, Milford Haven	**221**
New Sloop, Hakin	**238**
New Tavern, Sandy Haven	**254**
Newport Arms, Old Bridge, Haverfordwest	**46**
Newport Castle, Hakin	**239**
North Gate, North Street, Haverfordwest	**57**
Oak, Grove Row, St. Thomas' Green, Haverfordwest	**119**
Observatory Hall, Hubberstone	**250**, 253
Odd Fellows' Arms, Cartlett, Haverfordwest	**34**
Odd Fellows' Arms (Rose and Willow), Honeyborough,	**173**
Old Black Horse, Prendergast, Haverfordwest	**36**
Old Inn (1), Prendergast, Haverfordwest	**37**
Old Inn (2), Prendergast, Haverfordwest	**38**
Old Packet House, Hakin	**232**, 235
Old Rosemarket Tavern, Rosemarket	**151**
Old Seaman's Arms (Seaman's Arms), Quay Street, Haverfordwest	**71**, 76
Old St. David's Arms, Barn Street, Haverfordwest	**127**
Old Three Crowns, Haverfordwest	132
Old Tuns (Three Tuns, Three Tuns and Thistle), Tower Hill, Haverfordwest	101, **104**
Old(e) (Lower) Three Crowns (Times Square), High Street, Haverfordwest	**75**
Orange Tree (Champers, Golden Lion), Charles Street, Milford Haven	**217**
Packet House (New Inn, Milford Hotel, Nelson Hotel, Lord Nelson Hotel), Hamilton Terrace, Milford Haven	**197**
Peddlars'/Fiddlers' Arms, City Road, Haverfordwest	**128**
Pelican, Freystrop	**142**
Pelican, High Street, Haverfordwest	**80**
Pelican, Prendergast, Haverfordwest	**36**

Pembroke Arms, Dark Street, Haverfordwest	**100**
Pembroke Arms, Hakin	**232**
Pembroke Arms, Hill Street, Haverfordwest	**116**
Pembroke Castle, Neyland	163, **170**
Pembroke Yeoman (Upper Three Crowns), Hill Street, Haverfordwest	**112**, 139
Penry Arms, Portfield Gate, Haverfordwest	130, **131**
Picton Castle (Brunel Quay Hotel), Neyland	162, **163**, 164
Pier Hotel, Marine Gardens, Milford Haven	**195**
Pill Inn, Hook	**146**, 148
Pilot Boat, Hakin	**235**
Plaisterers' Arms, Castle Back, Haverfordwest	**58**
Plaisterers' Arms, Milford Haven	**194**
Plasterers' Arms (Haverfordwest Tavern), Dew Street, Haverfordwest	**89**, 110, 120, 128
Plough and Harrow, Prospect Place/Cartlett Rd., Haverfordwest	**32**
Plough, Hakin	**244**
Plough, Hill Street, Haverfordwest	**114**, 120
Plough (Bear, Champion), Market Street, Haverfordwest	**105**
Plough, Shipman's Lane, Haverfordwest	**120**
Plough, Priory	**186**
Plough, Uzmaston	**135**
Plumbers' Arms, Prendergast, Haverfordwest	**36**
Plume and Feathers, Old Bridge, Haverfordwest	**46**
Prince of Wales, Hakin	**238**
Prince of Wales, Merlin's Bridge	123, **137**
Prince William, Dale	**260**
Priory (1), Priory	**186**
Priory (2), Priory	**186**
Quay, Quay Street, Haverfordwest	**74**
Queens Hotel, Cartlett, Haverfordwest	**24**
Ra Café Bar (Lion Spirit House/Lion Vaults, White Lion (2), The Bar), Dew Street, Haverfordwest	**83**
'Raggy Down' (Sailors' Home), Marloes	**264**
Railway, Cartlett, Haverfordwest	**24**
Railway (Cromwell Arms), Barn Street, Haverfordwest	**127**
Railway, Johnston	90, **180**
Railway Inn/Hotel, Victoria Road, Milford Haven	17, 196, **204**
Railway Tavern, Front Street, Milford Haven	**201**
Rat Tavern, Market Street, Haverfordwest	**105**
Rats Island Tavern, Dew Street, Haverfordwest	**89**
Recruiting Sergeant, Milford Haven	**194**
Red Cow, St. Thomas' Green, Haverfordwest	**120**
Red Lion, Quay Street, Haverfordwest	**74**
Rifleman, ?Castle Square, Haverfordwest	**71**
Rifleman, St. Thomas' Green, Haverfordwest	83, 110, **117**
Rising Sun, Broadway	**276**
Rising Sun, Freystrop	**143**
Rising Sun, North Street, Haverfordwest	**57**
Roebuck, Neyland	**160**
Roebuck (White Hart), Steynton	160, **184**

Rope Walk Castle, Hakin	**232**
Rose and Crown, Victoria Road, Milford Haven	**204**, 223
Rose and Shamrock, Hakin	**240**
Rose and Willow (Odd Fellows Arms), Honeyborough	**173**
Ross and Wexford Arms, Hakin	**237**, 239
Royal, Broad Haven	62, 267, **273**
Royal, Charles Street, Milford Haven	82, **218**, 250
Royal Cellar Bar, Dark Street, Haverfordwest	**101**
Royal Exchange, Bridge Street, Haverfordwest	**61**
Royal Oak, Bridge End Square, Haverfordwest	**45**
Royal Oak, Dew Street, Haverfordwest	**89**
Royal Oak, Slebech	**133**
Royal Victoria/Victoria, Merlin's Bridge	**140**
Royal William, Haverfordwest	**20**
Royal William, Marloes	**263**
Royal William, Milford Haven	**229**
Royal William, Neyland	**159**
Rule and Compass, Freystrop	**141**
Sailmakers' Arms, Hakin	**232**
Sailors' Arms (Jolly Sailor), Quay Street, Haverfordwest	**72**
Sailors' Home, Hakin	**240**
Sailors' Home ('Raggy Down'), Marloes	**264**
Sailor's Return, Hakin	**239**
Salutation Hotel (County Hotel), Picton Place, Haverfordwest	**30**, 48
Salutation, Neyland	**173**
Sawyers' Arms, Drawbridge Lane, Haverfordwest	**75**
Seaman's Arms (Old Seaman's Arms), Quay Street, Haverfordwest	**71**, 129
Shamrock, Hakin	**235**
Shepherd's Arms, Uzmaston	**135**
Ship (Brig, Black Lion), Dale	**260**
Ship, Bridge Street, Haverfordwest	**61**
Ship, Hill Street, Haverfordwest	106, **114**
Ship, Neyland	**159**
Ship Aground, Cartlett, Haverfordwest	**32**
Ship and Brig, Hakin	**240**
Ship and Castle, Bridge St./Castle Squ., St. Martin's, Haverfordwest	**65**
Ship and Castle, Llangwm	**147**
Ship and Castle, Milford Haven	**229**
Ship and Line, Freystrop	**143**
Ship at Launch, Hakin	**245**
Shipwrights' Arms (1) (Carpenters' Arms (1)), Hakin	**237**, 245
Shipwrights' Arms (2), Hakin	**243**
Shipwrights' Arms, Neyland	**160**
Silverdale, Johnston	**181**
Sir Benfro, Hubberston	**254**
Sir Charles Whetham, Pill, Milford Haven	187, 196, 199, **208**
Six Bells, Tower Hill, Haverfordwest	**104**
Sloop, Dale	**260**
Sloop, Hakin	**236**, 237

Sloop, Milford Haven	**194**
Sloop, Sandy Haven	**254**
Sloop and Railway, Dartmouth Street, Milford Haven	**221**
Smiths' Arms, St. Martin's, Haverfordwest	**59**
South Wales Hotel, Neyland	**160**, 164
Spirit Shop, Hakin	**238**
Spirit Shop (Trafalgar), Charles Street, Milford Haven	196, **220**, 228
Spirit Vaults (Gibbs' Gin Shop), High Street, Haverfordwest	**77**
Spirit Vaults, HamiltonTerr./Dartmouth St., Milford Haven	**201**
Spread Eagle, Tiers Cross	**188**
Spring Gardens Brewery, Mariners' Square, Haverfordwest	98, **99**, 106
Square and Compass (Carpenters' Arms), Cartlett, Haverfordwest	**22**
Square and Compass, Old Bridge, Haverfordwest	**49**
Square and Compass, Neyland	**159**
Square and Compass, Slebech	**133**
St. Bride's Hotel (New Inn), Little Haven	**265**, 271
St. David's Arms, Hakin	**245**
St. Dogmell's Arms, Hakin	209, 233, **238**, 239
Stable, Burton	**155**
Stag, Bridge Street, Haverfordwest	**62**, 273
Stag, Neyland	**160**
Stag and Pheasant, Prendergast, Haverfordwest	**41**
Stannard's Wine Vaults (Wine and Spirit Stores), Old Bridge, Haverfordwest	**45**, 46
Star, Castle Back/Queens Square, Haverfordwest	**58**
Stonemasons' Arms, Merlin's Hill, Haverfordwest	**123**
Swan, Dale	**260**
Swan, Holloway, Haverfordwest	5, **52**, 118
Swan, ?Tower Hill/Dew St., Haverfordwest	**104**, 267
Swan, Little Haven	**267**
Swan, Pill, Milford Haven	**207**
Taberna, Herbrandston	**252**, 262
Talbot, St. Mary's Street, Haverfordwest	**101**
The Bar (Lion Spirit House/Lion Vaults, Ra Café Bar, White Lion (2)), Dew Street, Haverfordwest	**83**
Three Compasses, Hakin	**246**
Three Crowns (Weary Traveller), Hubberstone	242, **249**
Three Crowns, Milford Haven	196, **229**
Three Crowns, Waterston	16, **178**
Three Cups, Broad Haven	**272**
Three Horseshoes (Griffin), Dale	**262**
Three Horseshoes (George's), Market Street, Haverfordwest	**107**
Three Horseshoes, Llangwm	**147**
Three Horseshoes, Merlin's Bridge	**140**
Three Horseshoes, Tiers Cross	**188**
Three Lamps, Cartlett, Haverfordwest	**33**
Three Mariners, Broad Haven	**272**
Three Mariners, Dale	**260**
Three Mariners, Conduit, Hakin	**246**

Three Mariners' (Hotel Mariners, Mariners'), Mariners' Square, Haverfordwest	20, 68, 88, **93**, 110
Three Tuns, Hakin	**237**
Three Tuns (Old Tuns, Three Tuns and Thistle), Tower Hill, Haverfordwest	101, **104**
Three Tuns and Thistle (Old Tuns, Three Tuns), Tower Hill, Haverfordwest	101, **104**
Tiddley (Weary Traveller, Travellers' Rest), Freystrop	**142**, 143
Times Square (Old(e) (Lower) Three Crowns), High Street, Haverfordwest	**75**
Trafalgar (Spirit Shop), Charles Street, Milford Haven	**220**
Travellers' Rest (Weary Traveller, Tiddley), Freystrop	**142**, 143
Travellers' Rest, Neyland	**173**
Trooper's, Nr. Llangwm	**150**
Tudor Cellar Bar (Hideaway Bar), Hill Street, Haverfordwest	**116**
Turk's Head, City Road, Haverfordwest	**127**
Tylers Arms, Cartlett, Haverfordwest	**25**
Union Hotel, Milford Haven	**201**
Union Tavern, Quay Street, Haverfordwest	**72**
Upper Three Crowns (Pembroke Yeoman), Hill Street, Haverfordwest	77, 92, 111, **112**, 116
Victoria/Royal Victoria, Merlin's Bridge	**140**
Victoria Hotel, Priory Road, Milford Haven	220, 234, **228**
Victoria, Middle Street, Milford Haven	**219**
Victoria, Robert Street, Milford Haven	**227**
Viking (Great Eastern, Warrior), Neyland	**165**
Vine, Merlin's Hill, Haverfordwest	**120**
Vine, St. Martin's, Haverfordwest	**59**
Vine, Johnston	**181**
Warrior (Viking, Great Eastern), Neyland	**165**
Waterford Pacquet (Wexford and Waterford Packet), Hakin	205, 225, **241**
Waterford, North Street, Haverfordwest	**57**
Waterloo, Little Haven	**271**
Waterloo, Milford Haven	**194**
Waterman's Arms, Hakin	**232**
Waterman's Arms, Quay Street, Haverfordwest	**72**
Waterman's Arms, Milford Haven	**191**
Weary Traveller (Travellers' Rest, Tiddley), Freystrop	**142**, 143
Weary Traveller (Limeburners' Arms), Jubilee Row, Haverfordwest	**34**
Weary Traveller, Johnston	**179**
Weary Traveller (Three Crowns), Hubberstone	**249**
Weary Traveller, St. Martin's Place, Haverfordwest	**93**
Weary Traveller, Waterston,	**177**
Welcome Traveller, Tiers Cross	**187**
Wellington, Prendergast Hill, Haverfordwest	**36**
Wellington Tavern, Hazelbeach,	**175**
Wexford Tavern, Hakin	**239**
Whale (New Inn), Portfield Gate, Haverfordwest	**130**
Whale, Charles Street, Milford Haven	**221**
Wheatensheaf (?Wheatsheaf, St. Martin's, Jolly Seaman, Falcon), North Street, Haverfordwest	**57**
Wheatensheaf, Milford Haven	**191**

Wheatsheaf, Prendergast, Haverfordwest	**36**
Wheatsheaf (?Wheatensheaf, Jolly Seaman, Falcon, North Street), St. Martin's, Haverfordwest	**57**
White Hart, Dale	**260**
White Hart, Hill Street, Haverfordwest	**111**
White Hart, St. Mary's Street, Haverfordwest	**102**
White Hart, Solbury Cross	**190**
White Hart (Roebuck), Steynton	**184**
White Horse, Dew Street, Haverfordwest	**83**, 88
White Horse, Prendergast, Haverfordwest	**36**
White Lion, Bridge Street, Haverfordwest	**61**
White Lion (1), Dew Street, Haverfordwest	**89**
White Lion (2) (Lion Spirit House/Lion Vaults, Ra Café Bar, The Bar), Dew Street, Haverfordwest	**82**, 267
White Lion, Priory Street, Milford Haven	191, 196, 204, 206, **223**
Wine and Spirit Stores (Stannard's Wine Vaults), Old Bridge, Haverfordwest	45, **46**
Yard of Ale, High Street, Haverfordwest	**78**
Yarmouth Arms, Hakin	**240**

ALSO FROM LOGASTON PRESS

Castles and Bishops Palaces of Pembrokeshire

by Lise Hull

Within 50 years of their arrival, the Norman invaders had built a line of earth and timber castles on the southern side of the Preseli hills that was to become the 'Landsker line', with a second clutch of castles to the north of the Preselis. In time, stone castles were integrated into the line of defences. This guide covers all the castles, from mighty Pembroke and enriched Carew to the lowliest motte or ringwork, together with bishops palaces. A series of chapters detail the county's military history from 905 to the Civil War, after which each site is given its own entry detailing its construction and history, together with a note about specific location and access arrangements.

Lise Hull has been exploring and studying the castles of Pembrokeshire for 20 years. She holds a Masters Degree with Distinction in Heritage Studies from the University of Wales, and a Master of Public Affairs degree, specialising in historic preservation, from Indiana University.

Paperback, 240 pages with over 100 black and white photos and plans.

Price £7.95

ISBN: 1 904396 31 3 (978 1 904396 31 4)

ALSO FROM LOGASTON PRESS

Pubs of Narberth, Saundersfoot & South-East Pembrokeshire

by Keith Johnson

This covers all existing hostelries in Narberth, Saundersfoot and South-East Pembrokeshire (almost, but not quite, the old Narberth Hundred licensing district), along with many that have come and gone. It also includes details of the use of south Pembrokeshire coal in the wider brewing industry and information on the Narberth wine merchants James Williams.

Keith Johnson was born in a Pembrokeshire pub –the Carew Inn – where his parents were licensees in the 1950s. He has spent most of his working life as a journalist in west Wales, either on the *Western Telegraph* or the *Carmarthen Journal*, and currently combines freelance writing with editing *Pembrokeshire Life* magazine.

Paperback, 208 pages, 150 black and white photographs, drawings and cuttings.

Price £9.95

ISBN: 1 873827 21 6 (978 1 904396 21 6)

ALSO FROM LOGASTON PRESS

The Architecture of Death – The Neolithic Chambered Tombs of Wales

by George Nash

This book is concerned with the 100 chambered tombs in Wales that have significant remains—there are as many or more that are believed to have disappeared either due to depredation over time or of which only the barest hint remans.

An opening chapter details the background to the Neolithic, or new stone age, when these tombs were built. It covers the climate and vegetation of the period, the changing cultural influences, the trade contacts by sea with Ireland and Brittany and thence further afield, as well as overland through what became western England. The culture and beliefs of the people are considered, the scant evidence for their settlements contrasting with the often dramatic remains of the monuments for their dead. The five different styles of chambered tombs are described—Portal Dolmens, the Cotswold-Severn Tradition, Passage Graves, Gallery Graves and Earth-Fast monuments—with thoughts as to why the varied styles developed in the way and locations that they did. The chapter also contains a brief overview of the antiquarian investigations of the 1700s and 1800s. There is still much to consider: for example the bones found in some tombs often prove to be the assorted remains of a number of individuals. Does this mean that people were initially buried elsewhere and subsequently moved to a main, central tomb, with bones being lost in the process? Was it just the social elite who were buried in these tombs, and if so what happened to the rest of society?

The bulk of the book is a gazetteer to the 100 sites, with copious plans and photographs, along with a description and summary of what is known from the various archaeological excavations and research that has taken place over the years. The sites are grouped into eight core areas, running clockwise round Wales from the Black Mountains on the border with Herefordshire, through South-East Wales around Newport, the Gower Peninsula, South-West Wales, Harlech, the Lleyn Peninsula, Anglesey and North Wales, together with a few isolated monuments.

George Nash is a part-time lecturer at the Department of Archaeology and Anthropology, University of Bristol. He is also a Principal Archaeologist at Gifford (Chester). George has researched the Neolithic and Mesolithic over most of Europe and is currently part of an international research team working on a Neolithic tell site in southern Romania. He is also undertaking excavations around the Neolithic burial site of Arthur's Stone in Herefordshire.

Paperback 256 pages with over 250 illustrations.
Price £17.50
ISBN 1 904396 33 X (978 1 904396 33 8)

ALSO FROM LOGASTON PRESS

Romanesque Architecture and Sculpture in Wales

by Malcolm Thurlby

This is the first comprehensive study of Romanesque Architecture and Sculpture in Wales. As the project progressed, more and more Romanesque work was found, much to the joy of those of us who revel in this style. Unsurprisingly some of the most lavish survivals of this work are found in the cathedral of Llandaff and in the abbeys and priories of southern Wales (and to a lesser extent in central eastern Wales), where the Normans penetrated early on and where relative security allowed work to proceed. St. David's was rebuilt in 1182 in a very late Romanesque style after an earthquake largely destroyed the previous building erected some 65 years earlier. But many of the smaller churches across south Wales also have elements of Romanesque work, notably in their fonts.

Yet much survives in north Wales too, largely thanks to the patronage of Gruffudd ap Cynan and his aspirations on the European stage. In decyphering the work of Gruffudd ap Cynan, for example, there are few people better placed than Malcolm Thurlby, for he can bring his huge knowledge of the Romanesque to draw out the wider story—making comparisons with work across Europe in terms of overall design, and more locally to ascertain from where the masons and sculptors were drawn. Thus the book is not just about the individual examples of the style, but about why certain work has adopted the particular design and ornamentation that it has, with the ability to now read 'backwards' from what we can still see to the mind of the patron who was commissioning the work those centuries ago.

The book takes the building of Llandaff cathedral in 1120 as a juncture in the development of the Romanesque in Wales, its appearance being on a massive and lavish scale. Thus chapters deal with Romanesque work prior to 1120, the creation of Llandaff cathedral and its effect, notably in southern Wales, the work of Welsh patrons in, mainly, north and west Wales, and then a chapter devoted to the unravelling of Romanesque St. David's, rebuilt when Gothic was well established in France and had been successfully introduced into England and Wales.

Malcolm Thurlby was born in England and decided that art and architecture was to be his line of work when shown the richly carved doorway at Kilpeck Church in Herefordshire. He is now Professor of Visual Art at York University in Toronto and the author of many articles in a variety of journals. He has also written *The Herefordshire School of Romanesque Sculpture*, first published by Logaston Press in 1999 and reprinted several times. .

Paperback 400 pages with over 500 black and white photographs and 16 colour plates.
Price £17.50
ISBN 1 904396 50 X (978 1 904396 50 5)